"The current economic crisis has underlined how traditional means of managing people are no longer effective. Too many businesses underperform because they can no longer count on the commitment of their workforce. Only by treating employees as key stakeholders and engaging them will organizations be successful. This timely book provides a practical roadmap for companies to create an engaged workforce and is essential reading for all business leaders."

Professor Klaus Schwab, Founder and Executive Chairman,
World Economic Forum

"This is an important contribution to leaders and managers across all types of organizations. I believe readers of this book will be more confident and better equipped to address the issues their organizations are facing."

David MacLeod, Chairman of the UK Government-sponsored Employee Engagement Task Force and co-author of the influential report to the UK Government *Engaging for Success*

"This book highlights in a very understandable and comprehensive way, one of the most important HR concepts of our age, 'engagement'. During difficult times, we need more than ever to engage our workforce, to get them involved and committed. This book shows how to do it, and is a 'must read' for all line managers and HR professionals."

Cary L. Cooper, CBE, Distinguished Professor of Organizational Psychology and Health at Lancaster University Management School, UK

"A must read, timely and practical primer on how to engage any workforce – warts and all."

Will Hutton, author of *Them and Us: Changing Britain – Why We Need a Fair Society*, Principal at Hertford College, Oxford, UK, weekly columnist at *The Guardian* and *The Observer* Newspapers

"An engaging book about engagement! Linda and Geoff have produced an authoritative book that makes the business case, the emotional case and developed an easy to understand model that will allow HR practitioners and line managers to accelerate implementation. Recognizing there is no 'one size fits all' approach, the book is full of practical case studies that will inspire and enthuse."

Dean Royles, Director, NHS Employers

"The topic of employee engagement has caught the imagination of researchers and practitioners. But for many it is not clear what exactly it is, how you measure it and more importantly if, when and why it is related to productivity. In this well researched, easy to read, and eminently practical book Linda Holbeche and Geoff Matthews answer all the central questions about engagement. The book is topical, very up-to-date and highly practical."

Adrian Furnham, Professor of Psychology, University College London, writer on leadership and management topics and regular columnist for the *Sunday Times*

"This book is a major contribution to helping managers take action to improve employee engagement in their business context. It's packed with ideas and advice for managers who want to foster commitment and energize their organizations. The authors' ideas around creating a new employment relationship built on engagement will have wide currency in the years ahead, and are as necessary as they are revolutionary for all business executives."

Mike Cullen, Ernst & Young Global Managing Partner – People

ENGAGED

UNLEASHING YOUR ORGANIZATION'S POTENTIAL
THROUGH EMPLOYEE ENGAGEMENT

LINDA HOLBECHE
AND GEOFFREY MATTHEWS

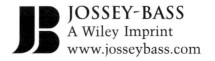

JOSSEY-BASS
A Wiley Imprint
www.josseybass.com

This edition first published in 2012
Copyright © 2012 John Wiley & Sons Ltd

Under the Jossey-Bass imprint, Jossey-Bass, 989 Market Street, San Francisco CA 94103–1741, USA
www.josseybass.com

Registered office
John Wiley & Sons Ltd, The Atrium, Southern Gate, Chichester, West Sussex, PO19 8SQ, United Kingdom

For details of our global editorial offices, for customer services and for information about how to apply
for permission to reuse the copyright material in this book please see our website at www.wiley.com.

The right of the authors to be identified as the authors of this work has been asserted in accordance
with the Copyright, Designs and Patents Act 1988.

Reprinted July 2012

Library of Congress Cataloging-in-Publication Data
Holbeche, Linda.
  Engaged : unleashing your organization's potential through employee engagement / by Linda
Holbeche and Geoffrey Matthews.
     p. cm.
  Includes bibliographical references and index.
  ISBN 978-1-119-95353-1 (cloth)
 1. Employee motivation. 2. Employees—Attitudes. 3. Management—Employee participation. 4.
Organizational behaviour. I. Matthews, Geoffrey. II. Title.
  HF5549.5.M63H65 2012
  658.3'145—dc23
                                                                              2012004082

A catalogue record for this book is available from the British Library.

ISBN 978-1-119-95353-1 (hardback), ISBN 978-1-118-33822-3 (ebk),
ISBN 978-1-118-33820-9 (ebk), ISBN 978-1-118-33823-0 (ebk)

Jacket design: www.rawshock.co.uk
Set in 10/14.5 pt FF Scala by Sparks Publishing Services Ltd – www.sparkspublishing.com
Printed and bound in Great Britain by TJ International Ltd, Padstow, Cornwall, UK

CONTENTS

FOREWORD

Today's volatile global economy has created both opportunities and risks for companies around the world. Most are under increasing pressure – in terms of costs and also their ability to attract and retain great people – from a wider range of global competitors than ever before. An organization's greatest asset is its people, but only if they are engaged. If they are willing to give that extra discretionary effort, the benefits to the bottom line can be substantial. Companies are increasingly recognizing this potential and the need to foster a new kind of relationship with employees. This book, offering a practical slant on employee engagement, is therefore well timed.

Our own research has proven that there is a business linkage between an engaged workforce and a better service for our clients, which in turn leads to greater job satisfaction and increased opportunity and reward for our people. Business strategy must therefore be focused squarely on shaping a culture that motivates employees to go the extra mile, leading to a greater competitive edge. It sounds simple enough in theory, but it's not always easy to pinpoint what it is that successful businesses are doing to create these high engagement levels. The case studies involved in this book all have their own story to tell and help add pertinent and practical insight to the theory. They have achieved exactly what the title outlines – unleashed potential.

Globalization presents huge opportunities, but a new breed of manager needs to be able to manage effectively across borders. This requires a shift from a 'one-size-fits-all' style of management to one that is more inclusive. Engaging an entire workforce is a complex challenge, but doing it over multiple geographies is even more so. It is one of the greatest business challenges of the 21st century. Creating inclusive leaders requires taking a new look at tried and tested programs to develop the right talent to manage across borders in both developed and emerging markets.

At Ernst & Young we are always looking at how to build on our global people strategy to increasingly engage our people through empowering them as they move through their career lifecycle. All geographical areas will have to meet the same high level of management standards to ensure a consistent global proposition for our people, but different approaches will reflect differing local perspectives. We want all employees' relationship with the firm – whether they stay three months as an intern or 30 years as a partner – to last a lifetime. In an increasingly networked world, it's these relationships, connections and experiences that deliver great results for our people and our clients.

No strategy can be implemented without involving line managers. This book rightly concentrates on how they can drive engagement through establishing a psychological contract, or a non-contractual relationship, with all employees. Business strategy cannot be set without consulting with line managers throughout the whole process. In turn, line managers will need to demonstrate that they can get the best out of their teams through sensitivity to local markets, through making everyone feel valued, and through being adept at harnessing diverse opinions to produce better results for customers or clients. By doing so, line managers can cut through the complexity with a people strategy that fits their specific market.

This book is a major contribution to helping managers take action to improve employee engagement in their business context. It's packed with ideas and advice for managers who want to foster commitment and energize their organizations. The authors' ideas around creating a new employment relationship built on engagement will have wide currency in the years ahead, and are as necessary as they are revolutionary for all business executives.

Mike Cullen
Ernst & Young
Global Managing Partner – People

FOREWORD

Given the extent of the challenge facing our economy we can only expect to succeed if we harness the full capability and potential of all our people. Nita Clarke and I through the last four years writing *Engaging for Success* and in the follow-up work have seen wonderful examples of employees delivering outstanding organizational outcomes. They illustrate the point that this can be achieved if we create the right conditions at work. When we get it right it is a win for the organization, a win for the country and a win for the employee.

Linda Holbeche and Geoff Matthews' book is an important contribution to help organizations set about improving their levels of employee engagement. They have included practical help and insights through case studies, ideas for action and in how to follow up and act on engagement surveys. This is an important contribution to leaders and managers across all types of organizations. Linda and Geoff are experienced and knowledgeable leaders who have significantly contributed to this issue in a number of ways including by being experts contributing to the Government-sponsored Task Force on this topic.

I believe readers of this book will be more confident and better equipped to address the issues their organizations are facing.

David MacLeod
Chairman of the UK Government-sponsored
Employee Engagement Task Force and
co-author of the influential report to
the UK Government *Engaging for Success*

INTRODUCTION

When we decided to write this book, we wanted it to be a resource for managers. While much has been written about employee engagement in the Human Resources (HR) world, there's been far less for leaders and supervisors 'at the sharp end'. So if you are reading this book, you are interested in, or at least a little curious about, employee engagement. Or you may want to understand more about what it is, what drives it and what difference it can make to business success. You may be an executive who knows that your organization is capable of higher performance, but you can't understand why this is not happening. Or you may be a line manager who wants to get to grips with what might engage your team, especially in today's challenging times.

You may have read about employee engagement, but wonder if it is genuinely a new concept or a case of the emperor's new clothes. Or you're a manager in Communications or HR who wants to know how to pinpoint your policies and practices to areas that will make the most positive impact on employee engagement. Alternatively, you may just want to think about your own level of engagement with the work you do, in particular about how you can become more engaged and derive more pleasure from your work.

We've written this book for all of you. We want the book to be useful and thought-provoking, and most of all we hope it will prompt ideas you can put into action. That's why we've included several case studies and checklists in boxes, which you can apply straight away or refer to later if you want to read on without interruption. So you can read this book all in one go or use it as a resource to come back to again and again.

In essence, we cover:

- why you should want employee engagement
- what steps you need to take to get it
- what you need to do to measure it
- what it looks/feels like when you've got it
- what organizations and line managers can do to stimulate engagement
- what benefits you get from it.

We have many people to thank for their kind support and willingness to share their ideas and company practices. Sadly we cannot mention everyone, but we would nevertheless like to express our particular appreciation to the following for their help in developing the case studies and other contributions that appear in the book:

- Krista Baetens and Sarah Keizer of ING Bank
- Cris Beswick
- Wayne Clarke and Ceri Ellis of Best Companies
- Eric Collins of Nampak Plastics Europe Ltd
- David Clymo of Schindler Group
- Rita Cruise O'Brien
- Charles Donkor of PricewaterhouseCoopers
- Jean Halloran and Cynthia Johnson at Agilent Technologies
- James Furber of Farrer and Co.
- Andrew Lycett and Sarah-Ellen Stacy of RCT Homes
- Carol McCarthy of Infosys
- Graham Valentine of Choy-Valentine
- Oscar Zhao of Blue Focus
- Peter Ziswiler of Sika AG.

We are also delighted to feature examples of interesting practice from Bentley, Birmingham City Council, Boots Opticians, British Gas, Cadbury's, Cougar Automation, Effectory, Goodman Masson, Google, Innocent Drinks, Instant, John Lewis Partnership, Luminus Group, Marks and Spencer, Marriott Hotels International, Medtronic, Merck Serono, The Nationwide Building Society, New Charter Housing Trust Group, NHS Dumfries and Galloway, Orchid Group, Royal Bank of Canada, Sainsbury, South Tees NHS Trust, Standard Chartered Bank, Tesco, UKRD, Unilever, the Universities of Chester and of Leeds, and White Stuff.

We are most grateful to the different companies surveying employee engagement for generously sharing their research and suggestions, and for the thought-provoking work of many leading researchers, practitioners and professional bodies around the world that are seeking to develop leaders and make workplaces more effective.

We are especially grateful to Mike Cullen, Global Managing Partner – People at Ernst & Young, and to David MacLeod, co-leader of the UK Government's Engaging for Success Taskforce, for their forewords to this book.

We would also like to thank the editorial, production and marketing teams at John Wiley and Sons for their wise counsel and active support, in particular Michaela Fay, Natalie Girach, Sam Hartley, Nick Mannion and Claire Plimmer, as well as Tom Fryer at Sparks Publishing Services.

Above all we are infinitely grateful to our partners and families who showed no end of patience, encouragement and (most of all) engagement.

Linda Holbeche and Geoff Matthews
April 2012

CHAPTER 1

Introduction

To say that we're living in uncertain times is to understate the case. Who could have foreseen some of the dramatic political upheavals and global events that have taken place since the Millennium? Or the discrediting of some of our most visible business leaders and the dramatic closure of several major corporations? Or that social media, designed to connect dispersed populations, would become a tool for mobilizing social protest to unseat governments and topple autocratic leaders? Who would have thought that the credit-fuelled economic model of globalization would implode, revealing the shakiness of supposedly 'rock-solid' banks?

Many of yesterday's 'certainties', 'facts' and 'truths' risk looking more like hypotheses or wishful thinking in the light of current developments. Even if the turbulence following the recent financial crisis eventually comes to be seen as a temporary aberration, there is no doubting that the trend towards faster and faster change will be ongoing. Back in the 1990s, Richard D'Aveni coined the phrase 'hyper-competition' to describe the competitive dynamics of the business world (D'Aveni, 1994). He argued that all competitive advantage is temporary and is based on continuous creative destruction, improvement and out-manoeuvring competitors. Today, D'Aveni's prediction is a reality; barriers to entry have collapsed in many sectors as a more connected world allows competitors to spring up from nowhere. It is not surprising, therefore, that for organizations in every sector, speed, innovation and agility are becoming the key capabilities for survival and sustainable performance.

Another aspect of this new era is the way companies create value. Since the late 1970s, when much mass production manufacturing progressively moved from the West to developing economies in Asia, companies in western economies have increasingly competed on the basis of mass customization, using the potential of high technology and intelligent systems to obtain and use detailed knowledge of the customer – his or her likely wants and preferences – to gain competitive advantage on the basis of their customer insight, service and innovation. However, the so-called 'knowledge economy' knows no geographic boundaries and is no longer a mainspring just of western economies as was originally assumed would be the case. The gamble taken by US and UK politicians and policy makers in the 1980s was that developed countries would always be pre-eminent as 'high skill, high pay' economies. Now that other nations also have access to high skills and high technology, western economies risk having to compete on a high skill, low pay basis (Brown et al., 2010). Continuous innovation will therefore be the key means of maintaining competitive edge.

Of course, to succeed in today's more knowledge- or service-based economies, it's not enough to have flexible business models, structures and processes. People are the source of production and of innovation. Their skills, behaviours and mindsets need to be agile too. Agile employees are multi-skilled, flexible people, capable of rapid decision-making and continuous learning. They are resilient and able to work within adaptable structures. Surviving and thriving in the longer term involves getting the 'right' people focused on the 'right' things and engaged in the collective effort. Consequently, in recent years we have seen an explosion of Human Resource initiatives relating to so-called 'talent' – how to attract, motivate and retain the people on whose skill and will business success depends.

Above all, it is *engaged* employees – who are aligned with organizational goals, willing to 'go the extra mile' and act as advocates of their organization – who are most critical to business success. And yet, survey after survey indicates that employee engagement with organizations is generally low. As Judith Bardwick, author of *One Foot out the Door* (2007, p. 13), puts it:

> *A not-so-funny thing happened on the way to the 21st century: hardworking Americans overwhelmingly stopped caring about their jobs. After years of massive layoffs and countless acts of corporate callousness, people from all fields and backgrounds – but especially the young and educated – got the message: the company no longer values them. Expecting the worst to happen, they saw no reason to give any organization their all. As a result, as many as two-thirds of today's workers are either actively looking for new jobs, or merely going through the motions at their current jobs. While they still show up for work each day, in the ways that count, many have quit.*

While the above describes the situation in the USA, we would contend the same scenario is being repeated in many workplaces across the globe.

The rising importance of employee engagement

It is for that reason too that 'employee engagement' – a term barely heard before the late 1990s – has become a major issue for businesses large and small. That's because high-performance theory places employee engagement, or 'the intellectual and emotional attachment that an employee has for his or her work' (Heger, 2007), at the heart of performance – especially among knowledge workers. The relationship between the individual and the organization provides the context in which employee engagement is created.

Employee engagement is characterized as a feeling of commitment, passion and energy that translates into high levels of persistence with even the most difficult tasks, exceeding expectations and taking the initiative. At its best, it is what Csikszentmihalyi (1998) describes as 'flow' – that focused and happy psychological state when people are so pleasurably immersed in their work that they don't notice time passing. In a state of 'flow', people freely release their 'discretionary effort'. In such a state, it is argued, people are more productive, more service-oriented, less wasteful, more inclined to come up with good ideas, take the initiative and generally do more to help organizations achieve their goals than people who are disengaged.

Employee engagement has been linked in various studies with higher earnings per share, improved sickness absence, higher productivity and innovation – the potential business benefits go on and on. For instance, a Corporate Leadership Council (CLC) study found that companies with highly engaged employees grow twice as fast as peer companies. A three-year study of 41 multinational organizations by Towers Watson found those with high engagement levels had 2–4 per cent improvement in operating margin and net profit margin, whereas those with low engagement showed a decline of about 1.5–2 per cent.

Company data also highlight links between engagement and performance. **Marks & Spencer**, the famous UK retailer, includes several questions relating specifically to engagement in its annual survey of its 80,000 employees. The scores of the stores with the highest and lowest levels of engagement correlate strongly with their sales figures, mystery shoppers' scores and absence rates (Arkin, 2011).

So interested was the UK Government in how employee engagement affects productivity that in 2007 the Department for Business (BIS) commissioned a review to investigate the links. Business leaders from all sectors of the UK economy, HR professionals, academics, union leaders, trade bodies and other interested parties took part. As David MacLeod, one of the authors of the resulting report *Engaging for Success: Enhancing Performance through Employee Engagement* (also frequently referred to as 'The MacLeod Report') put it, 'the job is to shine a light on those doing it well so that more employers understand the benefits of working in that way and really embrace it' (in Baker, 2010). One interviewee for the MacLeod report concluded that:

Engagement matters because people matter – they are your only competitive edge. It is people, not machines that will make the difference and drive the business.

(MacLeod and Clarke, 2009, p. 137)

How engaged are employees?

It seems that even in 'normal' times only a minority of employees are fully engaged at any one time, with almost as many actively disengaged. Various UK studies suggest that more than 80 per cent of British workers lack real commitment to their jobs, with a quarter actively disengaged. Despite the conclusion by BlessingWhite Research in its *Employee Engagement Report* (2008) that US workers are among the most engaged worldwide, research of nearly 8000 US workers by Harris Interactive in 2010 found that only 20 per cent reported feeling very passionate about their jobs. Even back in 2003, a Gallup poll reported that only 19 per cent of British employees were engaged and that 20 per cent were actively disengaged. The cost of this was then estimated at between £37.2 billion and £38.9 billion (Flade, 2003).

Today's tough times are likely to create even greater engagement challenges, with potentially serious consequences for organizations and the economy. HR consultancy Aon Hewitt reported in June 2010 that 46 per cent of the companies they surveyed had seen a drop in engagement levels – a 15-year record. Similarly, research in 2010 from the professional body for HR professionals in the UK and Ireland, the Chartered Institute of Personnel and Development (CIPD), found that only three in ten employees were engaged with their work (Alfes et al., 2010). It also discovered that:

- only half of people say their work is personally meaningful to them and that they are satisfied with their job
- fewer than one in ten employees look forward to coming to work all of the time, and just over a quarter rarely or never look forward to coming to work
- just under half of all employees say they see their work as 'just a job' or are interested but not looking to be more involved
- approximately half of all employees feel they achieve the correct work/life balance.

Research has found that employee engagement is on the decline and there is a deepening disengagement among employees today (e.g. Truss et al., 2006; Bates, 2004). Flade (2008) estimates that the cost of disengagement to the UK economy in 2008 alone was £64.7 billion. This declining level of engagement has a number of implications for businesses:

- It reflects a weakening of trust, which is an essential precondition for employee engagement. The deep recession and ongoing economic turbulence have strained the relationship between employers and employees. Public trust in business leaders, markets and institutions has been undermined and this mistrust has extended to within organizations. Now, people may be more inclined to distrust first rather than trust, and are less willing to give discretionary effort.
- The longer-term risk to the retention of key people. With high levels of unemployment, it's easy to dismiss this in the short term; but recruitment firms are aware of wide-scale, pent-up career frustration and predict that, as soon as the jobs market improves, there is likely to be significant employee turnover.
- Those employees who stay may no longer give their discretionary effort, with potentially damaging consequences for performance. The longer the downturn goes on, and the tougher the measures taken to keep organizations viable, the greater the risk of employee relations becoming more difficult and employees themselves simply 'hunkering down' and doing the minimum necessary to get by, but no more than that. Given that tough times are when businesses need the best from their people in order to succeed, this is really the worst of all worlds.

So it's clearly important – but what exactly is employee engagement?

Defining terms

Definitions of employee engagement abound and there is no single standard definition, since various experts place emphasis on different aspects of the subject. Some focus on what drives engagement, while others consider the effects of engagement. Some look at specific players involved, such as the role of the supervisor, or the part played by top management; other definitions consider the state of engagement, or how it feels to be engaged.

In the following sample of definitions, some of the differences of emphasis are obvious. Employee engagement is:

- the individual's involvement and satisfaction with, as well as enthusiasm for, work (Harter et al., 2002)
- employees' relationship with the organization, its leadership and their work experience (Towers Watson, 2008)
- a heightened emotional and intellectual connection that employees have with their job, organization, manager and co-workers (The Conference Board, 2006)
- a positive attitude held by the employee towards the organization and its values (Robinson et al., 2004)
- a set of positive attitudes and behaviours enabling high job performance of a kind that is in tune with the organization's mission (Storey et al., 2008)
- the connection and commitment that employees exhibit towards an organization, leading to higher levels of productive work behaviours (Vance, 2006)
- the extent to which employees commit to something or someone in their organization, how hard they work, and how long they stay as a result of that commitment (Corporate Leadership Council, 2004).

In other words, engagement is both a cause and effect. It involves a relationship between the organization and the employee. It builds on several more familiar workplace concepts such as employee commitment, job satisfaction and organizational citizenship; however, engagement goes beyond all of these since it connects these positives with improving business outcomes and performance. The concept builds on early studies carried out after the Second World War that found links between employee morale and worker speed and reliability in the mass-production economy.

But employee engagement is not to be confused with employee satisfaction. Satisfaction levels can be raised to a very high level – but the effect on the business might actually be negative due to cost, the entitlement mentality created or worker complacency. In contrast, engagement is about what the engaged employee will do in relation to the organization. Engagement is seen firstly as an 'attitude of mind', a set of positive attitudes, emotions and behaviours enabling high job performance of a kind that is in tune with the organization's mission. For us, employee engagement is about winning commitment by transforming the bond between the employee and the organization so that someone really is ready to offer their head, hands and heart to the job. But what constitutes engagement is something we'll explore in more detail in Chapter 3.

In some ways, saying that employee engagement is important to productivity is stating the obvious. Intuitively we know this makes sense. We've all met people who are engaged in what they're doing, who are willing to make extraordinary efforts on behalf of their organization. We've also probably seen the opposite, where the dead hand of cynicism and disengagement kills off the spark of ingenuity, energy or innovation.

> Engagement is seen firstly as an 'attitude of mind', a set of positive attitudes, emotions and behaviours enabling high job performance of a kind that is in tune with the organization's mission.

What does engagement look like?

While we may all have a sense of what engagement looks like, research by the UK's Institute for Employment Studies (Robinson et al., 2004) found that engaged employees:

- look for, and are given opportunities to, improve their performance – and this benefits the business
- are positive about the job and the organization
- believe in and identify with the organization
- work actively to make things better

- treat other people with respect and help colleagues to perform more effectively
- can be relied on and go beyond the requirements of the job
- see the bigger picture, even at personal cost
- keep up to date with developments in their field.

In short, employee engagement is easily the most likely and desirable focus for developing the employment relationship between individual employees and their employers.

The employment relationship has often been described as one characterized by exchange (Rousseau, 1990; Guest, 1997; Coyle-Shapiro and Kessler, 1998). This assumes a two-way relationship, one of reciprocity and mutual benefit. As well as an explicit exchange of work in return for pay and benefits, there are also more implicit or subconscious social exchange processes occurring within the workplace. These are invisible, but no less powerful – and, as a consequence, the employment relationship is increasingly conceptualized as involving a 'psychological contract'.

Unlike a legal contract, the psychological contract focuses on the individual (and hence more subjective) nature of the employment relationship. It represents the individual's expectations about the overall employment 'deal' – what obligations the employee owes the employer and vice versa. These can include expectations about job security, how work is assigned, what is a reasonable level of work pressure or about how career progression will occur. Long-standing custom and practice will reinforce the psychological contract, but it remains something that can easily be undermined, and with it, overall levels of engagement.

Social exchange theory argues that when one party gives something to another, it expects the other party to reciprocate by providing some contributions in return (Blau, 1964). From an employer's point of view, engagement is about employees exerting extra 'discretionary effort' to help the organization succeed. Employees, on the other hand, want worthwhile and meaningful jobs. If the balance seems fair, there is a good possibility that employees will be engaged. Even if conditions deteriorate somewhat, a strong psychological contract that feels fair will keep employees engaged with their employers – in some cases for quite some time, if managers take the right steps.

What does disengagement look like?

Conversely, symptoms of disengagement are more commonplace. Gallup distinguishes between employees that are 'actively engaged', 'not engaged' (i.e. average performers) and actively disengaged (Flade, 2006). In most studies, the latter two groups are reported as being in the majority. You may have heard the (probably apocryphal) story about the CEO of a large international corporation who called in management consultants to survey his workforce because he was concerned about low levels of morale and productivity. The consultants surveyed the entire workforce and after considerable analysis were able to present the findings to the CEO. 'Well,' said the lead consultant, 'you're extremely fortunate to have such a talented and capable workforce. They're all using their initiative, showing leadership and demonstrating teamwork, and are concerned about doing a good job. The only problem is that they're not doing that at work.' The talents and energies of those employees were being used to benefit their families and communities, as scout leaders, school governors, etc., rather than being applied at work. The challenge of course is to create the work context in which people want to make their greatest contribution.

In various studies, scholars suggest that it is the psychological contract that mediates the relationship between organizational factors and work outcomes such as commitment and job satisfaction (e.g. Guest and Conway, 1997; Marks and Scholarios, 2004). Typical organizational factors of employment relationships – such as job security, performance management, human capital development, opportunities for growth and the firm's core philosophies of Human Resource Management (HRM) – may have a profound impact on the development of perceived mutual obligations (Rousseau, 2000; Sparrow and Cooper, 2003; D'Annunzio-Green and Francis, 2005). As long as the 'obligations' that the employee feels are owed by their employer continue to be met, the employee is likely to reciprocate with good performance.

If one or other party, more commonly the employer, unilaterally changes the terms of the psychological contract, the other party, usually the employee, may perceive that their psychological contract has been breached or violated. According to Coyle-Shapiro and Kessler (2000), the extent of the balance/imbalance appears more important to the nature and health of the contract than the specific content of the contract. When employees perceive that the terms of their psychological contract have been breached, they reciprocate by withdrawing or making less effort on behalf of their employer. Symptoms of psychological contract breach – such as emotional exhaustion, higher turnover intentions, turnover behaviour, and lower job satisfaction, trust and commitment – are now increasingly associated with employee disengagement.

In other words, if people perceive that their psychological contract has been broken by their employer – for instance if their workload is significantly increased, or they work in a high-pressure environment or because their own job may be at risk – people are unlikely to remain engaged. And if employees more generally become disengaged, there can be negative consequences for productivity and innovation.

> When employees perceive that the terms of their psychological contract have been breached, they reciprocate by withdrawing or making less effort on behalf of their employer.

Some of these consequences may initially be quite subtle. For instance, in 1998 one of us carried out a brief retrospective study of a merger between two pharmaceutical companies that had taken place in 1991, in which Company X had acquired Company Y. The HR Director was one of the few members of senior management from Company Y to survive the merger. Several months after the merger, the rate of productivity among the research scientists formerly of Company Y had dropped significantly. None of these employees was at risk of losing their job, but many did not yet know exactly where they would be assigned. The HR Director was asked by the Board what was going on. He used the phrase 'they're burying their babies' to describe the way employees were keeping their best ideas to themselves in case they wanted to leave the company. Without trust, there was little basis for rebuilding a psychological contract with the new organization. Moreover, individual psychological contracts in this case were influenced by group perceptions about whether there was an equitable and viable basis for a social contract with their new employer.

A win-win relationship?

Mainstream people management practices are built on the assumption that what is good for the employer is always good for the employee. These take an instrumental view of employees, who are generally portrayed as 'consumers' of HR practices or of employer brands. For instance, the CIPD argues that engagement works by bringing together the objectives of employees and employers to the benefit of the organization, creating a win-win situation. Similarly, in what Tsui et al. (1997) describe as the 'mutual investment model', there is a mutually beneficial transaction between an employer willing to ensure the wellbeing of the employee (e.g. health and wellbeing, career opportunities, and training and appraisal) and an employee who knows what is expected and offers up the appropriate behaviours to meet those expectations. High mutual obligations are significantly more likely to lead to better outcomes for the organization, such as higher employee commitment and the associated benefits of discretionary effort, pro-social organizational behaviours and so on.

In practice, the goals of employers and employees may not be perfectly aligned. For example, there is some research suggesting that many employees – even at executive level – would prefer to trade off some of their income for a reduction in working hours. Moreover, such a balance of interests is even less likely to be achieved in a context of downsizing and ever-increasingly tight control of resources by employers, as a result of which employees who 'survive' redundancy are expected to take on heavier workloads. Whereas the traditional employment relationship model of industrial relations consisted of 'regulated exchange' and collective agreements between management and employees (Sparrow, 1996, p. 76), today's workplaces are far less regulated and the employee relationship with the employer is more individualized. As a result, employees are more likely to find their part of the 'deal' becoming unbalanced. In such a context, how mutual is the employment relationship and how much influence can individuals exercise within it? Or does it lead to a workplace culture of disgruntled compliance rather than enthusiastic commitment?

In contrast, engagement is about how responsive an employee is to their organization. We recognize that different people will be engaged by different things and a good many may not be open to being engaged with their organization at all. For instance, an employee may love their work and like their colleagues, but have no regard for their supervisor or the organization as a whole. In the university sector, for example, it is not uncommon to find academic staff who are highly engaged with their work and enjoy collaborating with their international peers, but who are scathingly critical of their own institution and its management. If the individual is engaged with their work but not their organization, should this matter? Arguably, yes, if their lack of commitment to the organization manifests itself in unhelpful attitudes or disparaging remarks that undermine any sense of common purpose among their immediate colleagues.

That's the point about discretionary behaviour: it is discretionary and cannot be 'forced' out of people. This puts the onus on the employer to create the conditions in which employees are prepared to 'connect' and give more of their discretionary effort. This includes taking into account the organizational culture: while the people within it (especially senior managers) create the culture, they are also shaped by it. It is hard to remain engaged and keep 'going the extra mile' when no one else does. All these potential engagement challenges require a proactive, leadership response – but employee engagement is a shared responsibility between the 'right' kinds of leaders, managers and HR practitioners, as well as employees themselves.

What do employees want?

According to a study of 90,000 employees in 18 countries by HR consultancy Towers Watson (2008), engaged employees are not born; they're made. Most employees care a lot about their work. They want to learn and grow. They want stability and security, and, with the right opportunities and resources, they'll commit to a company. They care deeply about a work-life balance – which does not mean slacking off. They want to give more and get a measurable return for their effort. And, as we shall discuss in later chapters, most employees want to feel valued and involved. Above all, they want work with meaning and purpose.

The American writer Studs Terkel (1974, p. xiii) sums up what is probably a common desire across generations:

> *Work is a search for daily meaning as well as daily bread; for recognition, as well as cash; for astonishment rather than torpor; in short – for a sort of life, rather than a Monday–Friday sort of dying.*

When Terkel first wrote this in the 1970s, scientific management practices were being applied to white collar office work for the first time, thanks to technology. Also known as 'Taylorization' (after F.W. Taylor, who pioneered the time and motion studies that formed part of this approach), these practices were originally applied in manufacturing environments such as the Ford Motor Company. Taylor apparently said:

> *Hardly a competent workman can be found who does not devote a considerable amount of time to studying just how slowly he can work and still convince his employer that he is going at a good pace.*

This observation shows that the underlying principle of Taylorization is a lack of trust. Instead, work was broken into its components, with skilled/decision-making work separated from the routine. Such fragmentation allowed greater control, with decision-making becoming the preserve of management. As a result, many people found their ownership of the work process, and the quality of their work experience, diminished. Conversely, other people found themselves 'work-rich'. The resulting trend – still visible today – is towards heavy workloads, shorter lead times and higher work demands.

So Terkel's comment is likely to apply now more than ever. With the generational change occurring, Generation Y and 'Net Gen' employees are increasingly looking for work where they are more actively involved and listened to; they want to identify with their workplace and not simply see it as somewhere to spend the working week. In Chapter 3 we will explore in more detail what many employees appear to find meaningful at work.

Added to this is the greater insecurity in the workplace. Whereas being made redundant was once seen as rare, and mostly affecting older workers, many employees will have experienced this at least once in their lifetime – and in some cases, more than once. Added to this is the trend towards flexibility at work: with more use of temporary workers, contractors and outsourcing, the risk is that employees become more concerned with worrying about their future than about their work. Taken together, these trends prompt the question 'just how is flexibility to make a more engaged human being?' (Sennett, 1998, p. 45). We shall examine this question more specifically in the next chapter.

> Engaged employees are not born; they're made. Most employees care a lot about their work. They want to learn and grow.

The business case – what's the evidence?

Organizations therefore need to be able to adapt to a new context – the people economy. And, given today's fast-changing environment, organizations also need to be agile: to swiftly turn decisions into actions, manage change effectively and as part of 'business as usual', focus intensely on customers, and optimize the value of knowledge and innovation. Employee engagement is the vital ingredient in all these capabilities. It is the link between strategic decision-making and effective execution, between individual motivation and product innovation, and between delighted customers and growing revenues. For the UK parent of an international aerospace business, the benefits of staff engagement are multiple:

- Better understanding of problems is spread across the workforce – it is essential to have an effective problem-solving culture.
- Teams of committed employees are helped to grow and develop, evaluate issues, and make decisions.

As a company spokesperson put it, 'this is not an optional extra – it is the UK's only source of possible competitive advantage in this global business'.

Engagement is important and cannot be taken for granted. The former CEO of GE, Jack Welch, has been quoted as saying that 'no company, large or small, can succeed over the long run without energized employees who believe in the mission and understand how to achieve it'. Here are some more of the many 'soft' or hard-to-quantify reasons for taking employee engagement seriously:

- It unlocks people's potential and raises their involvement in the business.
- It increases motivation, productivity, quality and innovation in the workplace.
- It can raise job satisfaction and psychological wellbeing, and help people get through downturns with a positive attitude and retain them in the upturn.
- It increases the employees' sense of pride so they become stronger advocates for the organization, improving its brand and reputation.
- It can help pull together different workforces as part of the post-merger integration of two organizations.
- It links clearly with employees' willingness to stay working with their employer and their advocacy – a disposition to spread the word about what a good place the organization is to work in and for, and do business with. (Disengagement has a similar effect – in the opposite direction. For instance, one fast food chain suffered damage to its brand image when a video of a disgruntled employee being very unhygienic in his handling of the food products was shown on YouTube.)

Another 'soft' factor is the so-called 'cost of quality'. This isn't the price of creating a quality product or service; it's the cost of *not* providing a quality product or service, perhaps because the employee is so disengaged that they do not care enough to do a good job. Every time work is redone, the cost of quality increases. That's because if a service needs to be reworked, such as the reprocessing of a loan operation or the replacement of a food order in a restaurant, this represents a cost that would not have been expended if quality were perfect. In customer-facing situations, the risk of financial penalty of poor service is higher given that it is estimated that customers tell at least another seven people about the dreadful service they have received.

However, for those looking for irrefutable proof that engagement leads directly to performance, the picture can be frustrating. The wide variety of definitions of employee engagement is reflected in the many ways it is measured, as we shall consider in more detail in the next few chapters. Engagement is usually measured by how people behave at work – described in terms such as 'committed, enthusiastic, open-minded, focused, helpful, caring, vocal and positive'. What is less clear is whether engagement is an output of an individual's intrinsic motivations or an output from a series of activities or processes – and if so, what are these?

Attempts to provide harder evidence of the value of engagement abound. A large body of research explores how clusters of Human Resource practices appear to impact on employee engagement and performance (Huselid, 1995; Guest, 2002; Purcell et al., 2003). By and large these studies are inconclusive with respect to tying down specific and universal causal linkages, but there is a strong consensus that certain 'clusters' of practices work effectively in some situations, some of the time.

Many survey providers claim to have found a strong correlation between engagement levels and productivity, profitability, customer service and innovation. More generally, high levels of engagement promote retention of talent, foster customer loyalty and improve organizational performance and stakeholder value (SHRM, 2011a). Other studies suggest that engagement accounts for roughly 40 per cent of observed performance improvements. It is true to say that the data does not state there is a clear causality at work; nevertheless, the closeness of the relationship is such that many major organizations have concluded the financial benefits from engagement make it a key business imperative:

- Highly committed employees try 57 per cent harder, perform 20 per cent better and are 87 per cent **less likely to leave** than their disengaged colleagues (Corporate Leadership Council, 2004).
- When employees are highly engaged, their companies enjoy 26 per cent higher employee productivity (SHRM, 2011a).

- Companies with a highly engaged workforce **improved operating income** by 19.2 per cent over 12 months; those with low engagement saw **operating income decline** by 32.7 per cent (Towers Watson, 2008).
- Engagement levels are predictors of **sickness absence** – highly engaged employees miss 20 per cent fewer days of work (SHRM, 2011a).
- Top-quartile engagement scores correlated to 2.6 times **earnings per share** compared with those in below-average engagement. Those in the top quartile averaged 12 per cent higher profitability (Flade, 2006).
- Companies with highly engaged employees enjoy 26 per cent higher employee productivity, have lower turnover risk and are more likely to attract top talent. These companies also earned 13 per cent greater total returns to shareholders over the past five years (Towers Watson, 2010b).

Many studies conclude that highly engaged employees tend to support organizational change initiatives and are more resilient in the face of change. During today's challenging times, in which many organizations are downsizing or implementing other cost-reduction measures, it becomes more important than ever to understand how to maintain or enhance employee engagement.

In some sectors, executives do not need persuading to take employee engagement seriously. A good deal of research in the banking and retail sectors points to a strong link between engagement, customer service and satisfaction, as well as associated revenue and profitability levels. In such sectors there is a clearly identifiable service-profit value chain. As a spokesperson for **HSBC** put it:

Employees' intellectual capital is the business's greatest asset. We need to work to keep their interest and involvement in the company high. We need to recognize these contributions through questions, feedback and suggestions.

Similarly, a spokesperson for the UK supermarket firm **Sainsbury** pointed out that:

Employee engagement drives customer service – we can predict store performance by reference to its engagement scoring, the higher that is the better the store will do.

The well-known work on the employee-customer-profit chain at the US department store **Sears** (Kirn et al., 1999) tells a compelling story about how improvements in employee attitude (about the job and about the company) drive employee behaviour and retention. This then drives service

> During today's challenging times, in which many organizations are downsizing or implementing other cost-reduction measures, it becomes more important than ever to understand how to maintain or enhance employee engagement.

helpfulness and perceived merchandise value, leading to customer impression, retention and recommendation, which in turn leads directly to operating margin, revenue growth and return on assets. In the case of Sears, a five-unit increase in employee behaviour led to a 1.3 unit increase in customer impression, which led to a 0.5 per cent increase in revenue growth. So skilled was the analysis of employee data, and the implementation of related policies and actions, that Sears was able to use employee and customer survey data to predict business results.

A public sector equivalent of the private sector service-profit chain model has been produced based on research carried out in Canada (Heintzman and Marson, 2006). In public sector organizations the bottom-line results of private sector value chains are replaced by trust and confidence in public institutions. Heintzman and Marson argue that engaged employees drive citizens' service satisfaction, which in turn drives increased trust and confidence in public institutions. They base their model on the top public sector reform challenges, namely:

- modernizing human resource practices
- service improvement
- strengthening citizens' trust in public institutions.

Engagement challenges and approaches therefore appear to apply across sectors and geographies, even if there may be differences in what specifically works where, and for whom. So adopting a proactive approach to employee engagement brings benefits to stakeholders. For instance, in the UK's **National Health Service**, it has been found that patients recover better and live longer where staff commitment has increased (Dawson, 2009). In **Bromford**, the Housing Association (fifth in the UK Best Places to Work list in 2007), a spokesperson describes engagement in action:

> *Achieving 100% tenancy occupancy was, we thought, an impossible target, but employees set it as their own target and they did it – colleagues expect more of themselves than do their managers.*

IES research (Robinson et al., 2007) suggests that the business benefits of employee engagement include greater customer loyalty, better productivity, improved employee retention, positive advocacy, performance and receptivity to change.

Of course, a key feature of engagement is that there are 'win-win' outcomes for all concerned, so employees benefit too. They experience enjoyable work, health and wellbeing, and self-efficacy. What's not to like?

Conclusion – an engagement deficit?

So we can conclude that employee engagement makes a significant difference to business results, even though the exact causality is not always clearly understood. We argue that engagement reflects the state of the employment relationship and, at an individual level, the psychological contract. In the current environment, that engagement is likely to be at risk.

Employers therefore cannot afford to be complacent if they wish to retain and motivate valued employees. Yet strangely, the MacLeod Report found strong evidence of an 'engagement deficit' among many UK senior executives – and we doubt whether UK managers are alone here. In some cases it's because leaders and managers are unaware of employee engagement, or do not understand its importance. In other cases, leaders understand its importance but appear ill-equipped to implement engagement strategies – especially if these might challenge their power base. The issue seems to lie in their unwillingness to 'walk the talk' on values and truly relinquish command and control styles of leadership in favour of a relationship based on mutuality (MacLeod and Clarke, 2009).

This suggests that if leadership and management styles are to be conducive to improving employee commitment, they must evolve to meet today's challenges. Changing workforce dynamics, a more educated workforce and different motivators by generational group mean that old-fashioned 'stick and carrot' incentives are less likely to work. Likewise, the longer-term demographic shift and a more diverse workforce (gender, ethnicity, age, etc.) precludes 'one size fits all' solutions to attracting and retaining people. When competition for skilled staff eventually returns, an inability to engage effectively will lead to haemorrhaging of talent from slow-responding companies.

In this new era, employers will need to be smarter about how they develop employment relationships based on adult-adult, rather than parent-child, relationships. They will need to ensure mutual benefits (as well as risks) for both organizations and employees in engaging for sustainable high performance.

Persuaded? In the next chapter we shall consider why engagement is so elusive and look at what gets in the way of employee engagement.

Checklist

- Which groups or individuals are critical to your organization's success? How engaged are these people?
- What do you consider to be the critical people risks in your organization?
- How well do managers in your organization (especially top management) understand the importance of engagement to business success?
- How proactive are your organization's strategies to increase employee engagement and retention?

CHAPTER 2

In Chapter 1 we hope we convinced you that employee engagement is important – not only to the business but also to everyone who forms part of it. If organizations are to be sustainably successful in the 21st century, they will need to be 'lean' and 'agile'. This new agility is about gaining competitive advantage by intelligently, rapidly and proactively seizing opportunities and reacting to threats. Business models will need to be more adaptable to fast change, while leaders and managers will need to be capable of strategic anticipation and effective execution. However, to succeed in the global marketplace, just having the right strategy will not be enough. Success requires the 'right' kind of willing and able people, focused on the 'right' things and engaged in the collective effort. Employee engagement is the next frontier in achieving sustainable high performance in this new era.

Over the next two chapters we shall look at what various studies suggest are the main drivers of employee engagement, as well as what drives the opposite – disengagement. Gallup (2010) proposes that in the minority of 'world-class' organizations, the ratio of engaged to actively disengaged employees is 9.57:1. We would contend that these low levels of employee engagement – which are mirrored in so many organizations – mean that we have reached a point where a fresh approach is essential: employee engagement is not simply 'nice to have', but is a critical component of future business success.

So first we're focusing on disengagement. This may seem strange, but we think it's important to consider some of the underlying reasons why work in today's organizations so often turns people off. Our argument is that it's no good just trying to 'fix' engagement with an 'initiative of the year' approach. This is too simplistic; it ignores what may be really causing the problem, and risks missing the real issues and engendering employee cynicism instead. We're going to be arguing that people are affected by wider social change and that the whole context of the employment relationship is being transformed. Increasingly there are tensions and conflicting needs between what organizations want and what employees need. There are also shifting perceptions about how much institutions, and their leaders, are to be trusted. We're going to look at the changing employment landscape through the eyes of employees and also of managers, since these are the key players in the employment and engagement relationship.

The changing engagement landscape

Of course, the question of how far the goals of employees and their employers are aligned is not a new one – and much has changed in the last three decades of economic liberalization and globalization, and related trends towards privatization, outsourcing, workplace flexibility and the individualization of the employment relationship. Milton Friedman (1982), one of the leading proponents of neo-liberalism, argued that the doctrine of 'social responsibility', that corporations should care about the community and not just profit was pure socialism, highly subversive to the capitalist system and could only lead towards totalitarianism. This free market philosophy gradually took root in most aspects of Anglo-American society. Scase (2006) described the 1990s as the 'Age of Individualism', built on self-interest, entrepreneurialism, consumerism and wealth creation. We contend that we may be reaching a 'tipping point' where these trends have reached their limits.

The recent financial crisis has clearly illustrated the inherent risks of an economic system based purely on a market-driven, short-termist, bottom-line mindset. Corporate strategy guru Michael Porter argues that the purpose of the corporation must be redefined as creating 'shared value', not just shareholder value (Porter and Kramer, 2011). Thus companies will need to be able to reconcile social and business goals, and move from short-termism to sustainability. Recent trends – such as the call for increased business regulation (e.g. Sar-

> The recent financial crisis has clearly illustrated the inherent risks of an economic system based purely on a market-driven, short-termist, bottom-line mindset.

banes-Oxley, de-risking the banks), bonus deferrals and claw-backs, and 'say on pay' votes for investors – all point towards the need for a more 'balanced' ethical and equitable business model. When the recession hit in 2008/09, the fact that so many companies found creative ways to reduce labour costs (such as through short-time working) rather than automatically laying off employees suggests a more acute awareness by employers of the need to protect and keep talent than was evident in the downturns of the 1980s and 1990s.

Diverging interests

Back then, the employment landscape was being transformed by the trend towards de-unionization, more casual workers and organizational re-engineering. It was also transformed by the growth of managerialism, or giving managers 'the right to manage'. 'Star' executives such as Lee Iacocca, Jack Welch or Sir Ian MacGregor were lionized on both sides of the Atlantic, and the increasing focus on management was matched by the blossoming of MBA programmes at business schools, the growth of management consulting and the increasing influence of prominent consultant 'gurus' such as Peters and Waterman (1982) or Hammer and Champy (1993). The private sector managerialist ethos was strong and a steady flow of managerial talent went from the private to public sectors to spread these methods, not least in the UK under the 'New Labour' government.

But such approaches meant that the interests of senior managers and employees increasingly diverged, just as the pay gap itself widened ever further between leaders and the led: in 1950, US CEOs earned 24 times the average worker's pay; by 1990 it had risen to 122 times and by 2009, 550 times (Hutton,

2011b). So much of this change process was gradual, subtle and mostly hidden from view. These accelerating imbalances of wealth, opportunity and good fortune came to be taken for granted and were seen as 'normal'.

Just how far the goals of employers and employees had drifted apart is reflected in the significant restructurings of businesses since the 1980s. Under pressure to optimize shareholder value, managers focused on short-term business enhancements that drove up share value, such as mergers and acquisitions, restructurings, outsourcing, divestments, off-shoring and greater use of technology and automation. So while share values improved as a result of restructurings and layoffs (with executives often rewarded in the process through stock options or share plans), for many employees the consequences of reorganization and the flattening of career structures usually included a loss of job security and clear career path.

The commoditization of work

The division of labour and commoditization of work that was ushered in by mass production in manufacturing in the early 20th century has now extended across much of the workplace. Since the 1990s, white collar work – especially in sectors such as banking – has been similarly revolutionized by the new generations of information and communication technologies. Back office operations have been centralized and a new form of 'front-line' facility has been developed in the form of 24-hour, customer-servicing call centres that may be several time zones away from where the customer is actually located. Former white collar work has become embedded in online tools, so compartmentalizing and de-skilling jobs. This has had the effect that it is more difficult for employees to have a sense of pride in the job when they are no longer responsible for the whole task and instead address a small piece of a complex value chain. The high turnover rates of call centre staff is unsurprising, therefore, when they are responsible for handling customer concerns but are frequently not fully trained or empowered to resolve them.

The predictions in the 1970s that technology would both liberate people to enjoy lives of leisure and also engender – to quote one title – 'the collapse of work' (Jenkins and Sherman, 1979) have, in practice, been proved faulty. In fact technology has been used to achieve the exact opposite for many white collar workers (i.e. an intensification of work), leaving other less 'technology-savvy' workers with poor employment prospects. Equally, we now have the spectre of a new 'lost generation' of young, well-educated people leaving school or higher education with few or no prospects of a meaningful career. In mainland Europe, Spain has been worst affected, with almost half of its young people unemployed – sparking the *Indignados* protest movement that has since spread elsewhere, such as in the 'Occupy' protests. In the UK, everyone has become familiar with the term 'NEETs' – 'Not in Education, Employment or Training' – that can apply to up a quarter of youngsters in some cities. The ranks of the marginalized have grown, creating what Guy Standing (2011) has described as 'the precariat'.

So we have people who are work-rich and those who are very work-poor. For those in work, thanks to the possibility of remote access to emails and the internet – via laptops and other mobile devices – work has no real boundaries of time or space. Increasingly, therefore, work spills into every waking moment. For professionals a working day can seem full of an endless stream of emails, meetings and bureaucratic demands, while the 'day job' gets squeezed in round the edges. Long working hours are commonplace and the UK's Health and Safety Executive (2007) noted work-life imbalance as one of the principal causes of stress. Madeleine Bunting (2004) argues that ambitious employees in particular risk becoming 'willing slaves' as they strive to respond to potentially unreasonable employer demands in the hope of getting on in their careers.

In these circumstances, it becomes a questionable assumption whether what is good for the business is automatically good for employees. And who acts as steward, safeguarding the interests of business and of employees? In Personnel, yesterday's 'staff manager' has mostly become today's 'business partner' – with the change in name reflecting the greater emphasis on meeting the goals of the business rather than the traditional focus on attending to the

> For those in work, thanks to the possibility of remote access to emails and the internet – via laptops and other mobile devices – work has no real boundaries of time or space.

welfare of employees. In practice, power in the employment relationship is more one-sided, with the employer arguably holding the largest share.

Mutuality?

Under the old, paternalistic psychological contract, employees might expect job security in exchange for hard work and loyalty to their employer, and promotion on merit or seniority. Such mutual expectations reflected a longer-term relationship between employer and employee. During the period of significant business transformation from the late 1980s onwards, this psychological contract came to be seen by employers as an expensive obstacle to labour flexibility and, consequently, many of its 'terms' were jettisoned. Jobs were no longer for life and, with flatter organization structures, opportunities for promotion up a hierarchy became fewer. Instead, under the terms of the 'New Deal' (Herriot and Pemberton, 1995), the onus was increasingly on employees to make themselves 'employable' by developing the skills required to be marketable within or beyond the employer organization.

Consequently, instead of mutuality of interests, the risks in the employment relationship have largely passed to individuals whose ability and willingness to be flexible may be the crucial determinant of their success in an increasingly ephemeral workplace. Loyalty to the firm has become eroded as companies change hands (and names), offices are replaced by 'hot desks', and the certainty of job descriptions is replaced by the need just to keep up with the task of the moment. These 'high velocity' workplaces 'offer no ongoing relationships, no safe haven, no personal space' (Victor and Stephens, 1994, p. 481). This appears to have reduced people's expectations about the extent to which they can rely on or trust others – including their employer – to protect their interests.

In practice, despite the rhetoric, mutuality of interest between employees and employers seems to have quietly disappeared in many places. Nowadays, many senior managers are specifically rewarded for driving down employment costs by finding alternative ways to get work done more cheaply, for instance via technology or outsourcing. Reward and promotion practices have led to increasing polarization between 'core' workers and those on the periphery, as well as widening pay differentials between top managers and those at the bottom of the hierarchy (Hutton, 2010b). Such extremes of reward blow the myth that 'we're all in this together'.

The growing engagement gap

If employee engagement is elusive enough in 'good' times, it is – not surprisingly – even rarer in today's challenging economic environment. This has also created a new leadership challenge: an increase in complexity, ambiguity and uncertainty, and a heightened potential for anxiety and mistrust. All are key elements of the new leadership terrain.

Insecurity

For many employees, working life today feels more threatening and insecure. Tough times, in particular, show for many employees just how skewed the employment relationship has become. With budget cuts impacting both the public and private sectors, employees are likely to be experiencing a complex cocktail of noxious ingredients: work intensification and demands for 'more from less', less autonomy, ongoing job insecurity, and uncertain financial futures. An increased focus on performance management, incentive pay and goal alignment can add to this sense of insecurity, especially when tools like forced distribution ratings are used to expose individual performance to minute inspection. Technology has enabled more and more monitoring in 'real time', which increases control over daily work: as Totterdill (2002) comments:

> There has been a disturbing decline in the levels of autonomy which employees had previously enjoyed at work. This reflects pressures of technology, externally driven targets and erosion of participative working methods.

More generally, deep organizational changes have a profound impact on people within organizations; if change results in job losses, the psychological contract between employers and employees can be seriously damaged. In such circumstances, many employers struggle both to lose cost and surplus capacity, and still keep employees engaged, committed and high performing.

Without job security, then, it is extremely difficult to engage people. Defined back in 1943, Maslow's 'Hierarchy of Needs' suggested that basic needs such as food and shelter, followed by safety (including job security), will take precedence over other higher level needs such the opportunity to be appreciated by others or to use one's creativity (Maslow, 1954/1987). So if people are insecure, they tend to focus on the basics, such as whether they have a job at all. It is only when these needs are satisfied that people look for more meaningful ways of engaging. And even though some individuals may find the effects of change positive, more generally people find change unsettling: 58 per cent of respondents to the CIPD Employee Outlook (2009) reported being anxious about the future, even though their own job was not at risk. Robbins (1999, p. xvi) points out some of the effects of downsizing on survivors, which he likens to a sickness:

> With budget cuts impacting both the public and private sectors, employees are likely to be experiencing a complex cocktail of noxious ingredients: work intensification and demands for 'more from less', less autonomy, ongoing job insecurity, and uncertain financial futures.

Symptoms of this sickness include job insecurity, perceptions of unfairness, depression, stress from increased workloads, fear of change, loss of loyalty and commitment, reduced risk-taking and motivation, unwillingness to do anything beyond the required minimum, feelings of not being well-informed, and a loss of confidence in upper management.

Not surprisingly, the main thing employees want from their employer in today's turbulent times is job security (SHRM, 2011b). After this, employees want the opportunity to use their skills and abilities so that they can prove their value to employers and develop their employability, should they need to take their skills and abilities elsewhere.

Reputation

Company reputation, good or bad, is one of the external factors that influences employee perceptions and feelings about their employer. 'Big brand' companies have sometimes found their own reputation to be at risk because of their dependence on the practices of companies in their supply chain: working conditions in factories in some of the low-cost subcontractors in developing economies have ultimately rebounded on the client company's brand reputation. Similarly, in the financial services sector in particular, the tarnishing of company reputations following the banking crisis is reported to have damaged employee morale. Financial services employees have even described to us their embarrassment about owning up to being a 'banker'.

Some academics argue that there is reverse causality with respect to employee engagement: if the organization is successful and has a good reputation, employees are more likely to identify with the organization and feel good about working for it. If they are engaged, they are likely to be active advocates of their organization and recommend it to others as a place to work. If employees feel pride in their organization, they are more likely to commit to it. However, employees cannot be 'forced' to engage, and, as Professor Nigel Nicholson (2011) points out, 'people's commitment to an organization is provisional and based on engagement; they no longer automatically wear the company badge with pride'.

Loss of job satisfaction

The widening engagement gap has been accompanied by shrinking levels of job satisfaction. The CIPD's Employee Outlook survey in January 2010 revealed that the proportion of UK workers satisfied with their job had dropped from 48 per cent six months earlier to 35 per cent (CIPD Research, 2010). Younger workers were particularly unhappy at work, with job satisfaction among 18–24-year-olds plummeting to 5 per cent from 44 per cent. In the public sector, cuts to budgets, pension rights and jobs were leading to staff insecurity and hostile industrial relations. Similarly, Mercer's 2011 global survey showed a marked decline in commitment and job satisfaction since 2006

(Mercer, 2011). It suggested that more than half of the UK's employees were unhappy at work, with more than a third seriously considering leaving their jobs. Mercer observed three broad groups of employees emerging from the results of the research:

- **Assertives**, who feel positive about their employer but are making decisions in their own self-interest. These people provide discretionary effort and go the extra mile for their employer and themselves.
- **Passives,** who feel indifferent and possibly like victims; these people may struggle to go the extra mile either for their employer or for themselves.
- **Good citizens,** who feel good about their employer and are loyal irrespective of how bad things have been. Their self-interest is low.

Among the 'passive' group, only 46 per cent got a sense of personal accomplishment from their work while even fewer (37 per cent) said they were proud to work for their organization. Just 47 per cent said that, considering everything, they were satisfied with their job. Of course, employee apathy and disengagement can undermine business performance, especially in a post-recession period when companies need commitment from their workforce and energy to drive business growth. In addition, this research suggests that those seriously looking to move were potentially high performers, since they scored 54 per cent for personal accomplishment, 48 per cent for pride in their organization and 48 per cent for satisfaction. So arguably, the most vital employees from the employers' point of view are those most likely to leave.

Individual employees generally have to watch out for their own interests and how well they can do this depends to a large extent on their personal market value at any one time. Employee self-interest can rebound against employers: if their future is in doubt in their own organization, there is less incentive for employees to offer their best. Staff may avoid jobs that make them less marketable elsewhere, or do them with less enthusiasm. Worse still, in sectors where demand for talent is high (e.g. new technologies, emerging markets), employers cannot control the market for talent. Employers can no longer expect loyalty and employees with the right skills may 'jump ship' without hesitation for a better offer.

Clearly employers are going to have to continue to work hard to rebuild motivation and commitment among workforces bruised by job insecurity, pay freezes or cuts, as well as increases in workloads, stress and conflict.

> Individual employees generally have to watch out for their own interests and how well they can do this depends to a large extent on their personal market value at any one time.

Lack of meaning at work

So even though these shifts in the employment landscape may now be considered 'business as usual', employees themselves at some level may be experiencing a sense of loss or alienation about their situation. In Chapter 1, we cited American writer Studs Terkel's comment that 'work is a search for daily meaning as well as daily bread' – but the reality is that, for many, this is becoming more and more of a challenge in today's organizations. Back in 2004, one of us carried out some research to explore in more depth a curious recurring phenomenon emerging from an annual survey of UK employees from about 2000 onwards. The survey, known as *The Management Agenda*, had been carried out by a management school since the mid-1990s, and its aim was to explore how employees were experiencing the workplace (Roffey Park, 1998–2012). Clusters of themes started to emerge from analysis of open-ended responses to a variety of questions. These all appeared to reflect a sense that employees felt something had been lost or was missing from their working lives. We decided to investigate further and held a series of self-nominated focus groups attended by people from a wide range of sectors and in a variety of white collar jobs.

This more detailed study became known as 'the search for meaning at work' (Holbeche and Springett, 2005). We explored what people meant by 'meaning' and, from their stories, it seemed that for many people, this was about connecting with others through time, having a sense of higher personal purpose and a heightened understanding of what is really important – of what it is to be human. Meaningful moments appear to elevate people's focus and their desire to give to others and fulfil themselves.

Of course, it could be argued that the search for meaning is perennial and simply part of the human condition; moreover, it may become accentuated by certain situations and at different life stages. However, our study suggests that the search for meaning at work was becoming more acute for many UK employees during the first decade of the 21st century. More people reported in our 2004 survey that they were looking for meaning at work (70 per cent), than in life in general (46 per cent). Eighty-two per cent of 20–30-year-olds in our sample appeared to be looking for more meaning in their lives.

Some of the things that people felt were missing in their work lives reflected the general backdrop to contemporary society:

- A lack of work-life balance as people generally spend longer at work than on other parts of their lives. Many people were working long hours and felt under heavy workload pressure, as a result of which they felt that other important aspects of their lives were 'squeezed out'.
- Change and the 'dog-eat-dog' ethic in many workplaces led to a loss of connection, making relationships more transactional and mistrustful.
- Reported higher levels of employee cynicism over a range of issues, including 'hollow' ethical policies such as diversity and corporate social responsibility.
- The general public, and employees in particular, were becoming increasingly distrustful of authority. 'Fat cat' pay issues and corporate scandals were causing people to doubt the purpose of their organization and the integrity of leaders.
- The community as a whole has undergone a moral/values transformation in recent decades to a more commercial, secular society. Many people are experiencing the lack of community spirituality – they want to fill a 'God-shaped' hole.
- The pressure to be perfect reflected in a plethora of 'alternative' therapies and self-help books and groups, with the implication that individuals should fend for themselves in order to 'fit the mould'.

Clearly, issues affecting work and employee engagement are not easy to compartmentalize. On the whole, people working in larger organizations appeared to experience less meaning than those in small organizations. Many people (39 per cent) experienced tensions between their own values and those of their organization. Women (44 per cent) were more likely to report that they experienced these tensions than men (35 per cent). Among the main destroyers of meaning in the workplace were factors such as short-termism, transactional relationships, lack of congruence by leaders or failure to 'walk the talk' on values.

We found strong correlations in the data. When work and the workplace lack meaning, morale suffers and people start to look for other jobs or consider self-employment. Change also becomes more difficult to manage. Conversely, when people experience greater meaning, they appear to be 'in flow', able to give of their best and willing to change. This is why we argue that employee engagement is closely related to personal meaning, and why we are convinced that sustainable performance will not be achieved by metaphorically whipping people harder. If employees are to experience meaning and engagement at work, the employment relationship must be of high quality, and built on a platform of mutual trust and respect.

The 'meaning at work' study also suggests that, while this search for meaning may be the primary goal of human beings, irrespective of social and economic position, the ways that people seek to fulfil this goal are changing. It seems that many no longer find meaning through their work role alone, or by the products and services they select. They now seek to create meaning by engaging in relationships within communities – of which organizations are just part. The communities they select are different from the communities we are used to. People are rejecting communities based on roles and rules, instead preferring communities that they help to co-create.

Changing expectations of younger workers

While there is a risk of stereotyping, it is clear that there is a generational shift in expectations of work. With the post-war Baby Boomers moving into retirement, the workforce balance is shifting towards Generation X (generally born in the 1960s and 1970s) and Generation Y (or 'Millennials' or 'Net Gen', generally born in the 1980s and 1990s). A study by PricewaterhouseCoopers (PwC, 2008) highlighted not only the change in attitudes in those joining the labour market but also the increased impact their demands will have as employers in many parts of the world compete for an ever-shrinking supply of young workers.

Tamara Erickson, a leading expert on the multi-generational workforce, argues that each generation is influenced by the context they experienced in their formative childhood and teenage years (Erickson, 2010). So Millennials (sometimes also dubbed the 'Facebook' generation) will already have been exposed to a wider variety of sources of information and access to events than previous generations. PwC discovered that 85 per cent were already members of social networks such as Facebook, and generally have greater exposure via the Internet to the volatile nature of world dynamics and higher awareness of the inherent short-termism of business than previous generations. We contend that such experiences are likely to shape their expectations about work, the nature of employment and careers, and the kind of employment relationship they will expect. Certainly PwC's research revealed the importance to Millennials of corporate social responsibility (CSR), with 88 per cent saying that they would favour employers whose values with respect to CSR reflected their own. Yet this survey of more than 4000 graduates worldwide did not indicate a propensity to change jobs faster (notwithstanding the image that Millennials have) or to turn their backs on established careers and businesses. But – importantly – they valued training and development more highly than anything else offered by employers.

Perhaps not surprisingly, given such expectations about personal growth, research by

> The bottom line for managers is that they will need to be more 'savvy' in being attuned and responding to the expectations of their staff, especially as long-term demographic trends lead to a shrinking workforce that will be more susceptible to a desire to change their job if their needs are not being addressed.

Ashridge Business School and the Institute of Leadership and Management (2011) found that many UK graduates believed they had taken the wrong type of work, or were progressing at a slower pace than they had hoped for. More than half (56 per cent) of graduates wanted their managers to be a coach/mentor to them, but only 26 per cent of graduates actually felt that they received this support.

The current recession may be a tough reality check for all workers, but we would contend that younger workers want a better work-life balance than their parents had, and that with a more and more educated workforce comes a desire for greater freedom and independence in the way they work, rather than direction and control in the way that they are managed. There may need to be some compromise on the parts of both younger workers and their managers. Younger workers may need to accept that in today's tough times they may need to absorb extra workload, while managers may need to work hard to keep younger workers engaged and developed. If not, high turnover of younger talent is likely when there is a more substantial return to times of growth and high employment.

Of course, within any generalization there are as many exceptions as those who are true to type. But with the increasingly multi-generational nature of many workplaces, it is unlikely that a one-size-fits-all vanilla 'engagement' initiative will succeed. The CIPD/Kingston Business School engagement study (Truss et al., 2006) found that engagement levels tended to go down as length of service increased – an indication to employers that they need to ensure that longer-serving employees continue to be exposed to new and interesting challenges. People in their forties and fifties had the highest levels of workplace stress and were most likely to find it difficult to achieve a work/home life balance. Further, those with caring responsibilities for children were less likely to be engaged. Employees aged under 35 were significantly less engaged with their work than older workers. The bottom line for managers is that they will need to be more 'savvy' in being attuned and responding to the expectations of their staff, especially as long-term demographic trends lead to a shrinking workforce that will be more susceptible to a desire to change their job if their needs are not being addressed.

More specific engagement factors

Just as with generational differences, so there is an all-round danger of over-generalizing about engagement. While consultancy models may categorize employees as 'engaged', 'agnostic' or 'disengaged' – and suggest that efforts should be focused more on the 'engaged' and the 'agnostic', while the profoundly disengaged should be 'dealt with' through the performance management process – we would argue this is probably too simplistic. People are rarely wholly engaged or disengaged – individuals' needs are very personal and attitudes can shift, sometimes rapidly. Any engagement effort should therefore recognize that people are human beings first and foremost, and be geared to creating a sense of connectedness between the employee and the organization that leads to a (positive) change in how they view it, and how they act as a result.

In addition, there are also secondary context- or job-specific factors that can affect levels of engagement.

Context-specific

The CIPD/Kingston Business School engagement study (Truss et al., 2006) highlights contextual influences on engagement such as role and occupation; management style; communication and involvement, and opportunities for flexible working. Size of organization may be a factor influencing engagement, although this is subject to ongoing debate. What is clear is that the life-cycle stage of a business can affect engagement, such as when a small or medium-sized enterprise (SME) becomes successful, expands and moves out of its entrepreneurial, start-up phase. At this point, the way the firm is led and managed, the nature of communication, and employee involvement in decision-making often change, with sometimes negative effects on engagement. As new people join the company, the nature of collective engagement may change further.

Job-specific

Changing working patterns are also likely to have an impact on engagement. For instance, the CIPD/Kingston study found differences in engagement levels according to working pattern and hours – with full-timers significantly more engaged than part-timers, while employees who worked average working weeks were more engaged than their colleagues on shifts or on a rota. This suggests that employers need to work harder with people who are not necessarily at work during 'standard' working times, ensuring that they too receive communications, are managed effectively and have opportunities to grow and develop in their jobs.

Person-specific

Aside from differences by generational group, research has found that women, in general, are more engaged than men – but they also tend to do different kinds of jobs. Employees with a disability were less engaged due to a range of negative factors, including bullying and harassment, not being listened to, the stress of work, a feeling of less control over their work, and higher levels of anxiety.

What we can conclude is that the organization first and foremost has the power of influence over a range of factors that impact on engagement. Any absence of mutuality of interest is likely to rebound on firms when the economic recovery eventually comes. Likewise, this raises the question about what sort of leadership is needed in this changing environment.

But whose job is engagement?

Of course we recognize that the organization may, or may not, be able to control external factors that can affect employee engagement, such as how it is perceived externally – its reputation. We also recognize that people engage themselves: while organizations must lead on creating the right conditions, they can't force this. And although it may be hard to motivate other people (because motivation is largely intrinsic), it is frighteningly easy to demotivate them. A public sector-focused study (CIPD, 2010a, p. 5) states that:

> *Survey evidence shows that trust, a sense that employees will be treated fairly, and confidence that management will deliver on its promises – the three con-*

stituents of a positive psychological contract – have for some time been in short supply in the public sector.

However, we argue that the organization has the primary responsibility to create the conditions for employee engagement and performance. While HR practitioners can help create some of the tools and practices to increase employee engagement, it is *managers*, given the nature of their role, who are in the best position to directly affect engagement on a daily basis and it is mainly (though not exclusively) through managers that employees have a relationship with the 'organization'. The quality of line management impacts on almost all aspects of working life. Line managers play the primary role in creating the workplace climate and therefore directly affect engagement on a day-to-day basis. They have the job of ensuring that people have interesting and challenging roles. They are responsible for managing and recognizing performance, and for helping staff develop.

Outdated approaches to leadership and management

Hamel and Breen (2007) noted in *The Future of Management* that, for all the huge strides that have been taken in terms of living standards and individual expectations over the past 150 years, many of the world's largest firms still operate essentially the same 'command and control' management model that was introduced during the Industrial Revolution and has been with us ever since. Traditionally, would-be senior managers in the US have prepared for responsibility by taking an MBA, while in the UK, accountants often end up running organizations. Octavius Black, CEO of the MindGym, argues that neither of these routes prepares individuals for a world in which the ability to read a balance sheet and a P&L is no longer sufficient: 'the numbers are still relevant, but they aren't a differentiator any more'. As Black points out (Saunders, 2011):

We have done competitive advantage from strategy and from technology. What's left is competitive advantage from your people and the line manager is critical to that. Get your people to flourish and your organization will perform better.

It is senior executives that 'set the tone' of engagement in an organization, whatever its size, according to a global engagement survey of more than 1000 multinationals (Melcrum Publishing, 2005). The attitudes of senior managers in particular appear to act as barriers to engagement and lead directly to a disengaged organizational culture (MacLeod and Clarke, 2009). For instance, in the CIPD/Kingston study (Truss et al., 2006), barriers to engagement included senior management invisibility and an obsession with targets, reactive decision time, bureaucracy, and rigid communication channels. In a Towers Watson report (2008), only 10 per cent of employees agreed that senior management treated them as if they were 'the most important part of the organization'. Similarly, in CIPD's (2009) Employee Outlook survey of 3000 UK employees:

- less than half (42 per cent) agreed with the statement 'Senior managers have a clear vision for their organization'
- 48 per cent said they were not consulted by senior managers about planned changes
- 35 per cent felt that senior managers were not to be trusted.

In this respect the UK seems to lag behind many other countries, according to a global survey that found that the relationship between senior management and staff was positive in only 30 per cent of UK organizations, compared with 43 per cent in America (ORC International, 2011). Rory MacNeill, Managing Director of ORC International's Employee Research division, comments (2011):

> Employers in the UK must look at their approaches and put measures in place to improve perceptions of management. If they don't, they risk a continuing downward engagement trend.

Similarly, the Hay Group's *Climate Change* report, based on attitudes among staff in 12 sectors, suggested that as much as one-third of an organization's business performance was dependent on a positive working climate (Hay Group, 2011). The report argued that the lack of this is costing the UK financial services sector alone £8.5 billion annually in reduced profits.

'Toxic' managers

If this wasn't bad enough, a lack of engaging management is an all-too-com-
mon feature of many studies. A survey by the UK's Chartered Management
Institute estimated that ineffective management could be costing UK businesses more than £19 billion per year in lost working hours (Pearson, 2011).
The study of 2000 employees revealed that 75 per cent of workers wasted
almost two hours in every working week due to inefficient managers. The
most time-wasteful management practices included unclear communication,
lack of support, micro-management and lack of direction. In other studies,
typical employee complaints about managers included:

- never around or too busy to spend time with me
- micro-manages everything I do
- avoids conflict and difficult decisions
- more focused on own career goals than mine.

For many managers, especially those who have been promoted into functional
roles on the basis of their technical excellence, the task of managing and developing people can seem daunting, riddled with complexity and an interference
with the 'day job'. Some struggle to mobilize the skill and will of those around
them in ways that make a significant, positive difference to the business. IES
research suggests that many managers are poor at developing relationships
with staff (Robinson et al., 2004, p. 58). The behaviours of 'disengaging managers' are described as follows:

- lack of empathy and interest in people
- failure to listen and communicate
- perceived as self-centred
- doesn't motivate or inspire
- blames others, doesn't take responsibility
- aggressive.

They are variously stereotyped as a 'micro-manager', 'muddler', 'blamer',
'bully', 'egotist' and 'pessimist'. In particular, such managers are perceived to

lack flexibility, both conceptual and emotional – consequently they find it hard to see things from others' perspectives or value differences, which is a bedrock capability of innovation. In some cases, managers don't even recognize the importance of employee engagement; it is seen as a 'nice to have' or to be outsourced to someone else, such as HR.

> For many managers, especially those who have been promoted into functional roles on the basis of their technical excellence, the task of managing and developing people can seem daunting, riddled with complexity and an interference with the 'day job'.

As Judith Bardwick (2007) points out, when people work for a manager who does not care about their people as individuals, focuses on their weaknesses and not their strengths, and doesn't communicate or listen to their input, employees are neither committed nor engaged. They are much more likely to feel resentful, frustrated and under-valued. The old cliché – that people don't leave their organization, they leave their manager – has some truth to it. In other words, managers hold many of the keys to sustainable engagement and performance but they are often ill-equipped to use them. The result is no discretionary effort, high turnover of employees and customers, falling sales, and declining profits and shareholder value.

Hamel and Breen (2007) are therefore not alone in suggesting that 'management is out of date', and that a paradigm shift is needed. Goffee and Jones (2009) also argue that, with the growing dependence of businesses for their success on 'smart' or 'clever' knowledge workers, traditional management approaches will not work. 'Old' management and leadership styles, based on a convention of low trust/high control, sit uneasily against a paradigm of 'volunteer' workers who are expected to be accountable and empowered, willing and able to create shared learning and intellectual capital.

What about managers themselves?

This burden of responsibility for engagement is a heavy one for many managers. They are often accused of being barriers to change but leading teams in difficult times is all the harder if managers are themselves 'in the dark' and feel as disempowered as their staff. And while there is growing awareness that, in today's flatter organizational structures, 'command and control' management methods are counter-productive with smarter workers, and that other conventional methods of motivation (e.g. pay for performance) are becoming exhausted or even ineffectual, many managers struggle to rise to the challenge of getting their employees to continuously deliver 'just that bit more' for the business.

The challenges of managing and motivating staff are made more difficult in today's leaner organizations with their wider spans of control and more diverse and widely distributed workforces, with more and more workers working offsite (for instance from home or dispersed internationally). With increased pressure on managers, there is less time to get to know individuals and find out what makes them 'tick', or to socialize with teams. Add to that the complexity of working with a multi-generational workforce, each of whom may have different expectations of careers, their boss and their relationship with their organization, and the manager's task is far from easy.

Bunker mentality

How are managers responding to the engagement challenge? Management capability is really put to the test in tough times. While there is some encouraging practice, many managers are reported to have adopted something of a bunker mentality and their default position appears to be micro-management. Especially when managers appear to withdraw, or become more 'command and control' in their approach, employee engagement is likely to be the major casualty. Krista Baetens, Managing Director and Regional Head of Corporate and FI Lending, Asia Commercial for the Dutch bank **ING**, points out the dangers of micro-management:

> *One of the drivers for disengagement is when you have no control over your workload or working hours; when you as an employee have no impact on how you manage your time, your job – to me, that is micro-management. Often in crisis situations you observe a tendency for micro-management. I think this*

is probably one of the worst things to do because it allows people to completely shift their responsibility and accountability to someone more senior without any excuse: because when you micro-manage, you are sending an implicit message to your staff saying 'I don't trust you'. I feel this is disengaging and it exposes the company to rather large risks because people may care less or feel less ownership. When you cut that umbilical cord of trust, I find it may be quite detrimental to employees' engagement.

Sometimes line managers feel held back from above and lack the authority to act on things that would make a difference to employees. Matters are made worse when senior management fails to provide clear direction. Of course this can be difficult when an organization is struggling to survive or is in some kind of strategic 'holding pattern' until things pick up. In many cases, legal restrictions and employment law mean that employers are restricted in what they can and can't do, which can inhibit flexibility, innovation and free thinking. In unionized environments, many managers are concerned about the increasingly rigid relationships with unions and are fearful of getting embroiled in complex defensive negotiations with them. There may also be a skills issue here; many line managers lack good people management skills, such as the confidence and ability to coach their teams.

So just when high touch and genuine connection are needed, many managers are adopting more formal and impersonal approaches.

Lack of consultation

Lack of staff involvement and consultation seem commonplace. In one major professional services firm (PSF), decisions are made by partners. The risk to partners' personal livelihoods means that difficult decisions are not always taken. Conversely, the owner-manager of another firm is quick to make decisions but not in consultation with others, so his decisions are not always easy to implement. He leaves to other managers the difficult task of getting staff onboard after a decision has been made. Ironically, his fear that involving staff will slow down the decision-making process often leads to lack of employee engagement and slower implementation. In public sector organizations, where cuts are underway and where there is an 'obsession with cost reduction targets', engagement becomes strained. For instance, many NHS employees report that the organization has become too task-focused and that teams are suffering because of this.

So just when good communication and a clear focus on customers are needed, it seems that many organizations obstruct the 'voice' of their employees and end-customers through:

- bureaucracy/red tape
- rigid communication channels
- management by email
- inconsistent communication streams, especially when staff work on different shifts or are not co-located
- badly managed ideas and suggestion schemes
- ideas not acknowledged or responded to.

On the other hand, some senior managers may be trying too hard to demonstrate visibility and concern, and there is danger of over-correction. For instance, in one organization a squad of well-intentioned senior managers caused consternation by turning up at a team meeting unannounced and left in their wake nervous jitters, with employees asking, 'Why are they here? Why us? Are we next?'

Even when jobs are not at risk, lack of consultation can undermine employee engagement and trust. In several large pharmaceutical companies that were previously regarded as good employers, the loss of budgets for training and development, as part of cost-cutting programmes, was perceived by many employees as a rewriting of their employment 'deal' without consultation.

So what?

If the mutual bonds of commitment between employer and employee become weaker as they are put to the test in the current business climate, these bonds may break. While people may hang on to their jobs for the time being, they may be just doing enough to keep their jobs rather than giving their very best.

Trust – the bedrock of employee engagement – is very much undermined by poor management: people are more likely to keep their best ideas to themselves, especially if they don't trust their employer. As Steven Covey argues, trust always affects two outcomes – speed and cost (Covey and Merrill, 2006). When trust goes down, speed goes down and cost goes up. And in today's challenging times, trust is easily lost between managers and employees, especially when leaders become more 'command and control' in their approach. If there was a reasonably high level of trust present before the loss occurred, as is the case in some organizations that had previously won awards for their engagement practices, the consequences for all concerned are even worse, such as:

- reduction in discretionary effort
- reduction in willingness to take risks by employees
- defensive and/or disruptive behaviour from both parties; lack of communication and feedback
- lack of willingness to invest in relationships, possibly leading to a silo mentality
- increased stress levels among staff who generally wish to do a good job
- higher staff turnover
- a shift to behaviours that favour self-preservation such as watching one's back and justifying one's actions, or expressing opinions to curry favour
- increased monitoring, box-ticking and bureaucracy
- low morale and loss of engagement.

For instance, in one company, staff became so disengaged by 'command and control' management styles that a whole team left and took their best ideas with them to start up another company – in competition with the parent company they had just quit. That is why the importance of engagement and the impact of change on employees must not be under-estimated, or loyalty taken for granted.

In contrast, in another company, strong engagement existed before the crisis. When redundancies became inevitable, staff members were directly involved and HR helped managers handle the redundancy process – and got the restructure right. Consequently, the impact of redundancies was less. Staff whose jobs were lost thanked managers for the way the process had been handled.

Conclusion

Employee engagement is a barometer of the health of the employment relationship – and, if the findings of many studies are to be believed, there is something of an engagement crisis going on. The two-way relationship is unbalanced and seems tipped too heavily in one direction. The consequences of this may be less evident during a recession, where employees may be glad of any work – but they are likely to rebound strongly when economies recover. Organizations that disregard engagement – and especially employee voice and equity – risk losing their most talented people, and will have to rely on a disenchanted or even embittered workforce when they try to keep up with their competitors. It therefore becomes all the more urgent that employers find ways for staff to have a stronger sense of 'voice'. If they are asked for their views, and listened to, employees can help shape an environment where they feel more valued and committed.

We believe that focusing on engagement is a way to create workforce energy, not just satisfaction. This is not about relying on 'one size fits all' solutions such as incentive pay, or attempting to conform to unrealistic expectations that managers should become superhero leaders. In a corporate context where commitment has to be earned, and connectedness is more important than hierarchy, 'strong employee engagement can make the difference between an outstanding manager and a merely okay one', according to Octavius Black (Saunders, 2011). Mostly what is required is good management: delegation, communication, motivation, handling tricky relationships and connecting people. It's about managers developing effective social and psychological skills to be able to tap into the emotional side of work. It's also about developing a more creative, flexible and connected approach suited to the demands of today's complex global market. We shall consider what this means in more detail in Chapter 9.

And despite the difficulties, we believe it is possible to create a context where more people, more of the time, are engaged in their work and with their organization. In the next chapter we shall look at what appear to be the common drivers of employee engagement. And the good news is that, in themselves, these are not rocket science: the real skill lies in knowing which drivers matter most to which employees at any point in time, and then doing something to activate or improve these.

That, we argue, is the real art of employee engagement.

Checklist

- Pay attention to how your staff are coping with change and heavy workloads. Are there some things that you can encourage them to stop doing, to enable them to focus more on the things that matter, without becoming 'burned out'?
- Make a point of 'walking the floor', not in a formulaic way, but frequently – keep connected and in dialogue with people.
- Who do you consider your most key employees? Find out what motivates them and find ways to respond to their needs.
- How much are managers (especially top management) trusted by employees?
- What impact are current trust levels having on employee engagement and performance?
- What one thing might make a positive difference to rebuilding trust?

CHAPTER 3

So far we've looked at the business case for engagement. We've discussed the link between great business performance and the positive outcomes of employee engagement – discretionary effort or willingness to 'go the extra mile'. Research by various consultancies and survey providers – such as Effectory, the Hay Group, Gallup, Kenexa and Towers Watson, among others – suggests that engagement correlates strongly with organizational performance, in good times and bad. This is borne out by the experience of a variety of companies from different sectors, such as Campbell's and Standard Chartered. We've also considered data that suggests that at any given time, only a minority of employees are highly engaged. We've looked at some of the reasons why employee engagement is such an elusive phenomenon. We've argued that when the employment relationship becomes unbalanced, employee engagement is a likely casualty.

In this chapter we are going to flip the coin to look at what engagement is really about, and what appears to stimulate more employees, more of the time, to be highly engaged and produce great results. Achieving sustainable employee engagement, we believe, requires a more balanced employment relationship. So we will present an integrated model of what we consider are the key drivers of employee engagement, from both employer and employee perspectives.

Can anyone be 'engaged'?

But is it realistic to assume that every employee can become engaged? Voltaire said that 'work spares us from three evils: boredom, vice and need'. Of course, for some people, work is mostly an economic necessity that has to be endured. But we believe that for most people, work means more than this, and that they are intrinsically motivated to want to do a good job. Work is very important for a host of reasons: it provides people with a source of personal identity, fulfilment and achievement, and a feeling of belonging to a community. The secret to high performance and satisfaction – at work, school and home – is the deeply human need to direct our own lives, to learn and create new things, and to do better by ourselves and our world.

And despite all the changes that have taken place in the workplace, survey data suggest that most people still want to give of their best, and make every effort to do so – even, sometimes, at the cost of their own wellbeing. Social psychologist Christina Maslach argues that engagement and burnout are opposite poles of the same continuum (Maslach and Leiter, 2008). We argue that if employee engagement is to become more widespread and more sustainable, we need a paradigm shift in how we manage and work – so that employee engagement and 'love of work', rather than disengagement and burnout, become the norm.

> Despite all the changes that have taken place in the workplace, survey data suggest that most people still want to give of their best, and make every effort to do so.

But what really drives engagement, or at least creates the conditions for it? Herein lies the rub: just as there are many different definitions of employee engagement, so there are even more arguments advanced as to what drives engagement – and there is sometimes confusion between outcomes and drivers of engagement. Consequently, there is no one-size-fits-all definitive explanation. But even though studies suggest there may be subtle differences between sectors and across demographic factors, we believe there are some strong common themes. We propose an overall model that can help managers see what principally drives engagement in the workplace.

The main elements of engagement

So let's start getting to grips with what engagement is really about. As we have already pointed out, it is a product and a symptom of a relationship between employees and employers. Each party has different needs and engagement tends to be at its most powerful when both employers' and employees' needs are met.

An exchange relationship

In Chapter 2 we discussed the reciprocal nature of the employment relationship. But what do employees want from this relationship? In many cases, the expectations of employees from their work fall into the following categories identified by Khan (1990 , p. 692):

- **Intellectual** – am I able to grow; is my job stretching and interesting; do I have space; do I know what's happening; do my opinions count?
- **Emotional/affective** – do I care about the organization and its stakeholders and share its values; do I enjoy my work; am I cared for and valued?
- **Social** – is this an organization where I feel I belong, part of a good team; is my organization serving the community?

These, to us, are central, since if people are able to satisfy these needs, engagement becomes more possible. As we already saw in the 'meaning' study (see Chapter 2), employees of all ages and from many organization types said that they wanted interesting and varied work, the chance to achieve something worthwhile, to learn and experience personal growth, and to have the opportunity for career progression. People also wanted good communication, to feel involved but also have a degree of autonomy and control over their own work, and the freedom to balance work with other aspects of their lives.

For many people, their experience of meaning appears linked to their sense of identity and their ability to fulfil their goal of self-actualization through work. Where work offers people the opportunity to pursue this goal, and where people can identify with their organization and what it is trying to do, they are likely to be highly engaged. So these three categories – intellectual, affective and social – reflect an employee's rational and emotional needs for growth, inclusion, to be valued and treated as an adult, to feel part of something useful, and sufficiently motivated by the purpose their work serves to want to 'go the extra mile'.

But there are a number of moderating factors that can determine whether engagement is possible – or just mere aspiration. One is that of **fairness**. The Institute for Employment Studies (Robinson et al., 2004) argues that, first of all, a 'fair deal' must exist at work. If people feel treated fairly, they are ready to be engaged; if not, they are more likely to nurse their grievances than give of their best. Different factors can determine whether a 'fair deal' is perceived to exist, and whether an employee engages with their job, their organization, or both. Saks (2006) found that enriching and challenging jobs were a good predictor of how engaged someone was likely to be with their job. Fairness in the allocation of resources, in contrast, predicted how engaged someone would be with their organization.

The other key moderating factor is that of **trust**. When this exists between one person and another, a greater sense of security is created and so more openness to each other. Without trust, a sense of unpredictability exists, leading to anxiety and psychological withdrawal. So in a work context, when employees trust their employer, they will feel secure in their work relationship, avoiding the need to wonder if the employer will honour their word. They will be more ready to accept fresh demands from their employer (e.g. to perform additional tasks) and – given that trust is based on reciprocation – they will be confident that the eventual outcome will be as expected (e.g. that there will not be hidden extra tasks added later). Their employer will become more ready to entrust them with new tasks and so enhance their job. Over time, openness can increase, so creating a deeper-rooted relationship where employees will look out for their employer's interests and not just their own. Conversely, without trust, employees are much more likely to become disengaged, suspicious of their boss's intentions and look elsewhere for leadership.

Drivers of fairness

When it comes to fairness, the key principle is that of **equity**. This principle is crucial to employee engagement – the perception by employees that they are being treated fairly and justly. This is also the principle most at risk of being compromised in the current business climate, either because of conscious or unconscious discrimination at work, or when urgent business pressures cause corners to be cut in terms of reasonable treatment. Especially when tough decisions are being made – for instance about redundancies – people need to know that the process is fair.

Rewards are a real test-bed of the equity principle. A well-intended pay rise can lose all motivational effect if its value is not seen as reasonable compared to other colleagues', or is less than that offered by competing employers. Ironically, although organizations often place a heavy emphasis on external rewards, it seems that financial or material incentives (once they have reached an adequate level) do not play a significant role in increasing engagement. Indeed, Herzberg's (1987) research suggests that these may actually undermine it. For Herzberg, sufficient rewards are a 'hygiene' factor rather than a motivator, while insufficient rewards that are inherently unfair can become a source of active dissatisfaction. Khan (1990) argues that direct, specific monetary rewards actually reduce people's motivation to do creative work, while Pink (2009) proposes that heaping further rewards on someone does not proportionately raise commitment levels, and often undermines performance. More effective reward and recognition approaches take employee preferences into account – and, as a result, employees know they are appreciated. This can be as basic as managers and leaders remembering to say 'thank you' and 'well done'.

'Fair-proofing'
How then can the equity principle be applied in practice? Company HR practices and leader behaviour teach people what is really valued, for instance by what is condoned, who gets promoted or how senior managers are rewarded. Any 'say-do' gap between espoused company rhetoric and reality creates distrust and cynicism. In organizations that practise values-based leadership, values and behaviours are aligned, creating integrity and trust. Transparency is crucial to the building and maintenance of trust.

Equity is also about broader perceptions of fairness. For instance, when employees are enduring pay freezes or pay cuts, awarding bonuses to executives seems inappropriate. More generally, when leaders and staff interact socially, barriers can be broken down and more open communication can develop. This does not mean that CEOs and executives must spend all their time blogging or developing 'folksy' messages that convey a false familiarity; instead, it's about being genuinely accessible and open to hearing what people have to say.

Will Hutton (2010a), Principal of Hertford College, Oxford, argues that executives must lead the way in 'fair-proofing' their organization to ensure that it is fair to its own internal stakeholders (its employees). This involves going beyond current conventional 'best practice' with respect to leadership. So rather than simply appointing a strong board who are prepared to hold management to account for the achievement of declared business purpose, fair-proofing an organization involves also establishing a common understanding of fairness, i.e. due reward for 'discretionary effort'. Instead of simply exploiting every communication vehicle to impart the business purpose 'top-down' to staff and then encouraging feedback, fair-proofing involves paying equal attention to fairness and respecting 'the deal' from employees' experience and perspective. Instead of just applying the best reward practice, for instance, ensuring pay and promotion is earned through effort or result directly linked to business purpose, fair-proofing also involves establishing an equality of sacrifice, with no exemptions, and balancing short-term benefit forfeit with long-term benefit gain.

One consequence of fair-proofing, Hutton argues, is that there is a much stronger sense of shared purpose and more mutual risk/reward.

Employee voice

There is a strong association between equity and employees having a voice – being informed, being able to express their opinions to their managers and be heard – and engagement. The voice principle is most actively demonstrated in corporate communications and in high levels of employee involvement, participation and consultation. Employee voice is singled out in the MacLeod Report (MacLeod and Clarke, 2009, p. 33) as one of the top four engagement drivers (the other three are 'engaging leadership', 'engaging managers' and 'organization lives the values'). This occurs when 'employees feel able to voice their ideas and be listened to, both about how to do their job and in decision-making in their own department, with joint sharing of problems and challenges and a commitment to arrive at joint solutions'.

In recent times, the changing nature of communication, especially the role of social media, has heightened employees' expectations about how their organization should relate to them as individuals. Thanks to the communication immediacy of Twitter, Facebook and so on, people are now used to exchanging information and having their opinions heard continuously. Conventional top-down communication is no longer sufficient if real dialogue is required. This is an increasing issue – not only are younger people looking for more chances to have a say, but as the average educational level of workforces around the world increases, so employees are less ready to go along with a 'command and control' environment that does not tap into their ideas and contributions.

Consequently there is push from employees about changing the nature of organizational communication. Top managers need to create a culture where communications are credible, open and consistent, and where senior managers are more visible. A good example is the **Royal Bank of Canada (RBC)**, which restructured in 2004 (Moorcroft, 2006). Formerly, RBC's communication strategies focused on *informing* employees and creating awareness. The new strategy focused on *engaging* employees (and thus generating desired behaviours) that helped to create outcomes (measurable effects) that supported the organization's objectives. By helping employees have a better idea of how what they did impacted the organization, and by promoting behaviours that helped achieve organizational objectives, RBC started to reap the benefits through a highly engaged workforce, and is now regularly recognized externally as one of Canada's best employers.

> In companies with good communication, there is a constant flow of ideas up, down and across the organization.

In companies with good communication, there is a constant flow of ideas up, down and across the organization. In such contexts people are much more likely to be open to new ways of doing things. This requires managers who are not afraid of relinquishing control and who are willing to listen to people – but that interest and dialogue must be genuine. When people feel valued, well-informed, involved and fairly treated, they are more likely to be engaged and become more effective. That's why we're arguing that operating according to the principles of voice and equity is crucial to employee trust and likely to lead to employee engagement and performance.

So these principles of voice and equity appear to be central elements of engagement. People can love their jobs and enjoy working with their colleagues, but still become disengaged if they feel unfairly treated or that their views are ignored. In the current context, these key engagement drivers and principles are likely to be widely flouted. In a resulting low-trust, risk-averse work climate, innovation is a likely casualty: politics and fear will add significantly to the cost of doing business.

The importance of trust

Fairness, as we have seen, is therefore a key precondition for engagement. But another crucial requirement is trust. Trust is the primary defining characteristic of the very best workplaces (Great Places to Work Institute, 2010), yet trust in leaders appears low across the board, according to the CIPD's Employee Outlook survey findings (CIPD Research, 2011a). Only around one-third (34 per cent) of employees agree that they trust their senior management teams and 38 per cent disagree. Nearly half (47 per cent) of employees who strongly distrust their senior management are currently looking for a new job, compared to just 8 per cent of workers who strongly trust their leaders.

Cruise O'Brien (2001, p. 31) summarizes US research on trust as follows:

- People seem willing to award trust on the basis of fair treatment, respect and recognition for the contribution they make.
- People at the bottom of the organization are found to be continuous and careful 'intuitive auditors' in a process of assessment of those in authority.
- Deference to authority had been found to be based more on trust than on competence. People respond positively to even small acts of recognition like a 'job well done'.
- The durability of trust is based on integrity and consistency, which over time build on the basis of reputation.
- While the development of trust builds incrementally, distrust is much more catastrophic. Once trust is compromised, the effort to rebuild it is considerable.

Trust-building involves not only keeping promises, but also keeping appropriate boundaries and being sensitive to social and cultural cues. Trustworthy leaders are fair, for instance avoiding 'job creep' – which results in engaged employees who show discretionary effort ending up having to endlessly do more and more (Macey and Schneider, 2008). And when it comes to breaking bad news, trustworthy leaders are straightforward and honest while still retaining business focus; they demonstrate sensitivity and empathy.

> Trust-building involves not only keeping promises, but also keeping appropriate boundaries and being sensitive to social and cultural cues.

However, 'blind' or 'over'-trust on the part of employees can also be damaging. When employees trust other people without questioning – particularly when the relationship involves important matters – they are effectively abdicating personal judgement and responsibility. Since leaders (however well-intentioned) are human too, they can make mistakes – and so employees should retain a healthy scepticism even in a trusting relationship. A feature of a good, trustful relationship is that it is open, there is acknowledgement of mistakes, and mutual respect that allows decisions to be challenged. Andrew Lycett, CEO of RCT Homes (which features in a case study in Chapter 8) suggests that the real test as a leader is to be open with people when you make a mistake:

> *Recognize and apologize – make sure that people are encouraged to follow you by recognizing their effort and contribution and success. If your consistency does drop, get yourself back on track by admitting it.*

So good business ethics is not about avoiding mistakes but about dealing with problems, if they arise, in an ethical and transparent way.

Bridging the engagement gap through active partnership with employees

While organizations have the primary responsibility for creating engaging environments, employees too have their part to play. Though they're far from passive consumers of HR or management brands, much organizational effort appears to be based on the belief that employees are not responsible adults and that they need to be 'managed' into engagement and performance. We disagree with this view and concur with a new view of 'organizational effectiveness' (OE) (Francis et al., 2012) that highlights the importance of adult-adult employment relationships characterized by voice and equity. Instead of 'aligning' people to organizations by shaping them to organizational requirements – while simultaneously treating them as expendable resources – 'New OE' focuses on building trust, enablement and empowerment, with the employee 'deal' tailored as much as possible to the needs of individuals.

New OE recognizes that people want autonomy and can produce outstanding outcomes, given the right context. This calls for a potentially radically different mindset for employers and employees: one built on involvement, authenticity and mutuality. This can be seen, for instance, at **Unilever**, where the follow-up activity after an employee engagement survey is decided on by employees themselves. They make sense of the findings, identify the targets for improvement and devise the projects to deliver these improvements. Given that these projects are then resourced and delivered, employees are in no doubt about whether their views have been taken seriously by management.

So this is not just about leadership at the top. In contexts where speed and agility are required, leadership must become more distributed, with people at all levels taking resopnsibility for proactively making things happen. Co-creation requires that power is more widely distributed within organizations. This requires a new way of thinking for all concerned: the organization becomes a community of individuals looking to co-create, not a collection of human resources waiting to deliver.

Mutuality

At its core, New OE reflects a powerful ethic of mutuality. In a more active and collaborative partnership with employees, each party will demand more from the other, and the benefits and risks of the employment relationship will be more genuinely shared. Co-creation means involving people as human beings in the activities of the organization. This requires authentic and meaningful forms of participation, and greater transparency of process.

For instance, the success of **Google** has led to a minute examination of its working environment and company culture. Yet beyond the headline-grabbing tales of benefits such as games rooms and free food, a key to its success is its ability to leverage the involvement of its employees. Despite its meteoric growth, it strives to keep a small-company, unconventional culture that attracts people who are passionate about their work, enjoy working in dynamic small teams and want to push the limits of what information technology can do. As a result, everyone's ideas and inputs are welcome and valued, and anyone is free to ask questions directly to their top leadership at all-employee meetings.

We argue that pressure for such forms of participation is likely to grow. Social media and new technologies are subverting hierarchy, as well as changing people's expectations and the way they work and learn. People know what's possible and don't want to settle for less. They expect to be well-informed, to be consulted on changes that affect them, and to have fair access to development and promotion opportunities. Such a democratic form of partnership may represent a serious challenge to existing leadership and management practices and power bases. The implications for leadership styles are clear, as Peter Cheese (2011) points out:

> Instead of CEOs following old models of command and control, it's about empowerment, getting the best out of the team. It's not the big I am, the big ego CEO.

Yet the end justifies the means, since the outcomes will be more from less, innovation *and* also a more sustainable business practice.

Towards an integrated model of employee engagement

That's why the quality of work and working lives matters. And that's why the quality of the working environment, of management and of the nature of the 'deal' for employees are all pivotal to the maintenance of trust and mutual respect between employee and employer. Even if the rules of the game derive from the market place, human beings still thrive best in situations where market demands are counter-balanced by consideration for people.

While there are many different drivers of engagement, we would contend that these mostly fall into four areas of dynamic interconnection between individuals and organizations as follows:

- **Connection** – how strongly employees feel a sense of belonging with their organization, both in terms of sharing the same beliefs or values and in their readiness to follow the direction the organization is heading.
- **Support** – the practical help, guidance and other resources provided to help people do a great job. In particular how managers support employees in good times and bad.
- **Voice** – the extent to which people are informed, involved and able to contribute to shaping their work context.
- **Scope** – the degree of opportunity employees have to meet their own needs, to have control over their work and to play to their strengths. At its best, this reflects the two-way nature of an adult-adult employment relationship.

This is important, since (as described in Chapter 4) measurements of employee engagement frequently define many different drivers, and the problem for managers is how to make sense of them, or to know where to begin if they want to encourage higher engagement levels in their organization. As demonstrated in Annex 1, the above four points capture most of the drivers otherwise identified in engagement surveys and have the benefits of being easy to remember and enabling managers to judge quickly where they might need to take action in real time. This model is detailed further in Figure 3.1; at its heart is engagement and the two preconditions we have seen of fairness and trust. We will refer to this model repeatedly in this book as a way of exploring the main drivers of engagement, and the sorts of actions managers can take in response.

Another way of viewing the model is to think of a plant. In many respects, these four elements can be likened to how a plant is encouraged to grow. Connection is like the sun above, that the plant will strive to reach. Support is like the earth and nutrients that help foster growth. Voice is similar to cross-pollination and Scope is the provision of space in which to grow in the first place. All four elements of the above model are essential. Without Connection, an employee will lack direction and identification with the organization;

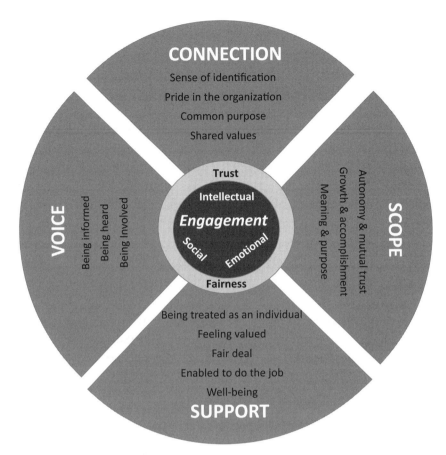

Figure 3.1 Employee engagement model. Source: Holbeche, L.S. & Matthews, G.P.

without Support, efforts may be discouraged, go off at a tangent or run out of steam. Without Voice, an employee may feel disregarded and excluded or – for lack of knowledge – waste time in duplicate effort; and without Scope, they may feel disempowered or unable to fulfill their potential. So let's now look in more detail at some of these 'core' aspects of engagement from the employer perspective.

1. Connection

We all know what it feels like to have a strong sense of connection, whether at school or college, or through belonging to a sports team, club or church.

Usually what makes it special is a sense of being with like-minded people, with the same goals and attitudes, and a shared commitment to achieve them. Work is no different, and the IES (Robinson et al., 2004) argues that if engagement is to occur, the employee needs to:

- identify with the organization and its values, and believe in its products and services
- understand the context in which the organization operates.

This is why a strong **sense of identification** is essential. Individuals who feel they belong and know how their efforts contribute to the success of the organization as a whole – regardless of seniority or sector – tend to be engaged and motivated, and feel pride in the organization. But as well as the 'what', there's the 'why' – employees need to know and care about what the organization is aiming to do. This is the power of a clear **vision**. Research on employee engagement found two common features in organizations with high performance: people knowing what to do and wanting to do the work (Sibson, 2006). Helping employees see how their job connects with the organization's strategy is the number one engagement driver identified by the Corporate Leadership Council. Robinson et al. (2004) argue that:

> An engaged employee is aware of business context, and works with colleagues to improve performance within the job for the benefit of the organization. The organization must work to develop and nurture engagement, which requires a two-way relationship between employer and employee.

Organizations with high engagement, high trust cultures tend to have a clear mission, vision and values, all of which are communicated to employees from the start of their employment and often before. Many key drivers of engagement are influenced directly or indirectly by corporate leaders. Clarity of business strategy, quality of top-level leadership and speed of decision-making can have a big impact. The MacLeod Report (MacLeod and Clarke, 2009, p. 75) concurs, arguing that one of the four main drivers of employee engagement is leadership, which:

... provides a strong strategic narrative which has widespread ownership and commitment from managers and employees at all levels. The narrative is a clearly expressed story about what the purpose of an organization is, why it has the broad vision it has, and how an individual contributes to that purpose. Employees have a clear line of sight between their job and the narrative, and understand where their work fits in. These aims and values are reflected in a strong, transparent and explicit organizational culture and way of working.

This 'line of sight' issue is reflected in many of the available survey instruments. **Standard Chartered**, an international bank focused on Asia, Africa and the Middle East, has carried out research on employee engagement among its 85,000 employees of 125 nationalities. The research shows that clarity on mission, as well as on organizational outcomes at team and individual level, are two critical variables for success. It also shows that the single biggest driver of engagement is the style of leadership employed by the boss (Cormack, 2011).

Kenexa found that the top of the four 'global macro drivers' of engagement detected through their surveys is 'leaders who inspire confidence in the future' (Wiley et al., 2010). Engaging leaders are strategic, anticipatory, proactive and people-focused, and can engage employees around a **common purpose** − which answers the 'why' question, or the reason for an organization's existence. Companies that combine and integrate market responsiveness, shareholder value maximization, innovation, employee engagement and stakeholder involvement around a clear business purpose significantly outperform those who do not, according to research by The Work Foundation (Bevan et al., 2005). Buytendijk (2006) also found that high-performing organizations have a strong sense of purpose internally and with external stakeholders. Springett's (2009) analysis of CIPD survey data also indicates that a strong sense of shared purpose leads to high levels of employee engagement.

Conversely, low levels of shared purpose indicate a fragmentation of efforts and, typically, little sense of strategic direction. Without a clear line of sight to purpose in people's day jobs, the motivational effect is unlikely to be achieved. Bureaucracy, inconsistent behaviours, policies and practices act as barriers and lead to employee cynicism and disengagement.

In Chapter 2, we saw the growing call for a more balanced view of what business is for: not only short-term maximization of profits, but also addressing wider stakeholder needs. To respond to this, corporate purposes need to bear in mind not only shareholders but also customers, employees and society as a whole, balancing the needs of all stakeholders (Basu, 1999). All decisions, including strategy, should flow from this purpose. Interestingly, though, research suggests that **customer purpose** may have a differentiating effect on levels of engagement. In 2002, Richard Ellsworth published data indicating that companies with strong customer purpose were significantly more profitable over a ten-year period than companies focused on maximizing shareholder value, or those trying to balance the needs of all their stakeholders (Ellsworth, 2002). The 'meaning' study (Holbeche and Springett, 2005) also found that customer purpose was the most engaging; it led to a strong sense of shared purpose among employees and a clear strategic focus, and unleashed creative capability inside organizations. Customer purpose also appears linked to a sense of collaborative community.

> Most people want to have a purpose beyond making money, even in challenging times: this is evidenced by the high commitment levels found by those working for charitable organizations, even in the most challenging environments of disaster relief or widespread disease.

More recently, employee survey data suggests there is increasing interest in purposes that are about creating a better world – for customers, stakeholders or society as a whole – and which seem to elicit the strongest shared sense of purpose (unpublished research by Springett, 2009). In other words, most people want to have a purpose beyond making money, even in challenging times: this is evidenced by the high commitment levels found by those working for charitable organizations, even in the toughest environments of disaster relief or widespread disease.

A key leadership task is to **design organizations** that provide people with line of sight to purpose (and customer), and increase the possibility of 'empowerment' – i.e. employees feeling willing and able to use their initiative to benefit the organization and its customers. In general terms, this involves flatter structures, broader roles, effective communication and information systems, appropriate (supportive) management styles, and continuous development. When decision-making is appropriate (i.e. at the lowest level possible commensurate with the nature of the decision to be taken) and when employees have the authority, tools, resources, skills and information they need to do the job, they are more likely to be proactive, responsible and accountable for their actions.

Leaders at all levels, but especially at the top of organizations, therefore have a key role to play in building cultures conducive to employee engagement. If senior management is to inspire engagement among employees and motivate them to go the extra mile, they must not only communicate a clear vision of the future but also:

- build trust in the organization
- involve employees in decision-making that will affect them
- demonstrate commitment to the organization's values
- tell stories that show people what is valued and why
- be seen to respond to feedback
- demonstrate genuine commitment to employee well-being (Melcrum Publishing, 2005).

At its most basic, this is about treating people as people, not commodities or costs.

It turns out that some leadership styles may be more conducive to this than others. Daniel Goleman and colleagues talk about the importance of 'resonant' leaders who, because of their emotional intelligence, can create an emotional bond with people in their organizations 'that help them stay focused even amid profound change and uncertainty' (Goleman et al., 2002, p. 21). In a content study of the impact of leadership style on employee engagement, Daniel Goleman (2005) and the Hay Group considered a range of six leadership styles defined by them and widely used in client organizations.

They found that four of the six styles – visionary (set vision and outcomes), coaching (develop the next generation), affiliative (people first) and democratic/participative (let's decide together) – create the kind of resonance that boosts engagement and performance.

The effect is that employees are clear about what's expected of them and what success looks like. When people can see how their efforts contribute to the success of the organization as a whole, they tend to be highly engaged. In contrast, the Directive (give directions, demand compliance) and Pacesetting (do as I do: keep up) styles of leadership correlate negatively with engagement across a large number of workplace environments. 'Command and control' management styles are therefore thought to be largely incompatible with staff engagement.

Of course, there is always a danger of stereotyping idealized leaders, and we don't believe such people exist. However, in this post-heroic age, we think there are many clues to be had – from the wealth of studies of engagement and from contemporary leadership theory – about how some managers are able to successfully engage other people. Forms and styles of leadership are variously described as 'moral', 'grown-up', 'differentiated' and 'prosocial' (Lorenzi, 2004). Goffee and Jones (2005), among others, argue that leadership demands the expression of an authentic self – people want to be led by someone real. People associate authenticity with sincerity, honesty and integrity. The authentic leader has confidence, hope, optimism and resilience, and also a moral/ethical, transparency orientation (Norman et al., 2005). Leaders are expected to 'walk the talk' and act as role models to others on values. Collins (2001) describes the defining characteristic of 'Level 5' leaders who help their organizations reach beyond 'good' to become 'great' as **humility**.

And in these more fluid times, there is a growing emphasis on developing collaborative communities of leaders at all levels – so-called distributed leadership. As we move away from these conventional leadership notions of control and the need for certainty, we will need to replace them by creating a sense of community and shared ownership that can enable leaders at all levels to emerge.

Shared values allow employees to feel a congruence between how they interact with the world and how other people do in the same organization. We've already seen the roles of fairness and trust as preconditions for engagement, and it is not surprising that '**Organization lives the values**' is another of the four main engagement drivers highlighted in the MacLeod Report (MacLeod and Clarke, 2009, p. 33):

A belief among employees that the organization lives the values, and that espoused behavioural norms are adhered to, resulting in trust and a sense of integrity.

The importance of this congruence between word and deed is echoed in the 'meaning' study. When we asked people what they felt would increase their sense of meaning at work, their responses included:

- developing leaders to have a more 'human' (not just 'business') focus
- corporate social responsibility practice
- closer alignment between organizational values and practice
- *really* focusing on customers
- work-life balance initiatives
- greater emphasis on teamwork and community.

The role of leaders as values role models seems particularly important. People want to work for ethical organizations and to see their leaders 'walking the talk' on values. They want to work with leaders and managers of integrity who set high standards, both personal and organizational, and who also provide the organizational support that employees need in order to be successful. They want to work for organizations they can be proud of, and can thus recommend to others.

Being ethical, showing integrity and treating employees with respect and fairness, is crucial to engagement. But it also pays to be ethical – ask any of the corporate leaders whose corporate and personal reputations have been tarnished recently! As we have already seen, the banking crisis and other scandals have resulted in generally lower levels of public trust in institutions, politicians and business leaders, leading to growing demands for better governance and stronger regulation. Ethical leadership has to start at the top, since the CEO and executives set the parameters for other people's behaviour. Trust in executives can have more than twice the impact on engagement levels than trust in immediate managers (BlessingWhite Research, 2011).

Not only are organizations increasingly held to account for their ethical business practices and values of their partners or suppliers, but also for their own **environmental and social stewardship**. Many organizations are attempting to demonstrate their values by embracing a commitment to philanthropy, volunteerism, corporate social responsibility (CSR) and environmental and social stewardship. There's a danger of tokenism, of course, and being ethical must be more than a PR exercise. It's important that employees have some choice about if, and how, they participate in such initiatives. But if such schemes are genuine and consistently delivered, they can enhance communities, build employee pride in their organization and make the world a better place.

> Many organizations are attempting to demonstrate their values by embracing a commitment to philanthropy, volunteerism, corporate social responsibility (CSR) and environmental and social stewardship.

Environmental and social stewardship – including a commitment to philanthropy and volunteerism – brings many tangible and intangible benefits. For instance, there is growing evidence that companies that really practise CSR enjoy higher profitability than their peers. UK retailer **Marks & Spencer** is leading the way in its sector on environmental stewardship with its famous 'Plan A' (so-called because there is no 'Plan B'), of which one goal is to make all its stores carbon-neutral in the near future. And as Tanith Dodge, HR Director of Marks & Spencer points out, her company's proactive approach to employee engagement – including factors such as employees' 'passion' for the M&S brand, their pride in working for an organization that is committed to sustainability, and their sense that the company cares about their well-being – is paying off in terms of improved business results, even when trading conditions are as tough as they are right now (Arkin, 2011).

So such real commitment not only helps communities but also enhances employer brands. It not only avoids visits from the Fraud Office, it also brings in talent. This is especially true for organizations seeking to recruit Generation Y and 'Next Generation' employees, who are likely to judge potential employers on their ethical and environmental credentials. Employers such as **PricewaterhouseCoopers** assign managers to projects working with aid agencies and charities to provide both sharp-end leadership training and also increase employee loyalty through feeling that they are working for a socially responsible employer. Above all, such commitment engages employees. 'Organization's reputation for social responsibility' is the third out of 75 drivers of engagement in the Towers Watson survey (2010b).

2. Voice

The next quadrant of the model picks up the principle of **Voice**. Most people have experienced what it's like where involvement doesn't exist, feeling left in the dark or ignored, and the refreshing difference when they are kept 'in the know' and are asked for their opinion. The starting point for this, then, is communication and sharing information. To quote Jan Carlzon, the former CEO of the Scandinavian airline SAS and who revolutionized its customer service: 'An individual without information can't take responsibility. An individual with information can't help but take responsibility.'

The IES research by Robinson et al. (2004) among 10,000 UK National Health Service (NHS) employees showed that 'opportunities for upward feedback' and 'feeling well-informed about what's happening in the organization' are key drivers of employee engagement. Moreover, the authors suggested that many of the drivers of engagement (and their resulting model – see Figure 3.2) are common to all organizations, regardless of sector.

Feeling **valued and involved** is central to the Robinson et al. (2004) model. Within this 'umbrella' a range of elements have a varying influence on the

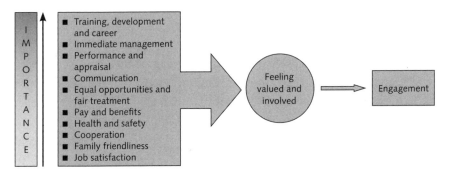

Figure 3.2 IES model of the drivers of employee engagement. Source: Robinson et al., 2004. Reproduced by kind permission of IES

extent to which employees will feel valued, involved and hence engaged. Some of these are what would be considered fundamental or contractual requirements of employment (the 'hygiene' factors), such as pay and benefits and health and safety. Others are areas where the organization must 'go the extra mile' to ensure employees feel valued and involved, such as effective communication, management and cooperation. Such consultation and participation in decision-making are especially important in times of change. Likewise, the MacLeod Report (MacLeod and Clarke, 2009) concludes that the main components of engagement are involvement in decision-making, freedom to voice ideas (that managers listen to), feeling enabled to perform well, having opportunities to develop in the job and feeling the organization is concerned for employees' health and wellbeing.

Similarly, the CIPD/Kingston Business School study found that line manager positives that impacted on engagement included 'treats me fairly', 'is supportive', 'listens to my suggestions' and 'makes clear what is expected of me' (Truss et al., 2006). In this study, the main drivers of employee engagement were having the opportunity to feed your views upwards, feeling well-informed about what was happening in the organization and thinking that your manager is committed to the organization.

We have already seen that trust is a precondition for engagement, and clearly this, combined with openness, is essential for engagement. It was W. Edwards Deming, the American expert who played such a key role in teaching the Japanese about quality, who encouraged them to see their businesses as systems, not hierarchies, built on what he called 'profound knowledge' harnessing the involvement of all workers. To foster this, he set out 14 principles for business effectiveness, the eighth principle being 'Drive out fear, so that everyone may work effectively for the company'. In doing so, he was getting organizations to involve their employees and so demonstrate **openness to new ideas**. 'Organization encourages innovative thinking' is in the top ten engagement drivers out of 75 in the Towers Watson (2010b) survey.

Increased transparency about the business fosters a sense of trust and allows employee involvement to draw on the ideas and experience of staff. To take one example, in one medium-sized catering company, the entire workforce was involved in the business planning process. There were presentations from the Board – who were open and honest about business results, what *managing change*

the strategic objectives were and how people could contribute to these. It was an interactive session, with staff contributing to the development of specific objectives and ideas about how these would be achieved. Staff were encouraged to be creative and come up with new ideas within a team environment. By treating staff like adults, management gained employee commitment and 'buy-in'. And though the business context is still challenging, business results for this company are improving and many of the successful new products have been originated by employees.

meaningful

> Consultation and participation in decision-making are especially important in times of change.

A precondition for Voice is to accept differences of experience, outlook and approach. These include visible and non-visible factors – for example, personal characteristics such as age, background, culture, gender, sexual orientation, disability, personality, working style, size, accent, language and so on. A 'one-size-fits all' approach to managing people therefore doesn't work, and acceptance of different personal needs, values and beliefs is essential. This is what **diversity** is about. CIPD defines managing diversity as valuing everyone as an individual – as employees, customers and clients (CIPD, 2011b). Employers are increasingly recognizing the importance of diversity in recruiting and retaining the skills and talent they need and the value of designing appropriate and fair people propositions in order to meet specific employee requirements. It's no longer a question of compliance but of meeting business needs by widening potential labour pools, leveraging the creative effect of mixing different views and ideas, and having a workforce that better mirrors society as a whole and so is better accepted externally, and has better insight into customer needs. Managing for diversity, then, helps organizations to:

- make sure their people policies and working practices are bias-free and fit well with business excellence models and initiatives
- create working environments in which people from all backgrounds can work together harmoniously by combating prejudice, checking stereotyping and stopping bullying, harassment, and undignified and disrespectful behaviour

- bring about cultural change
- have a workforce that is more creative and innovative.

Engaging managers **build teams** and encourage **team working**, as we shall explore in Chapter 9. If people are to see benefits in collaboration, there has to be both a shared platform of trust and also the opportunity for employees to develop valuable new skills through the team process. Individuals must be committed to the team, with a real desire to achieve team goals. This means that team members must be willing to share success and failure with the rest of the team. Accepting their share of responsibility for both means that team members must also be prepared to confront others who fail to deliver, or who blame others for things for which they are accountable.

Team members must be willing to help each other, but they should also be willing to learn from others and explore new areas outside their own environment. It is important that members understand the broader business context that their work is being conducted in and appreciate the different elements of the activities being carried out by others. This entails having a sense of other team members' priorities and requirements to ensure that work can proceed smoothly, without people making unnecessary demands on others through ignorance. They therefore have to be able to liaise across boundaries within their team and between the team and the rest of the organization, including their boss.

The team leader's role is both internal and external to the team. They must:

- act as coach and mentor to team members
- have excellent interpersonal skills, not just for communicating with the team but also for helping team members communicate effectively with each other
- be responsible for communicating the team's successes to the wider organization and building up a strong profile for the team throughout the business
- be visible, both to the team itself and within the organization as a whole.

3. Support

The third quadrant of our model – **Support** – highlights the vital role of line managers in enabling employee engagement. We can all recall bosses who encouraged us and challenged us to get out of our comfort zone, and who gave us a break to do something new and enriching. The encouraging word, the pat on the back and the concern for our needs are what helped to make us feel valued and important. The legendary co-founder of HP, Dave Packard (1995), recalled that:

> From the beginning, Bill Hewlett and I have had a strong belief in people. We believe that people want to do a good job and that it is important for them to enjoy their work at Hewlett-Packard. We try to make it possible for employees to feel a real sense of accomplishment in their work. Closely coupled with this is our strong belief that individuals need to be treated with consideration and respect. It has always been important to Bill and me to create an environment in which people had the chance to be their best, to realize their potential and to be recognized for their achievements.

This focus on 'creating the environment' and encouraging others is the essence of Support – and has been reflected not only in practices like the 'HP Way' but in the culture of companies across Silicon Valley and beyond.

While many factors can affect engagement, for most employees, the relationship with their line managers is the acid test of how they feel about the organisation, and how commited and willing they are to release discretionary effort. Whether they are first-level supervisors, front-line managers or senior leaders, **engaging managers and supervisors** are therefore central to the employee engagement challenge. If the relationship works well, employees reciprocate in two ways – through job engagement and organizational engagement. If that support is lacking, the psychological bonds loosen and employees may become disengaged. We've examined many studies of employee engagement carried out by academic institutions, commercial research bodies and management consultancies/survey providers. These highlight the impact of managers on engagement, for example:

- In the MacLeod Report, poor management is seen to lead directly to a disengaged organizational culture, with attitudes of senior managers in particular acting as barriers to engagement.
- The Work Foundation (2010) found that, for many employees, their line manager *is* their employer.

Internal company surveys such as UK retailer Marks & Spencer's own engagement data attest to the relative importance of line managers in driving engagement on a day-to-day basis:

- My manager and team work: 56 per cent
- Working conditions and job clarity: 31 per cent
- Communication: 13 per cent.

Managers play a key role in 'creating the environment'. This means propagating a positive climate and tackling the demotivating factors. Managers need to understand what makes people tick and, on a personal level, must build and maintain relationships of trust. Engaging managers facilitate and empower their staff rather than restrict them. According to the MacLeod Report (MacLeod and Clarke, 2009, p. 81):

> ... engaging managers offer clarity for what is expected from individual members of staff, which involves some stretch, and much appreciation and feedback/ coaching and training. The second key area is treating their people as individuals, with fairness and respect and with a concern for the employee's well-being. Thirdly, managers have a very important role in ensuring that work is designed efficiently and effectively.

Social support from line managers, whether informal or formal, is important. In companies that do this well, managers **treat people as individuals**, as full human beings. As Maslach et al. (2001) point out, support from managers can make the vital difference between employee engagement and burnout. At Standard Chartered Retail Bank, the task of managers in engaging employees is summarized as 'Know me, focus me, value me'. Engaging managers **show empathy and concern**, understand each individual's talents, interests and needs, and then match those with the organization's objectives – while at the same time creating personal, trusting relationships. Engaging managers enable employees to do the job: they provide tools and resources, feedback and coaching, and access to learning and development. They also recognize people's progress and achievements, and ensure that employees are appropriately rewarded and receive a fair deal.

A narrow focus on employee engagement without paying equal, or more, attention to the **wellbeing of employees** can lead to problems, such as sickness absence, according to Robertson and Cooper (2011). Research by Flade (2003) found that actively disengaged employees miss more than six days' work a year, while engaged employees miss fewer than three. Maslach et al. (2001) argue that workload, control, reward and recognition, fairness, shared values, and support are six key areas of work that drive both engagement – and burnout. Engagement consists of energy, involvement and efficacy, which turn into exhaustion, cynicism and ineffectiveness during burnout. Towers Watson (2010b) defines wellbeing as three interconnected elements of a person's work life:

- physical health – overall health, energy/stamina
- psychological health – stress/anxiety, intrinsic satisfaction, accomplishment, optimism, confidence, control, empowerment, safety
- social health – work relationships, balance in work and personal life, equity, fairness, respect, social connectedness.

Wellbeing is therefore a complex **health and safety** issue. But this is not simply a task for front-line supervisors; organizational care and concern for employee wellbeing is a key engagement factor in many studies. For instance, senior management's sincere interest in employee wellbeing is the number one engagement driver in the Towers Watson study, so it has to be authentically lived at all levels of the business. Similarly, a cross-sector survey by Towers Watson (2000) identified absence of workplace stress as one of the seven key factors affecting employee commitment. Another study, by Quantum Workplace (2011), identified that one of the five key senior management factors that set organizations with higher engagement scores apart from others is the provision of employee benefits that demonstrate a strong commitment to employee wellbeing.

But above all, managers are likely to have the most direct effect on the work-life balance of employees. Managers cannot force an employee to work longer hours, but the environment they create will affect employee stress levels and the extent to which employees are happy about being at work, rather

than spending time worrying
or feeling negative about work
when they are at home. Both
support from supervisors and
control in the form of day-to-

> Above all, managers are likely to
> have the most direct effect on the
> work-life balance of employees.

day employee control over workloads, and involvement in decision-making,
have been found to be positively related to employee engagement (Hakanen
et al., 2006).

4. Scope

In many respects, Support readily leads into the final quadrant of our model,
Scope. If Support is about 'creating the environment', Scope is about filling
it. Unlike many other studies, we argue that engagement is a shared responsibility between the individual employee and the employer. Ours is not a
paternalistic model; instead it proposes that really engaged employees work
within adult-adult relationships, in which risks, responsibilities and benefits
are mutual. Scope, then, is about providing the space where individuals can be
proactive, give of their best, take responsibility for making things happen and
be willing to change when necessary.

We also believe that when people have Scope they are more likely to build
new skills and capabilities that will enhance their employability, something
increasingly needed in today's uncertain world. Just how important this is to
employees is reflected in the Towers Watson (2010b) global employee engagement survey. The following were in the top ten of 75 engagement drivers:

- Improved my skills over last year (no. 2)
- Have excellent career advancement opportunities (no. 7)
- Enjoy challenging work assignments that broaden skills (no. 8)

And these factors seem to apply across cultures. In short, we think that when
people have Scope, the outcomes are win-win.

A key element of Scope is the work itself. How many well-qualified young
people start their careers in mind-numbingly dull jobs that are often all that's
left after technology has done the rest? No wonder there is high turnover

among young workers, even though there is a chronic shortage of job opportunities. Given that most employees want to find their work of at least some interest, poor job design often reflects lack of clear direction from the top and can lead to performance gaps and duplication of effort. Together with ineffective structures, poor job design seems destined to lead to rapid employee disengagement and early departure.

Conversely, good **job design** can create interesting roles in which people can use their skills. Since line managers are closest to the work that needs to be done, it falls to them to design roles in which individuals can experience some stretch, and have the appropriate level of responsibility, authority, resource, support and accountability to do the job well. While job descriptions can capture what needs to be done, managers need to be careful this doesn't become a straightjacket that impedes individuals. The downside, as Lawler and Worley (2011, p. 1) point out, is that:

> In an attempt to be clear about telling individuals what they need to do, they can be faulted for implying what they don't need to do and providing a convenient excuse for not doing things. When baggage handlers and flight attendants won't help the cleaning crew clean a late arriving plane so that it can leave on schedule because it's 'not their job', that's a real cost.

Job enrichment is key to creating interesting and developmental work. Hackman & Oldham's Job Characteristics model (1976) is still widely used as a framework to understand how particular job characteristics impact on job outcomes, including job satisfaction. The model states that five core job characteristics (skill variety, task identity, task significance, autonomy and feedback) impact on three critical psychological states (experienced meaningfulness, experienced responsibility for outcomes and knowledge of the actual results), which in turn influence work outcomes (job satisfaction, absenteeism and work motivation).

Autonomy is a key aspect of good job design. To a greater or lesser extent, most people want to feel able to control their destiny, to be regarded as responsible, capable and competent. They want to feel trusted to do a good job and have the chance to deliver without being micro-managed. Daniel Pink (2009) argues that every worker can become engaged if, having satisfied some of their basic security needs, they have scope to **grow and develop**. For this to happen, their job should provide space for:

- autonomy – the desire to direct our own lives
- accomplishment or mastery – the urge to get better and better at something that matters
- purpose – the yearning to do what we do in the service of something larger than ourselves.

When people can find **meaning and purpose** in their work, engagement is likely to be exponential.

While the desire for some autonomy at work is probably common to employees of all generations, it is especially strong in Generation Y graduates, according to research by Ashridge Business School and ILM (2011). What these people want most from their managers is respect, and to be trusted to get on with their work. They want collaborative work spaces and access to the latest and fastest technologies, where they can share, comment and collaborate as equals. They know they will have long working lives and embrace **lifelong learning**. More than half (56 per cent) of graduates in the Ashridge/ILM study want their manager to be a coach/mentor rather than someone who directs. By contrast, managers see regular feedback about performance (50 per cent) and setting clear objectives (49 per cent) as the most important behaviours. Building **mutual trust** is crucial to ensuring that employees can have the scope they need to give of their best.

Beyond growing in one's current job, **career development** matters to many employees, and organizations with high engagement tend to provide career tracks and opportunities at all levels so that people can further their own interests as well as those of their employer. Similarly, in many of the studies, training and development is linked with employees feeling valued and engaged; after all, employees know that they don't have a job for life, and part of the social exchange '**fair deal**' should be to equip employees not only for their current job but beyond it, potentially outside the company.

Some managers fear that training staff just increases their risk of leaving. However, this fear seems unfounded. Various 'great employer'-type awards such as 'Best Companies' suggest that high-performance organizations are good at developing employee skills and competencies, and tend not to have high labour turnover, which could otherwise make this investment in people uneconomic. They recognize that a thirst for improvement and growth by learning leads to new and better ways of working: skilled employees are more likely to stay with their employer precisely because they are being developed.

Conclusion

In this chapter we've looked at what appear to be some of the main drivers of employee engagement. Of course we recognize that engagement is an elusive state and that even the most engaged employee can quickly become disengaged. But a good engagement initiative reflects the fact that organizations are a composite of individuals. What engages different individuals will vary, depending on their role, life-cycle stage, personal interests, ambitions and goals. The role of good line management in recognizing and working with this is fundamental.

The question is, if employee engagement is so important and potentially at risk, what can be done to improve it? Over the next few chapters we'll be looking at how you can use surveys to get to grips more specifically with how employees are feeling, and about how to use information from surveys as a strategic tool to help pinpoint your actions. In Chapter 8 we'll consider what it means to build a culture of engagement, focusing more specifically on how to create **Connection**. In Chapter 9 we'll look at what it means to be an 'engaging manager' and how to provide **Support**. In Chapter 10 we'll look at how to build employee engagement, even if the going gets tough, and our emphasis will be on **Voice**. And, as the old proverb 'physician, heal thyself' reminds us, it is hard to be an engaging manager if you are yourself disengaged. That's why we'll round up the book with some suggestions about how you too can have **Scope** – and about how to reboot your own energy, wellbeing and engagement.

Checklist

- To what extent is employee engagement owned by business leaders and line managers, and a core part of the organization's people strategy? (It should not be a one-off exercise.)

- Which employee propositions make sense in your sector and your business? (There should not be a 'one size fits all' approach to engagement.)

- A good engagement initiative focuses on both the emotional element of the engagement relationship as well as the transactional. Where is the emphasis in your organization's initiatives? How can a better balance be achieved so that people find meaning in their work, regardless of how mundane the job might be?

- A key part of engagement is having a strong and dynamic vision, based on an uplifting purpose, one that makes it worth going for – one that excites people and makes them feel that coming to work each day is worthwhile. How uplifting is your organization's purpose, and how dynamic is the vision? How can roles be clarified so that people have line of sight to that purpose?

- Engagement drivers do not operate in isolation – they all interact and impact on each other. Which are the engagement drivers you can most directly influence?

- How can you open up communication – at both a rational and emotional level – about what keeps your workers from being engaged? (Don't confuse 'information' with 'communication'.)

CHAPTER 4

Near-empty offices late in the afternoon, a brisk trade in cynical jokes in the corridor and a general air of nonchalance – some of the all-too-frequent signs of a workplace that's 'switched off' and suffering from low engagement. But in another organization across town, the opposite can be seen: smiling faces, a buzz of energy everywhere and a 'can do' attitude whenever that little bit extra is asked of anyone. At its basic level, then, one can sense how far organizations are switched on. It's almost something you can smell in the air. But if that's so, why the need to survey employees to measure how engaged they are?

The importance of measurement

The reality is that – despite practices like 'managing by wandering around' – such assessments are, of necessity, selective and impressionistic. This is not to say they should be dispensed with – smaller organizations may well be able to rely on this as the way to 'feel the pulse', and clearly nothing can beat the richness of an in-depth conversation with someone to understand fully what's on their mind. But the UK's MacLeod Report on employee engagement (MacLeod and Clarke, 2009, p. 11) suggests that relying just on informal feedback becomes harder once an organization numbers twenty or more employees, and adds:

That is not to say that a sophisticated or expensive survey or questionnaire is always appropriate or necessary to measure engagement levels; many organizations supplement questionnaires with staff focus groups. For small organizations in particular the cost will almost certainly be prohibitive and may seem bureaucratic and burdensome. However, many leaders of small and medium businesses told us that once a business grows to a size where, in the words of one of the employers we spoke to, 'we can't all go to the pub together', gauging levels of engagement makes good business sense.

Clearly, then, the bigger the workplace, the more necessary it is to employ some sort of survey process to complement informal employee feedback – and these days, the vast majority of large organizations carry out periodic employee engagement surveys.[1] Surveying can have other benefits, such as surfacing issues that might not come out directly in discussion with staff. For example, employees with serious concerns (such as discrimination or harassment) may be reluctant to come forward and express their views openly, but are able to do so through survey feedback. Likewise, surveying might highlight otherwise unnoticed cases of managers who put a low priority on their people. Of course, everyone will have a view about what is the current mood in an organization, but given it is made up of many different individuals and so is a kaleidoscope of personal perspectives, it is impossible to understand exactly where the current strengths and challenges exist in an organization without resorting to some sort of survey process.

An effective survey therefore provides a baseline of how things stand at a point in time and allows internal comparison – for example, between one department and another, or between different types of employees (male/female, manual workers/supervisors, etc.). Hard facts are tougher to challenge than mere hunch, so solid data provides a more compelling basis for management to take action. As mentioned in the MacLeod Report (MacLeod and Clarke, 2009, pp. 4–5):

Many company leaders described to us the 'light-bulb moment' when an understanding of the full potential significance of employee engagement dawned. Tesco Chief Executive Terry Leahy has recorded his reaction when he realized that the company knew more about its customers than it did about its employees, and how the company then set about understanding what the workforce wanted, what motivated them at work and what workplace approaches would best build on those understandings, working in partnership with the retail workers' union USDAW.

This, then, is the benefit of surveying – to achieve a deeper level of insight that allows employee engagement and its underlying drivers to be better understood and addressed. Furthermore, by conducting surveys over time, it is possible to track progress – or to spot early on any issues that are arising.

As Wiley notes (2010b, p. 8), such strategic surveys can also help serve a number of other purposes – notably:

- providing a 'red flag' if there are potential workplace issues arising (e.g. increased employee perceptions that company values are not being respected)
- measuring progress towards the achievement of given strategic priorities (e.g. fostering an innovation culture, buy-in for a new business strategy, etc.)
- helping to become a best-in-class employer through measuring key outcomes such as retention, employee recommendation of the organization to friends and family, etc.
- potentially also creating predictors of future business performance.

While often overlooked, well-run surveys and follow-up actions can also have the side-benefits of increasing internal communication and of fostering employee commitment (because the process of being asked for their opinion makes people already feel more valued and involved).

Types of surveys and selection of a provider

Organizations can independently run their own employee engagement survey, which may be appropriate for smaller businesses that already have good levels of employee trust and just want a tool that is simple and inexpensive. Possible questionnaires for this purpose can be found fairly easily and some larger organizations (such as G4S, the world's largest security company) also run their own surveys as it is cheaper to do so (IDS, 2010). But construction of a suitable and effective survey is not straightforward and a 'home-grown' survey approach is not recommended for most organizations for the following reasons:

- Questionnaire design requires considerable care, or else questions can be poorly drafted and misunderstood by employees or create a biased response.[2]
- The survey may be inadequately validated and so fall short in terms of accuracy, reliability and robustness.
- There is a risk of organizations skewing the survey to focus too much on immediate concerns, rather than designing it to provide a balanced perspective of engagement levels and their different potential drivers.
- To run anything but a very simple survey requires a good deal of work, especially if the data is to be statistically validated, and the results presented in different formats to allow for ease of analysis and use. A poorly set up survey risks undermining its credibility.
- Employees may be suspicious of their employer running a survey in-house and have concerns about the confidentiality of their responses.
- It is usually not possible to compare the results of a home-grown survey with others, therefore precluding the use of external benchmarks to judge how well an organization is performing.

Fortunately, many survey providers now exist that can take care of this work for employers, with products that vary greatly in terms of sophistication and questionnaire length. Not only can surveys measure engagement levels and other aspects of work that can affect it, but often they can show which of the latter most closely relate to engagement through multiple regression analysis. Increasingly, then, the challenge instead is who to choose from the wide range available. One of the best-known providers is Gallup, whose core 12 questions – known as the Q^{12} – is popular because it is extensively tested and the combination of these 12 questions, plus any others an organization may add, means it takes little time for employees to complete the survey. The focus of the Q^{12} on the immediate work environment is especially valuable when employees work in groups and where front-line supervision has a noticeable impact on staff morale.[3] As a result, the Gallup survey is widely used for manufacturing, retail and customer service staff. In their bestselling study of successful management behaviours based on the Q^{12}, *First Break All the Rules*, Buckingham and Coffman (1999, p. 32) argue that the meta-analysis of their surveys showed that:

> For the most part, these twelve opinions were being formed by the employee's immediate manager rather than by the policies or procedures of the overall company. We had discovered that the manager – not pay, benefits, perks, or a charismatic corporate leader – was the critical player in building a strong workplace. The manager was the key.

However, it has been questioned whether the Q^{12} can provide the complete answer as to what drives engagement in all organizations (Hutton, 2009)[4] and not all survey providers anyway share Gallup's supervisor-centric view of what needs to be measured when assessing employee engagement. For instance, Gebauer and Lowman give a very different view, saying that Towers Watson's research points to the highest driver of engagement globally being 'senior management's sincere interest in employee wellbeing', commenting that 'this finding speaks to the enormous influence that a company's top leaders have on every member of the workforce' (Gebauer and Lowman, 2008, p. 15). Another survey provider, BlessingWhite, also commented that 'our findings suggest executive behaviours can have a greater potential impact on engagement than manager actions' (BlessingWhite Research, 2011, p. 3). So unlike the 'bottom up' view of Gallup, others argue that 'top down' factors such as overall business vision or direction can also have a critical impact on engagement. Of course these two views of the world are not mutually exclusive – in our view, both are important drivers of engagement and are each reflected in the model described in Chapter 3 as Support and Connection. Clearly, the best managers in the world will still struggle to motivate their staff if the organization as a whole appears to be going disastrously in the wrong direction, whereas the best-articulated company visions will not eradicate the corrosive effect of a supervisor who patently does not care about their employees.

Given there is no universally agreed definition of engagement (the Mac-Leod Report came across more than 50 definitions of what it meant), survey

Table 4.1 Comparison of questions used for the engagement index of two survey providers

Theme	Kenexa questions*	Towers Watson questions
Pride	I am proud to work for my organization	I am proud to be part of my organization
Satisfaction	Overall, I am extremely satisfied with my organization as a place to work	–
Retention	I rarely think about looking for a new job with another organization	It would take a lot to make me look for another employer At the present time, are you seriously considering leaving the organization?
Advocacy	I would gladly refer a good friend or family member to my organization for employment	I would recommend my organization as a good place to work
Alignment	–	I believe strongly in the goals and objectives of my organization
Motivation	–	My organization energizes me to go the extra mile I am willing to work beyond what is required in my job in order to help my organization succeed
Values	–	I fully support the values for which my organization stands

* (Wiley, 2010b, p. 57)

providers' views of what it means, as well as the questions used to measure engagement, will of course vary – as can be seen in Table 4.1, which shows what two leading providers use as questions to constitute their engagement index.

However, the MacLeod Report (MacLeod and Clarke, 2009, p. 10) rightly concludes that:

> *Despite there being some debate about the precise meaning of employee engagement, there are three things we know about it: it is measurable; it can be correlated with performance; and it varies from poor to great. Most importantly*

employers can do a great deal to impact on people's level of engagement. That is what makes it so important, as a tool for business success.

In practice, too, most third-party surveys have a lot in common when it comes to measuring engagement. The Society for Human Resource Management (SHRM) Foundation in the US identified ten common themes (Vance, 2006, p. 6) that are typically used to measure engagement in third-party surveys, namely:

- pride in employer
- satisfaction with employer
- job satisfaction
- opportunity to perform well at challenging work
- recognition and positive feedback for one's contributions
- personal support from one's supervisor
- effort above and beyond the minimum
- understanding the link between one's job and the organization's mission
- prospects for future growth with one's employer
- intention to stay with one's employer.

When looking at potential surveys, it makes sense, therefore, to check if they cover the four key dimensions of engagement described in Chapter 3, i.e. Connection, Support, Voice and Scope.

Likewise, as well as differing in the questions they may use, survey providers may also group them into different topics (or 'categories') for reporting purposes. So it is worth looking at this too, so that your organization chooses the right range of questions to address potential engagement drivers, and fit the sort of workforce and challenges you have. (See Table 4.2.)

Depending on your organization, therefore, it is worthwhile looking at different providers and the approach they take before making a final choice. Notable survey providers include Aon Hewitt, BlessingWhite, Effectory, Gallup, Hay, Inquisite, Kenexa, ORC, People Insight, PwC Saratoga, Scarlett Surveys, Sirota and Towers Watson.[5]

As part of choosing a provider, it is important that senior management have a clear and shared understanding about what they think is meant by

Table 4.2 Examples of engagement survey categories/drivers

Aon Hewitt	Towers Watson
Benefits	Career development
Brand alignment	Communication
Career opportunities	Competitiveness
Colleagues	Customer focus
Company reputation	Empowerment
Customers	Engagement
Diversity	Goals and objectives
Managers	Image
Pay	Leadership
Performance management	Operating efficiency
Physical work environment	Organizational change
Policies and practices	Pay and rewards
Recognition	Quality
Senior leadership	Performance evaluation
Sense of accomplishment	Stress, balance and workload
Training and development	Supervision
Valuing people	Working relationship
Work activities	
Work-life balance	
(Work) processes	
(Work) resources	

employee engagement and how they see it contributing to the business, so that the right survey can be chosen. For example, where are people on the continuum between high commitment and willingness to 'go the extra mile' versus active disengagement? Does it differ across the organization (by hierarchy or function/unit)? Doing this helps to clarify what the organization is striving for and therefore what to measure via a survey. Some examples of how companies have defined engagement are shown in Table 4.3.

A frank series of discussions at the top team level about where disconnects currently exist between business potential and actual performance, and where people are exceeding or falling short in their contributions, can also help clarify the broader intent of the engagement activities. For a manufacturing business, it may be that product reliability is holding back the company's image and so improved employee engagement could help turn this around by

Table 4.3 Examples of definitions of employee engagement

Dell	Royal Bank of Scotland	Shell
To compete today, companies need to win over the MINDS (rational commitment) and the HEARTS (emotional commitment) of employees in ways that lead to extraordinary effort (Vance, 2006, p. 3).	**Say.** Consistently speaks positively about the organization to colleagues, potential employees and customers **Stay.** Has an intense desire to be a member of the organization **Strive.** Exerts extra effort and engages in behaviours that contribute to business success (De Baere and Baeten, 2008)	The extent to which employees are proud to work for Shell, identify with and are inspired by our values and goals, and commit energy and creativity to the sustained success of the company

bringing about a stronger sense of quality focus and higher rate of employee suggestions. For a hospital, it could be that the need is to improve patient recovery rates. Higher engagement can improve teamwork (especially in the emergency room) and better diagnosis and problem-solving generally by staff. By linking the engagement survey topics with the key drivers for the business (such as may be set out in their strategy), a fuller framework can be developed that provides a context for the survey results and makes sense of it, given the nature of a particular organization.[6] This way, the survey is not simply seen as a data-gathering exercise, but can be put in a business context as a clear set of goals to be strived for that fit into an overall plan and can deliver longer-term organizational benefits. Likewise, the survey can then become an instrument to support the business, rather than a generic device that risks missing what matters most to the organization.

One area of potential confusion is between pure engagement surveys and more general 'best employer' surveys. While the latter can be valuable in benchmarking people practices against competitor employers and (in the case of good results) have value in recruitment advertising and enhancing employer branding, they do not necessarily directly address the question of employee engagement. Some do incorporate engagement surveys as part of their accreditation process, such as Aon Hewitt (for their Best Employer studies) and Best Companies Ltd in the UK (who run *The Sunday Times*' 'Best Companies to Work For' listing[7]). But before signing up for such a survey, be careful to check that it is not limited to evaluating HR practices. While this can help address some of the underlying factors influencing engagement (e.g. providing better career opportunities), engagement can often be impacted by issues outside the realms of HR and 'best employer' surveys may then risk falling short in providing the answers that can help create an engaged workforce. Good people practices aside, a key element of engagement (as discussed already) is Connection. Identifying with the business through a clear line of sight, aligned goals and having the right skills provides what Jim Haudan, the founder of Root Learning, calls 'the process of strategic engagement' (Haudan, 2008, pp. 169–231). As he warns, 'If you don't consider the strategic component of engagement, you may be measuring engagement in an incomplete way. In a worst-case scenario, you could have a lot of very happy people who feel engaged at work, but they may be doing things that are not part of the strategy that the organization is attempting to execute.' (Haudan, 2008, p. 176.)

When selecting a survey provider, then, the questions in Box 4.1 are worth bearing in mind.

As well as the time and cost of the survey, a critical consideration is the relationship developed with the survey provider. A good consultant will not simply administer a survey correctly but can help interpret the results, put them into

---

Box 4.1 Questions to consider when selecting an engagement survey provider

- How does the provider define and measure 'engagement'?
- What sorts of topics are covered by the survey questionnaire?
- How far do the questions and survey topics meet my organization's needs and key priorities?
- How unambiguous and actionable are the proposed questions?
- Is the survey really measuring engagement or just employee satisfaction?
- Does the survey collect quantitative data or can respondents also write in comments if so desired?

- Do the quantitative questions follow an agree/disagree scale and do they require a forced choice?[8]
- How far can the survey be tailored (e.g adding extra questions for an organization if they are particularly important)?
- How extensively has the tool been validated and tested?
- Can the survey results be compared to external benchmarks? What sort of benchmarks are available (by country, industry, workforce type, etc.)? How comprehensive is the data behind each benchmark (i.e. how many respondents and organizations)? How comparable to you are the organizations in the benchmark?
- (If needed) does the survey provider have international reach (i.e. are they able to provide meaningful benchmarks from different countries around the world)? Can they give international support (e.g. translate the survey into different local languages, have consultants in different countries to resolve local user questions, etc.)?
- In what format is the survey run (paper, online or smartphone, or all three)?
- How far can the data be broken down in the resulting survey reports (e.g. by team, business unit, department, country, etc.)?
- How easy are the reports to use and integrate into management presentations?
- Is it possible to generate special reports (e.g. for individual supervisors) highlighting those key areas where recipients should consider taking action?
- What other statistical tools are available to make sense of the data (e.g. regression analyses, quartiles, standard deviations, etc.)?
- What would be the survey costs (including potential hidden costs like ordering additional reports or cuts of data)?
- To what extent can the provider help with linkage research to explore how far survey data can be a leading indicator for business performance?
- Are there other customers that would be ready to share their experience of working with the proposed provider?

a broader perspective, and provide advice and guidance so as to make best use of the results generated. Without this personal rapport and customer understanding, there is a risk of the client being left with a lot of indigestible data that is time-consuming to understand and

> A good consultant will not simply administer a survey correctly but can help interpret the results, put them into a broader perspective, and provide advice and guidance so as to make best use of the results generated.

that hinders rather than helps achieve workforce insight. It's worth checking, therefore, the experience the consultant brings, whether they have worked in-house (and not just as an external advisor), and how other customers would rate their support.

What to cover in the survey

Once selected, an important activity early on with the survey provider is to finalize the questions to be used in the survey. Typically, the provider will have certain core questions that are especially correlated with employee engagement overall, but it is possible to add further specific questions (e.g. to enquire about current change issues, trust of management, commitment to internal values, etc.). Opinion research expert Peter Hutton cautions that generic questions from survey providers can seem quite 'vague and impressionistic' due to their being designed to apply in a broad range of situations (Hutton, 2009, p. 25). If this is so, they may need to be supplemented (or even replaced) by more specific questions; while these have the disadvantage of not being open to benchmarking against external norms, they can provide more precise and meaningful insight for a given organization.

In this respect, it can be worth in particular adding questions that measure progress on the key value drivers of the organization (e.g. in a retail environment, understanding how empowered sales staff feel, how strong a service mentality they have, etc.) or respond to a critical development in the organization, such as understanding employee attitudes due to a change of strategy or after a merger or downsizing (e.g. 'I am confident that the current reorganization of sales and marketing will ensure the company's long-term success'). All these questions can be valuable as a means of tracking progress towards strategic business- and people-related objectives. At **Standard Chartered**, a Gallup Q[12] is supplemented by ten further questions on topics important for the business, such as, for example, employee loyalty ('I plan to be working for Standard Chartered in three years' time') (IDS, April 2009).

Some selectivity in question topics is necessary, as it is impossible to measure every possible factor that may affect engagement; the Corporate Leadership Council's research points to potentially more than 300 'levers of engagement' (Vance, 2006, p. 19). While it may be possible to add specific questions by group if this is needed (e.g. just for employees working in a given division or country), bear in mind that a survey should not be too long – so focus on those questions that are essential (as opposed to 'desirable'). Typically questionnaires should take no more than 20 minutes to fill in, and ideally less – if a questionnaire is too long it will be time-consuming and deter potential respondents.

A further decision to take is whether to gather only quantitative responses (e.g. through a rating scale) or to set open questions where employees can write in their comments. Gebauer and Lowman (2008, p. 59) point out that 'carefully designed [open-ended] questions can elicit a wealth of information and serve as a kind of virtual focus group for managers', adding that suggestions gathered this way can be valuable as 'there is wisdom in crowds, meaning the collective insights of employees can be mined to isolate the best specific ideas for business improvement.' Written comments can also help clarify quantitative scores, and the frequency of words being used may give insight into an organization's culture or employee concerns. Leading expert on people at work Judith Bardwick (2008, p. 69) adds that:

Standard questions just don't explore the feelings people are experiencing. The standardized questions too often suggest the 'right' answer, and they don't provide any way for the person to describe the emotional component. The only way to get below the surface and understand employees' emotional temperatures is to ask open-ended questions that allow respondents to say whatever they really feel.

However, it's important to be aware that collecting qualitative data will noticeably add to the cost and time involved in running a survey, especially if there are multiple open questions or where the scope for comments is broad. As comments may need to be transcribed and/or translated, and then categorized and analysed to identify key trends, organizations need to allow adequate time and resources before adding such open-ended questions.

Furthermore, even if only quantitative questions are used, there are different ways of doing so. Peter Hutton takes issue in particular with the over-use of questions with an agree/disagree scale (Hutton, 2009). To get a better view, he argues other types should be considered, such as list questions (e.g. 'Tick which of the following apply ...') or asking employees to rank responses (e.g. 'Which from the following are the three most important issues for the organization to address?') to pinpoint more clearly where there are issues to address in an organization.

Take care also when working with a survey provider to make sure the semantics of the survey are clear – for example, will employees all understand terms like 'my organization' or 'senior management' the same way? Peter Hutton (2009, pp. 38–9) warns that terms like 'vision' can be even more of a minefield:

> The trouble is, these are management concepts and many staff will not necessarily understand the terms 'mission', 'vision', 'values' or 'objectives'. Moreover, they can easily be confused between group, corporate, divisional, departmental and individual objectives and goals.

Every effort, therefore, is needed to reduce ambiguity; the more specific the terms can be – such as referring to a particular tagline that may be used for the organization's strategy – the better. Similarly, are there expressions that are unique to the organization that need to be reflected in the wording (for instance, are employees referred to by a special name such as 'associate' or 'partner'?). Although not ideal, a glossary of terms at the start of the questionnaire may be useful to provide clarity for participants on the terms used. Finally, consider using different question styles if this helps – Hutton (2009, p. 39) suggests unawareness itself may be a barrier to engagement, in which case it may sometimes help to use a scale question about this (e.g. 'fully aware' through to 'never heard of') rather than the more typical agree/disagree format (i.e. 'strongly agree' through to 'strongly disagree'). All told, some time invested here will avoid respondents being left unclear as to how to respond and answering 'don't know' or incorrectly, rather than giving a meaningful response.

> It's important to be aware that collecting qualitative data will noticeably add to the cost and time involved in running a survey, especially if there are multiple open questions or where the scope for comments is broad.

Once the questions are agreed, a decision needs to be made about whether to group them in the questionnaire by survey category or to mix them in a random manner (and just use the survey categories for reporting purposes). IDS comments that the former approach can make the survey quicker to complete as respondents move from one discrete topic to another, but that the latter approach may force respondents to think more about each question separately and so deliver more considered answers overall (IDS, 2010, p. 5). There's no right or wrong answer here and a lot will depend on the range of questions planned, but it is obviously a topic that should be resolved after appropriate discussion with the survey providers.

It's important to agree as well with the survey provider how to code respondents so that they can be reported later according to different de-mographic parameters. Typical data collected is gender, age (by band), organi-zation level (e.g. manager), department/function, and location, but it may be useful to collect other elements such as skill group or specialism, or where someone is located (e.g. home-based, office, factory, etc.). However, the more such questions are asked, the greater the risk that employees may worry that this is a way of being able to identify individual respondents, so careful com-munication will be needed to explain why the additional data is needed and to reassure staff about survey confidentiality.

Finally, for online surveys, it is recommended to make access dependent on using individual one-time ID codes. This prevents employees completing the survey more than once and controls participation if some parts of the workforce are excluded (e.g. temporary staff, or if the survey is done on a roll-ing basis covering just a fraction of all employees) – but being able to do so relies on having comprehensive employee data beforehand to be sure that employees are notified correctly.

Setting up the survey process

Depending on an organization's size and geographic scope, setting up an engagement survey can be a significant undertaking. It therefore only makes sense to do so if the following factors are taken into account:

1 There must be management commitment both to the survey and also to share and act on its results. Senior executive sponsorship is key, but middle managers and first-line supervisors also need to be briefed so they can support the survey process and ensure employees feel reassured about taking part. Managers need to be ready to hear unwelcome feedback and then to respond to it. Doing this poorly (e.g. by hiding disappointing results or creating the impression that leadership is only paying lip-service to engagement) will be worse than not taking any action at all.

2 Employee representatives (e.g. works councils or trade union representatives) also need to be involved early on to ensure their buy in, and – in some countries – prior approval for running such a survey. Engagement surveys can be a welcome initiative in their eyes, because it helps quantify and reinforce concerns they may already be raising. But equally their support can evaporate if they get the impression that their role might be sidelined as a result, or that the survey process presents potential risks to employees in terms of confidentiality, management receptiveness to critical feedback, etc.

3 The survey must be understood in all locations, which may mean extensive translation into multiple languages so employees can make sense of and take part in the survey, giving answers that accurately reflect their opinions.

4 Data collection via the survey should be structured in such a way that it is possible to produce breakdowns and reports that reflect the details of the organization's structure, address managers' needs and deliver data that is meaningful and results that are actionable. At the same time, there is a risk

of over-producing reports (especially in large organizations), so get Communications or HR to check how far each report is needed – otherwise there is a risk of incurring a lot of added cost for data that is not really used.

5 Employees must have sufficient opportunity to take part in the survey. In a production environment, this may mean creating a special break where staff have the time to complete the survey and, for workplaces where staff may not have access to a PC (e.g. supermarket cashiers), it may mean offering paper questionnaires instead, or setting up booths where they can take part. For staff who are mostly travelling, it may mean enabling participation through smart phones instead.[9] In all cases, it's important to do this in an environment where staff feel they are not overlooked and can provide honest feedback without fear of the consequences.

6 Last, but not least, adequate resources and project management must be in place to ensure that the survey is well-run.

Top management may turn to Communications or to HR to help drive the survey process and follow-up activities. The advantage of Communications being the main support is that it can help create awareness about the survey and follow-up actions, as well as address some of the issues that might emerge from the survey results, such as increasing engagement through a stronger employer brand, explaining more effectively the organization's vision and mission, or enhancing internal communications cascades. There is considerable evidence too that good employee communication helps enhance employee engagement, and can even improve overall financial performance: Towers Watson reports that companies that are highly effective communicators had 47 per cent higher total returns to shareholders over the last five years compared with firms that are the least effective communicators (Towers Watson, 2010a).

In contrast, the benefit of HR being the main support is that many of the topics in the survey will be people-related anyway (e.g. culture, career opportunities, etc.), but then HR needs to pull together as a function to address what is needed to engage employees, preferably through what Whittington and Galpin (2010) call 'an integrated HR value chain' that comprises a series of practices that can help engage people all along the employment life-cycle.

If your HR organization is segmented in functional silos and struggles to collaborate, this will seriously undermine its effectiveness to deliver on this, because it they may come up with narrow solutions (e.g. a recognition plan for team worker of the month) as opposed to an integrated answer to what was possibly a much wider question, such as how to help create empowered teams. On the other hand, if the HR group has savvy business partners and people with organizational development skills, it can help develop holistic solutions that meet both people and business needs. The UK's Corporate Research Forum (CRF) concurs (Lambert, 2010, p. 5), suggesting that ideally:

> HR's role is primarily to help embed responsibility and skills in management at the micro level, i.e. teams, and at the macro level – leadership and culture – for which HR itself needs the requisite organization development and influencing skills. HR typically must work collaboratively with a suitably skilled internal communication function, and ensure clarity about respective roles.

But regardless of whether Communications or HR are chosen, in practice neither can handle the survey on their own: both need to collaborate (as mentioned above) and will need to involve other functions as well (e.g. IT, to support the running of an online survey), so clear assignment of roles and responsibilities, and good cross-functional project management, will all be required. CRF also stresses the importance of getting Communications and HR to develop a mutual understanding of each others' capabilities and potential contribution, given that 'historically, Personnel functions guarded information, while Communications' role has been to release it. The two functions typically need to undertake their own process of engagement to work together effectively' (Lambert, 2010, p. 44).

Employee engagement clearly 'raises the bar' for these functions and CRF (Lambert, 2010, p. 44) notes that:

> In practice, HR and Communications vary considerably in their ability to be both expert and persuasive guides [to management]. Much depends on the calibre and orientation of the heads of function – and colleagues partnering with business teams – including their ability to influence leaders on issues of behaviour and culture.

If these capabilities do not exist internally, it is important to have chosen an external provider whose own consultants can impact the organization effectively at the highest level. But whoever is finally chosen to support employee engagement work, it is vital that they are not seen to supplant management's overall ownership for this exercise. Otherwise, employee engagement risks being seen as some sort of 'nice to have' project for a staff function or third party providers rather than a key business process.

Timing and frequency of surveys

Survey timing is another important topic to resolve. Care needs to be taken to avoid running the survey at a time of year that conflicts with other priorities, such as the business year end or annual pay review, or when staff are likely to be on vacation – which will differ around the world given that summer and winter differ by hemisphere, and also taking account the effect of local religious and national holidays. Otherwise, the consequence will be a reduced participation rate. Survey timing may also need to be adjusted to optimize the use of the results in follow-up management action – for example, having the results in time for reporting in an annual business scorecard, or being able to access the survey analysis so suitable improvement goals can be set for the next business year. In terms of the length of the survey period, three weeks is recommended as a window in which people can respond; any less than this and there is a risk that employees may miss out because they are on vacation or travelling on business. A good participation rate depends on generating some excitement about the survey process: too long a survey period can undermine this, as employees may treat a distant deadline as a reason to put off responding right away and then subsequently forget to take part altogether.

Another question to consider is the frequency with which subsequent surveys will be held. This is something that may be asked by employees and it is worth having a clear idea about this beforehand. Typically, surveys are held annually, which allows enough time for follow-up actions to start to make a difference before measuring engagement levels again. Some organizations hold surveys more frequently (e.g. quarterly) but then typically either a subset of the organization is invited to respond at any one time or a narrower range of questions are used. For example, Sainsbury's supermarkets survey their staff via nine waves during the year so as to make sure they have a dynamic and more up-to-date view of employee opinions (IDS, 2009, p. 19). The benefit of this is that it provides more of a real-time sense of employee opinions; but if the survey samples are smaller (say, covering a quarter of the workforce), it may mean that the data is only statistically valid at the highest organizational levels (and so can provide less value for first- or second-level managers). Moreover, as it takes time to

Typically, surveys are held annually, which allows enough time for follow-up actions to start to make a difference before measuring engagement levels again.

affect engagement levels, frequent surveying may not show much underlying difference from one round to another. Furthermore, such frequent exercises carry the associated dangers of getting stuck in endlessly surveying and never getting round to taking action, and of focusing on short-term issues rather than deeper, more entrenched topics that are identified.

Holding surveys less frequently (c.g. every two to three years) obviously reduces the workload of running the survey and the associated survey cost, and allows more time for action afterwards. However, given that not all employees recall the results and follow-up from surveys anyway, reducing survey frequency may undermine the 'buzz' from the survey efforts and make staff feel less likely that their opinions are being heard. On the management side, too, the danger is that issues may be evolving in the workplace that are going unnoticed, and that the overall programme loses momentum anyway when there is an extended gap between surveys and it takes so long to see the fruits of the follow-up action. For those running the survey internally, a significant gap between surveys may see staff move and expertise get lost in the meantime, so added work and retraining may be required to get everyone ready when the survey is next run again. A longer cycle time between surveys therefore needs more care to ensure energy and focus on engagement does not go 'flat' over time, although (as the following case study shows), it is possible to follow such a timeframe and still have highly committed staff.

Case study: Schindler

Founded in Switzerland in 1874, the Schindler Group is a leading global provider of elevators, escalators, moving walkways and related services; its mobility solutions move one billion people every day all over the world. In 2010, it generated operating revenues of more than CHF8 billion. Behind the company's success are 43,000 employees in more than 100 countries, 59 per cent of whom are employed in the installation and maintenance of elevators and escalators. The company's vision – 'Leadership through customer service' – reflects the importance of ensuring uninterrupted mobility and was demonstrated notably during the Beijing Olympic Games and Paralympics, where Schindler had on-site service teams for the 175 Schindler escalators and elevators serving the Olympic Park and the 'Bird's Nest' National Stadium.

Given the service focus of Schindler, the company believes that only highly motivated employees lead to satisfied customers, and so to business success. Therefore, Schindler conducts periodic employee motivation surveys and creates action plans according to the results, in order to constantly improve the motivation level and sustain it above the national norm in each country. As part of this, Schindler carries out worldwide employee motivation surveys every three years. Nearly 85 per cent of its 43,000 employees took part in the last one in 2009, which showed improvement on all measures since the previous survey was conducted in 2006. The results of the global survey (which comprises around 70 questions) are used to measure engagement levels as well as gather employee feedback on key issues such as quality and safety. As of the last survey, Schindler had engagement levels in line with the Towers Watson High Performing Companies Index.

Another issue that sometimes arises is whether to delay or cancel a scheduled survey, e.g. due to exceptional business events such as an economic downturn, or if a lay-off has recently taken place. The usual concern is of course that scores may be lower in these circumstances – but effective leadership can bolster employee commitment and go

> Effective leadership can bolster employee commitment and go some way in helping to sustain engagement levels.

some way in helping to sustain engagement levels. Furthermore, data from a survey during an organizational change can highlight where commitment levels vary the most or where there are the greatest concerns in the workforce. If the survey is cancelled or deferred, the credibility of the process may well be undermined by giving the impression that employee views are only sought when they are positive, and this in turn may drive down engagement levels even further.

Launching and running the survey

Having set up the survey process, the next step is to launch and run the survey. Prior to and during the survey, communications are important to ensure that:

- there is awareness of the survey and the timeframe in which it is taking place
- the purpose of the survey is clearly understood, as well as what will be the follow-up steps afterwards
- employees feel encouraged to take part
- there is adequate reassurance about confidentiality of responses.

Ideally the survey should also be put into the broader context of the organization, such as linking it to striving towards certain business goals or becoming a best employer, so that it is not seen as a random activity by management. Some experts even suggest that ideally organizations should build around this focus group-tested 'messaging' about the engagement exercise (Macey et al., 2009, pp. 85–7). A tagline or brand for the survey (e.g. 'Your Voice', 'Speak Up', etc.) can, in any case, be useful so as to make the exercise more memorable and to help ensure that subsequent actions can be linked back – for example, 'We introduced a new set of company values in response to this year's feedback in the Your Voice survey'. As examples, Sainsbury's survey is called Talkback, while the **UK's Ministry of Defence** uses the tagline MOD Your Say.

Three key elements to support the survey launch are:

- **advertising** to make employees aware of the survey, e.g. workplace posters, flyers, adverts on cafeteria tray mats, adverts on workplace LCD screens, or giveaways (e.g. pens with the survey tagline)
- **notification** to tell employees how to take part, e.g. information through the intranet, email, postcards to employee home or inserts in payslip envelope
- **briefing** to clarify questions or address concerns, e.g. supervisors informing their teams (with the aid of speaking notes and Frequently Asked Questions – FAQs – if needed).

To encourage participation, some employers may also provide an indirect incentive to do so, such as a donation to charity for each response submitted.[10] While a survey is running it may be possible to monitor the response rate as it progresses and remind everyone of how this is progressing, so as to encourage higher participation levels. In doing so, care is needed to get the right message across so employees do not feel as a result that:

- awareness of participation levels means the survey is not confidential after all
- failure to participate might have a negative consequence
- management are somehow pressuring them to give a favourable response.

After the survey – turning results into action that makes a difference

Once the survey is complete, there will be a lot of curiosity from managers and employees about the results, and possibly some impatience to start taking action. At the same time, the survey results may seem such an impenetrable mass of data that it appears hard to know where to start, or what to do. Research suggests that a significant proportion of businesses fail to take action after their survey is held. The IPA (Involvement and Participation Association) in the UK tends to agree, having reported in 2007 that fewer than half of organizations knew what to do to encourage engagement (MacLeod and Clarke, 2009, p. 32). Getting started can be a challenge but, aside from missing the opportunity to improve business performance, not taking follow-up action is likely to reduce employee engagement by making staff feel that their inputs are being ignored.

To avoid getting stuck in this way, the following five steps are recommended so as to move forward:

1 Check
2 Calibrate
3 Commit
4 Communicate
5 Conclude.

These are also shown in Figure 4.1. This is what these mean in practice:

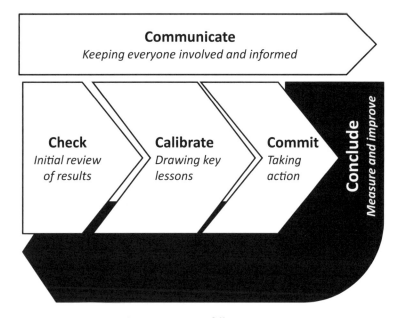

Figure 4.1 Survey follow-up steps

1   **Check:** Make a first review of the results to see if there are any problems with the data, and if there are major themes that come out of the results.
2   **Calibrate:** Dig deeper to be clear about what the key issues from the survey are, and use interaction with employees and other data sources to confirm the problems to be addressed.
3   **Commit:** Leadership teams agree on the key follow-up steps and take ownership for them so they are turned into action.
4   **Communicate:** An ongoing activity that begins before the survey, by making sure employees and managers understand the purpose of the survey and what the outcome of the survey process will be. Once the survey has taken place, the work involves making sure that employees know what came out of it, what you agreed to do and that they are kept informed as the follow-up actions take place.
5   **Conclude:** A final step that involves assessing what improved as a result of follow-up action, drawing lessons both for the next survey and for how to improve engagement and organizational effectiveness in the future.

We'll look at these five steps and how to make sure results turn into action in Chapters 5–7.

Conclusion

While it's often easy to tell people's overall engagement from how they behave, any serious attempt to assess, understand and improve workforce engagement in an organization larger than a small business requires survey work. By measuring and analysing people issues in a more specific and quantitative way, a survey brings such topics to the management table at the same level as discussions about (for example) finances or marketing. It enables managers to start to get a hold on what could otherwise be unclear or elusive workforce challenges. A survey also helps to make clear that people-related topics are not 'soft', but can be tracked and improved like any other part of the business. In that sense, the old adage that 'what gets measured, gets done' is true. But while a well-designed and run survey is important, further work is needed if one is to make sense of the data. This is the focus of the next chapter, where we'll look at how to get the most out of survey results and what can be done to sidestep the risk of 'analysis paralysis' that can sometimes prevent subsequent follow-up.

Checklist

- Do you have a clear idea about how engagement can contribute to your organization and its future effectiveness?
- What issues or engagement drivers do you need to monitor as a result in order to help your organization be successful?
- How well do you understand right now what makes your employees 'tick'?
- Do you already use employee engagement surveys, and how effective have they been?
- Is there sufficient management commitment to accept feedback (even if negative) and to take meaningful follow-up action as a result?
- Have there been past problems with surveys that need addressing in the future (e.g. quality of questionnaire design, employee confidence in confidentiality and in the survey leading to follow-up, etc)?
- Does your survey also allow for written comments to be added?
- Does your survey cover the four key dimensions of engagement (Connection, Support, Voice and Scope)?
- Aside from measuring engagement levels, what other potential business or workplace issues would you also want to cover in a survey?
- Can the survey data be broken down into reports that are understandable and actionable for local managers?
- How satisfied are you with your current survey provider? How far do you need them to be an expert advisor to you, and how effective are they in this?
- Do you involve employee representatives sufficiently in the survey process and seek their support for resulting actions?
- How adequately can you overcome potential barriers to participation (e.g. foreign languages, lack of access to a computer at work, etc.)?

- Do you have a project plan in place for running the survey and follow-up, and adequate resources to run the exercise? Are relevant internal groups sufficiently involved, such as Communications, HR or IT?
- Is the survey run often enough to be meaningful?
- Does the survey's timing run any risk of reducing participation levels (e.g. due to conflicts with holiday periods or work pressures)?
- Can the provider deliver results quickly enough to allow the data to be taken into account when setting priorities as part of the business planning process?

Notes

1 In the UK, the IPA has previously reported that 91 per cent of organizations use surveys to measure employee attitudes and perceptions, although this includes satisfaction and attitude surveys as well as engagement surveys (Jameson, 2009, p. 6).

2 For example, questions asking about how far employees act in an engaged way are better written in terms asking respondents what they observe when looking at other co-workers, which is more likely to be objective, than asking employees to report on their own behaviour, which will be subjective and prone to bias (Macey et al., 2009, p. 93). Bear in mind too that survey questions may be subject to copyright, in which case it is not possible to address this simply by 'lifting' questions from other surveys.

3 The original Q^{12} research mostly comprised retail operations (31 per cent), financial organizations (28 per cent), health care units (21 per cent) and education units (9 per cent) (Buckingham and Coffman, 1999, p. 259). In that sense, the original Gallup research tended to be oriented to organizations where customer focus was key and where people were more likely to work in teams – possibly explaining why the resulting Q^{12} focuses on the immediate work environment rather the wider organization.

4 For a review of the Gallup Q^{12}, see Hutton, 2009, pp. 69–83.

5 For details of further suggested suppliers in the UK, see IDS, 2010.

6 For more suggestions on how to develop an overall framework for understanding results, see Hutton, 2009, pp. 129–50.

7 For a review of the Best Companies Survey, see Hutton, 2009, pp. 91–100.

8 An agree/disagree scale has different possible responses (e.g. 'Strongly agree', 'Agree', etc.). Those with an odd number of possible responses allow a median (or neutral) choice (such as 'Don't know' or 'Neither agree or disagree'), whereas a forced choice scale has an even number of possible responses (say, four or six) that preclude a 'Don't know' reply. A forced choice scale removes uncertainty about what is meant by a median reply, but respondents may feel uncomfortable being pushed into replying one way or another.

9 The Bedfordshire police in the UK allowed its employees to participate in their engagement survey either online or using their work BlackBerrys (see IDS, 2010, p. 3).

10 For example, in return for each submitted survey, the Bedfordshire police promised to donate £2 to the charity 'Victims of Crime' (see IDS, 2010, p. 31).

CHAPTER 5

So now you've carried out a survey. After the effort to set it up and encourage everyone to take part, it might feel like most of the job is done – but in reality, this is where the real work begins. Within a few weeks of the survey closing, you will probably have received one or more reports with the results. At the same time, there may be a growing sense of anticipation in the organization. Employees gave their opinion weeks ago and are now beginning to wonder when they will see the results – and what they will say. Surrounded by reams of data, the danger is that the whole exercise can start to feel overwhelming and that it's difficult to make sense of it all, or know what to do next. However, the five steps described at the end of Chapter 4 can help you avoid this and instead maximize the benefits of your survey. As mentioned before, the five steps are check, calibrate, commit, communicate and conclude. This chapter will look at the first two, which are all about understanding what your employees are telling you.

Step 1: Check

Can the data be used?

Once you have the survey results, you'll obviously be keen to find out what they are saying. But before jumping into the details, it is important to check that each report seems correct. Mistakes can happen and it is a waste of effort analysing a report that is not right in the first place. For example, does the number of participants seem reasonable, given the size of workforce and expected response rate? Do any associated breakdowns of organizational data seem right (e.g. do the results for Europe include all relevant countries)? If not, check with the survey provider in case there has been a problem in defining or generating your report.

Bear in mind, too, that the number of participants also has an effect on the usefulness of your data. It may mean that, even if there are trends in the results, the data might not be statistically significant – and is therefore not a sound basis for drawing conclusions. Wiley (2010b) suggests a rule of thumb outlined in Table 5.1 for determining if changes in scores are statistically significant or not. This is important because the danger is that supervisors may read too much into changes in scores when they are not in fact statistically significant, and can therefore be misleading as indicators of what is really going on. In such a case, more qualitative ways of assessing engagement (such as focus groups) may be the only answer.

Another statistical indicator to watch out for is the degree of correlation between different elements in the survey results. Through multiple regression analysis, leading survey providers can help show what the correlation between different questions or survey topics is (e.g. how far engagement scores correlate with those for – say – performance management). A complete correlation would produce a regression coefficient of 1, but this is extremely unlikely to be achieved – in fact, anything above 0.3 is in practice significant. However, it is important to realize that such a statistical dependence does not imply causality, that these tools do have potential limitations and that, as surveys are (by necessity) selective in the questions they ask, they may potentially overlook other drivers of disengagement.[1]

Table 5.1 Guidelines for statistical significance in survey data

Numbers of respondents in the unit	Statistically significant percentage difference
5000+	3–4%
100–4999	5% or more
50–99	10% or more
<50	15% or more

Getting initial impressions from the survey results

After having done this initial check, the next step is to look at the survey response rate. On average, around two-thirds of those invited can be expected to take part, although a lower score might be expected the first time a survey is run, or if there are many participants who work offsite at customer locations – in which case, less than 50 per cent may realistically respond.[2] But a disappointing outcome here should be investigated thoroughly, because this may indicate misunderstandings about the survey's purpose, a lack of trust in the organization or scepticism about whether the survey will really lead to any follow-up action – especially if there have been other employee surveys in the past that did not trigger any consequences. If such a survey has been run in the past, a comparison between past and current response rates can be instructive. A rising participation level may show growing buy-in for the survey process, whereas a drop may reflect disappointment about a lack of follow-up on previous employee feedback.

The next step is to see what stands out from the results. Which questions scored particularly high or low? Are there any surprises, or data that possibly confirms suspected problems? Drilling down into the results is important too, especially as the aggregation of data for an overall report means that a lot of averaging of data has occurred that can that hide significant trends beneath the surface, e.g. between one department and another, or between different groups (e.g. male versus female, HQ versus front line staff, etc.).

When confronted with (say) a high overall favorable score, it may be helpful to dig into the underlying data to understand the strength of views. Is the score strongly positive (e.g. mostly respondents replying 'agree') or is it more lukewarm (e.g. mostly replying 'tend to agree')? Look out for questions with high rates of 'don't know' replies, which may indicate issues with the understanding of a specific question – or even that employees are reluctant to speak out and give a direct reply. Be aware too that higher levels of 'don't know' replies will lead to a corresponding drop in levels of positive and negative scores, and give the possibly misleading impression that people are more dissatisfied than they really are.

It's likewise important to avoid over-interpreting the responses to specific survey questions and to second-guess what participants had in their minds when they responded. Peter Hutton uses the example of a statement 'I intend to be working for the company in 12 months' time'. Although a high level of agreement with this could indicate considerable loyalty from employees, he argues it could just reflect that 'the job may be conveniently located; they may believe they would find it hard to find another job or they may feel that the pay is good, even though they dislike the work, and so on.' He argues that negative scores for more ambiguous questions can be even more problematic – with a statement 'I am satisfied about where the organization is going', he asks 'does disagreement mean that employees think they know where the organization is going but are dissatisfied with that direction, or do they just have no idea of where it is going?' (Hutton, 2009, p. 26).

> The trick, therefore, is to keep an open mind, given that responses are frequently only telling management *what* is felt by employees but not *why*.

The trick, therefore, is to keep an open mind, given that responses are frequently only telling management *what* is felt by employees but not *why*. Understanding the latter requires more investigation, so watch out for any possible personal biases when reviewing results. Focus on what the data says, noting what seems unusual, rather than already finding data to confirm one's existing views. If there are open-ended questions in the survey, these may provide more context for responses; otherwise, some of the methods described under 'Step 2: Calibrate' below may be required to flesh out what the responses really mean.

Possible factors leading to differences in data

Be aware too that data can vary by workforce segment (e.g. age, gender, position, length of service, department, country). So before concluding there may be an issue to address, a few examples of points to bear in mind are as follows:

- **Engagement scores are frequently affected by length of service and age:** Having chosen to join a new organization, recent hires tend to rate their employer very highly. Thereafter, engagement tends to drop off, although sometimes there may be a slight recovery in levels among those with longest levels of service. As regards age, many surveys point to engagement levels being lower among younger workers and higher among older staff. Engagement drivers may also differ by age group – younger staff may be more interested in training or career progression, older ones in job security or employee benefits.

- **Results will differ by sector:** This may be affected by the impact of the economic cycle on different industries; there does generally seem to be a variation in engagement levels by business type. For example, Kenexa's Work Trends Survey (2010) found that the best engagement results were in high-tech manufacturing and pharma/healthcare products, while communications services and transportation services came at the low end. Comparing results with a benchmark of others in the same industry can therefore be helpful in putting scores in context.

- **Scores often vary by job or organizational function:** For example, scores tend to be more positive in sales functions and less so in R&D, where staff may be more analytical and can see less directly the impact of their work on the success of the organization. There is often also a tendency for engagement levels to decrease with level in the organizational hierarchy. For example, the Kenexa Research Institute found that the Employee Engagement Index score for senior/middle managers averaged at 64 per cent, whereas the corresponding score of service and production workers was only 51 per cent (Wiley, 2010a). Aon Hewitt also reports that in the US what attracts and sustains people varies by function, as do their top engagement drivers. For sales it is 'manager understands what motivates me'; for manufacturing it is 'involved in decisions that affect my work'; in R&D it is 'appropriate amount of decision-making authority' and in customer service it is 'understand my potential career path in my company' (Aon Hewitt, 2010, p. 18).

- **Results may be lower in headquarters than elsewhere:** It is not uncommon for scores to be lower for HQ staff than in subsidiaries, as the latter may be more motivated by being closer to the day-to-day business, having fewer levels of management to deal with and seeing the results of their work more immediately. The environment is therefore more energizing than in a HQ role, where longer lead times and a potentially greater awareness of all the weaknesses and challenges of the overall organization may instil a greater sense of scepticism.

- **Scores will differ according to country:** Local cultural aspects will play a part in how respondents answer questions so that scores will vary by country. The Kenexa Research Institute reported in 2010 that a survey of 14 countries around the world produced an average Employee Engagement Index score of 56 per cent, but that respondents in India scored highest (at more than 70 per cent) while respondents in Japan came in at less than 40 per cent (Wiley, 2010a). This does not mean that employees are intrinsically more engaged in one country than another, but more often that cultural norms mean that employees will tend to answer the same question in more or less positive terms. Indeed engagement per se can manifest itself differently by culture – in a US setting, engagement may be seen more in terms of highly visible energy and enthusiasm, whereas this would seem out of place in some Asian settings (Macey et al., 2009, p. 25).

- **Engagement drivers will also differ by country:** Aon Hewitt reported that in its surveys, career opportunities came out as the top driver globally for employees, but the next highest driver varied by region. In Asia-Pacific it was brand alignment, in Europe it was people and HR practices, in Latin America it was recognition, and in North America it was managing performance (Aon Hewitt, 2011). Gebauer and Lowman (2008, pp. 13–15) point out that Towers Watson found the top engagement driver in Brazil was how far the organization rewarded outstanding customer service, in China it was the quality of opportunities for career advancement and in India the degree to which employees had input into decision-making in their department. To understand local differences, it is helpful to compare scores with local country norms, and then to involve local management and employees in working on the data, rather than drawing conclusions from afar that may be coloured by stereotyping or misunderstanding of what is actually going on.

As Gebauer and Lowman (2008, p. 59) comment, given the demographic diversity of survey results,

> *Many managers are tempted to eschew research and simply look for a universal silver bullet that consistently yields engagement. But there isn't one. For every*

company, for every employee group within the organization, for every individual, there is a unique combination of engagement drivers, and each driver has a different level of importance. That may sound overwhelming, but the goal for an organization and for individual managers is to know the combination of drivers that will be effective for particular employee segments within their workforce.

This means that action planning will need to involve some degree of tailoring to ensure these different needs are taken into account. Such segmentation could follow conventional lines (such as job type or gender), or less obvious ones such as lifestyle or behavioural groups. For example, using engagement and consumer research, **Tesco** grouped its staff into five employee segments ('want it all', 'live to work', 'work to live', 'pleasure-seekers' and 'work-life balancers'), and provided more tailored employment solutions to address their different needs.

Another element to consider is the interaction between the business situation and the survey results. While there is overwhelming evidence that increased engagement can lead to improved business results, employee engagement is not the sole driver of organizational performance. A general recession, a fast move by a competitor or a major product recall can all adversely affect business results and – depending on overall confidence in the organization – may impact the survey results as well. The engagement–business performance linkage is not therefore a simple one-way process; even so, organizations that have good levels of engagement and trust in their leadership are likely to see smaller setbacks in their scores than other businesses, and so be better placed to bounce back in the future.

Using yardsticks to evaluate your data

To get a complete picture, try also to look at the data from different perspectives. For example, how do the scores compare in absolute terms, and how do they stack up against any previous surveys? Can you compare the data to meaningful benchmarks? And does the data differ by workforce segment (e.g. age, position, length of service, department)? Table 5.2 shows some different ways in which you can evaluate your data.

Table 5.2 Means of evaluating survey data

Methods	Benefits	Potential challenges
Response rate (e.g. 81 per cent of employees took part)	Shows how representative the results are Level of score may sometimes also serve as an overall barometer of engagement	Important not to create a sense of coercion about survey participation
Absolute scores (e.g. 72 per cent favourable replies)	Easily understood Simple to use	Can be misleading (some questions may just tend to score high or low anyway)
Year-on-year trends (e.g. 2 per cent increase in favourable replies compared to the last survey)	Shows comparative progress over time Highlights declines or where improvement is absent	Needs large sample to be statistically meaningful
External benchmarks (e.g. own score is 3 per cent below country benchmark)	Overcomes potential cultural biases (a high score may be less impressive if there is a trend to score higher in that country or function anyway)	May not be available in all cases Benchmark needs to be meaningful (for example, is a cross-industry sample relevant for a company that only operates in one sector? Does a country norm have employers that are all in very different sectors from your own?)
Internal benchmarks (e.g. score for unit X is 2 per cent higher than overall company score)	More immediate organizational yardstick	Risk of creating too much internal competition Local cultural differences may mean external national benchmarks are a more meaningful benchmark than global company scores
Regression (key drivers) (e.g. the score for leadership has a X per cent correlation with overall engagement levels)	Shows factors that correlate most with engagement	More complex to explain/communicate. Important that correlation is not misunderstood as causality

Sharing initial results

How the data is fed back will necessarily vary by audience. Senior executives will be more concerned to find out about the key themes across their organization, about what is most driving (or impeding) engagement and how their results compare with peers or competitors. They will also want to understand the potential business risks implied by the results, what initiatives could help address this and where their sponsorship and involvement is most needed. In contrast, lower-level managers will want to dig more into the details to understand what is going on in the different parts of their organization, in order to comprehend the motivations and concerns expressed in the results, and then to start to think about what specifically can be done in response. But once these results have been initially digested by management, it's important to start sharing overall findings with employees (see Chapter 6) so as not to keep everyone waiting, and to begin to get staff involved in helping to understand and act on the results.

In all cases, when going through the data, keep a note of what issues start to appear. The goal at this stage is not to 'fix' them but to see patterns and potential prioritization of work. Remember also to look out for what has scored well: there's a risk of focusing on the negative, and not highlighting 'wins' from the survey that are positive news for the organization, or to show where follow-up action from past surveys has paid off in higher ratings this time around. Look closely at any data available on the key drivers of employee engagement, as action on these is more likely to have a bigger effect on engagement. Think too about how the impressions from the survey results compare with current business circumstances and priorities; are there overlaps and potential issues where some quick steps could help raise business performance? All of this takes time, and is best done through a combination of private work and joint discussion in management teams. By the time this has been reviewed once (and ideally twice) as a team, it should be possible to see a few top issues to address.

At this stage, make sure the management team are still behind the survey exercise – they need to be bought in throughout the survey process.

Step 2: Calibrate

Validating survey findings more fully

Now there should be a good first idea of what the results are saying; but the chances are, there are still areas of doubt. For example, many surveys only gather quantitative data: while this gives the 'what', the statistics may not provide the 'why'. Other sources can therefore be helpful to validate the conclusions drawn from the survey so that the statistics in the survey can be brought to life and data that might seem surprising or contradictory can be clarified. Some common methods, and their strengths and weaknesses, are described in Table 5.3.

> It can also be helpful to compare other sources of data with what is emerging from the survey, to see how consistent they are.

South Tees NHS Trust, part of the UK's National Health Service, has used focus groups very effectively to understand employee attitudes more fully. Although it uses the NHS National Staff Survey as a starting point, this is complemented by focus groups known as the 'Big Conversation', which involve a cross-section of employees and allow key topics to be explored in much more detail than the annual survey would allow. Participants are also asked two overall questions – 'What are the three best things about working in this division?' and 'What are the three things that could be better about this division?' By taking part, employees also feel like they are involved and have their say in the running of the Trust (IDS, 2009, pp. 32–3). Using such approaches to validate survey findings ensures that data is not misinterpreted and that ineffective solutions are not generated; it also makes employees feel they are part of the engagement process, as opposed to having solutions imposed on them, so creating greater buy-in for the future.

It can also be helpful to compare other sources of data with what is emerging from the survey, to see how consistent they are. How do survey results compare with what managers have been picking up from workplace conversations? HR departments can provide useful 'soft' data, such as observations from personnel officers dealing with employee grievances, feedback via employee representatives or by comments gathered through exit interviews held when staff terminate their employment with the organization. How far does this tally with survey results?

Possible correlations with other data

It's also worthwhile to see how scores compare with other indicators of organizational performance. For example, if engagement levels are declining, is this being reflected in accident rates, customer complaints or product defect levels? Be aware too that some metrics can be a *lagging* indicator: for example, employee disengagement may take a while before it turns into increased staff turnover, or before higher engagement is converted into increased customer satisfaction. As mentioned in Chapter 1, a number of organizations have found sufficiently strong correlation between engagement levels and organizational metrics that engagement can actually be seen as a *leading* indicator of future business performance. A good example is Kenexa's High Performance Model, which has been able to demonstrate the positive effect that leadership behaviours and workplace values have on employee engagement and so customer satisfaction (Wiley, 2010b, pp. 66–70).

Through linkage research, a strong correlation has been shown between practices such as employee involvement and training and their effect on employees (e.g. retention, teamwork), and so improved customer satisfaction and (ultimately) business performance (e.g. market share and profitability). Being able to demonstrate such a correlation in one's own organization and developing the supporting models, etc., requires significant investment, and is more effective when it is possible to measure such correlations at lower organizational levels. Hence, as leading survey expert Jack Wiley (2010b, p. 80) comments:

> *Branch banking and retail organizations are much more likely candidates for linkage research because they can treat branches or retail outlets as the unit of analysis. All three measures – employee, customer, and financial – are often available in these organizational settings.*

A good example is **Royal Bank of Scotland (RBS)**, which has its own human capital model that uses engagement survey feedback to serve as a leading edge

Table 5.3 Methods for clarifying survey results

Method	Details	Benefits	Potential challenges
Follow-up interviews	Individual interview (in person or by phone) to probe deeper and understand the meaning of the survey results	A one-to-one discussion allows confidentiality of responses and so more candid feedback Provides more time to drill deeper into topics	Risk of biased sample Requires neutral interviewer to allay possible respondent concerns about confidentiality The structure of the interview may skew the impression gained
Employee lunch/dinner with an executive	A group of employees are invited to have a meal with the CEO or another senior executive – the meal may be wholly informal or follow a rough agenda and have 'light touch' moderation	Brings front-line feedback to the eyes and ears of top management Employees can feel they are really being heard Opportunity for top management to clarify or dispel areas of confusion or concern	Only few employees will probably get the opportunity to take part Selecting participants may be sensitive Employees may feel intimidated by the setting and not be wholly frank with their remarks Executives may be tempted to go on the defensive rather than actively listen to negative feedback
Focus group	A small group of a dozen or so employees is invited to meet and answer questions to generate more thorough feedback on the issues arising from the survey	Allows 'deep dive' into specific topics Absence of an agenda allows flexibility as to what topics to explore and how to do so, and may allow probing of topics that may be awkward to cover in a session with managers Quick and reaches more people than interviews	Requires expert facilitation Risk of 'groupthink' and biased feedback Effectively only few employees can take part A reasonable number of meetings need to be held to ensure a representative sample

Poster session	Questions requiring clarification are put on large posters. Employees are invited to complete Post-it notes with their comments and to put these on the poster	Quick and easy to do Responses can be kept anonymous Can be run as a large-group event, generating energy and discussion	The pre-selected questions may not reflect what is uppermost on employees' minds
Town hall meeting	Data shared with employees in an open forum that allows questions and answers	Allows large numbers of employees to take part Survey sponsors are visible and available for questions	Risk of overloading the audience with excessive data Employees may be reluctant to raise issues in such a public forum Care needed to ensure session is seen as genuinely aiming to seek feedback
Large group meetings (e.g. 'world café', 'future search')	Large numbers of people brought together for a common meeting where they can work on identifying and resolving problems, in a mix of large and small work groups	Can tap into a wide source of knowledge Helps build up excitement and momentum about survey follow-up, and a stronger sense of common purpose Encourages consideration of 'out of the box' ideas	Requires careful planning and facilitation Depends on everyone being open to new and different ideas Risk of 'groupthink' or pursuit of unrealistic solutions

indicator for key elements of business performance (MacLeod and Brady, 2007, pp. 234–5). But even if it is not possible to establish a direct linkage between survey data and the business performance of one's own organization, clearly employee metrics (especially those related to engagement) do contribute to organizational success and so it is essential to spend time evaluating which are the key metrics and how they can be improved upon.

Avoiding 'analysis paralysis' – or addressing too many issues

The ability to 'slice and dice' data so many ways can lead to a disproportionate amount of time being spent on crawling through the results – whereas the ultimate goal is, of course, to take follow-up action. The analysis process should therefore be a question of weeks, not months – but by pulling together the survey analysis and including other additional sources of data, it is possible to calibrate the results to be sure of being on the right path. By maintaining momentum at this stage, it should be possible to avoid falling into the trap of 'analysis paralysis'.

The next step is to finalize conclusions with the top management team about what are the key issues from the survey and – importantly – what to do next. Tools such as a SWOT analysis or a fishbone diagram can help here, but ultimately the goal is to narrow down the findings and agree on a small number of issues to address that will make the most difference to future engagement levels and to the business overall. Put in practical terms, we would recommend a minimum of two and preferably no more than five action areas. This may seem quite small given that the survey may well have surfaced many potential issues for addressing. But it is unrealistic to try to tackle everything: employees do not necessarily expect it and going after multiple issues risks spreading resources too thinly, so that real progress will not be achieved. As Gebuaer and Lowman (2008, p. 67) caution, 'Not every insight requires action, even areas that received "low" engagement scores. The point is not to be outstanding in every single aspect of the employment deal. That's neither practical nor affordable.'

Action planning will also vary by organizational level. There will be a more natural division between the issues and actions being defined for the whole organization (as defined by the top management team) and those that can be addressed by middle managers and by first-line supervisors. Top management will tend to focus on setting and articulating the overall vision and direction, and in determining

> By maintaining momentum at this stage, it should be possible to avoid falling into the trap of 'analysis paralysis'.

programmes and policies for the whole organization, whereas middle and first-level management will focus on translating the direction and the programmes into the immediate workplace. In doing their work, middle managers can be aided by receiving ready-prepared reports or analyses that help them begin to identify priorities for action. At **Standard Chartered Bank**, managers receive scorecards that compare the results for their organization with other internal and external comparisons (IDS, 2009, p. 7), and so such gap analysis provides a foundation for their subsequent documented action steps, known as 'impact plans' (IDS, 2009, p. 28).

When identifying their follow-up actions, middle managers should consider the following points:

- Check first what the organization-wide priorities are so they know how much resource needs to be devoted to addressing these, and so their own plans can be aligned with these.
- Use the opportunity to discuss the survey results with their staff and get their input on what matters and possible actions in response. Some organizations delegate the survey analysis and action planning to employee groups, whose recommendations are then vetted by management. Alternatively, a series of dialogues can take place, where management have the final say but staff have the chance to offer their insights, make suggestions and help prioritize.
- When developing plans, it's essential not to dodge issues. It's easy to decide problems are too difficult or to park them with a different owner ('of course this is an issue only HQ can resolve') – but the resulting plan will lose credibility and relevance.
- At the same time, it's impossible to do everything, so avoid creating over-ambitious plans that are unrealistic and create disappointment later on.

In all cases, action plans should focus on the issues where follow-up work will most make a difference. It's obvious that they should address problems that are relatively easy to solve (especially if they have a high payback); these are good 'quick wins' that can be appreciated and also show early on that the survey process is already making a difference. This leaves the more difficult problems that require a good deal of effort before significant impact is seen. Because these have more risk and require more resources, care is needed to select and focus on the most worthwhile cases.

For first-line supervisors, bear in mind that the survey issues for this latter group are less likely to be about 'what' is done at work and more about the 'how'. So for example, while the survey may raise organization-wide issues about (say) work-life balance or customer focus, the supervisor's role is unlikely to be to develop programmes in response but – to take these two examples – more looking at how they can be applied more effectively with their team (e.g. giving staff more flexibility over how and when they work, or helping staff resolve customer problems). But given the major impact they have on the employee's working environment, supervisors therefore play a pivotal role in engagement survey follow-up.

Yet first-level managers may often not be doing these basics such as setting clear goals, giving ongoing feedback or removing roadblocks to their employees being able to do their job effectively – so this needs to be addressed through goal-setting and feedback for supervisors themselves. Good execution of core supervisory tasks such as providing support and development for staff, or helping employees understand how they and their goals fit into the overall organization, can therefore also help raise engagement levels (see Chapter 9).

Conclusion

Properly evaluating survey results can provide new insights into particular issues affecting a workforce or reveal more clearly what is on employees' minds. But it requires a judicious balance between exploring the data and not over-analysing it, and between spotting patterns and not jumping to conclusions. To avoid getting lost in unnecessary analysis, comparison to different yardsticks and supplementing quantitative data with qualitative input can help put results into a more meaningful context; however, it's important not to lose sight of the end goals of surveying (which are to identify a handful of key issues to address) and to be able to share results with employees at the earliest opportunity. Keeping up momentum is important so that action planning, communication and follow-up can take place soon afterwards. We will look at these in more detail in the next chapter.

Checklist

- Have the results been subject to an initial quality control before being analyzed?
- What initial messages can be drawn from the survey data and overall participation rate?
- Are there any factors that may be influencing the data (e.g. cultural differences, workforce demographics, etc.)?
- How do results compare to previous surveys or against other yardsticks?
- How can you collect additional 'soft' data to deepen understanding of what the survey results are saying?
- Do you see any patterns between the survey results and (for example) business performance or accident or attrition rates?
- Is there agreement on a focused set of two to five action points arising from the survey? Are there sufficient resources in place to carry them out?
- Are front-line managers able to handle employee questions about the survey and ready to get behind the resulting action plans?

Notes

1 For a fuller discussion of this, see Hutton, 2009, pp. 56–65.
2 The first time the global security company G4S held its engagement survey in 2009, it got a 29 per cent response rate. This was partly affected by the fact that around 80 per cent of its staff work on client sites (IDS, 2010, p. 19).

CHAPTER 6

In Chapter 4, we briefly outlined the five steps to move from survey to actions – check, calibrate, commit, communicate and conclude – and the last chapter covered the first two of these steps in detail. This chapter examines the remaining three steps. The first of these is 'commit', which is key to avoiding some of the problems found in organizations such as 'analysis paralysis' or lack of ownership for follow-up actions. We'll then look at 'communicate' – something that will have already started with sharing initial results, but becomes especially important when setting out action plans and making employees aware of progress being made. Finally, we'll discuss the fifth step – conclude – which is important to draw lessons from the engagement follow-up actions, and decide on what this means for future survey design and further action generally.

Step 3: Commit

The importance of top-level sponsorship for survey follow-up

By this stage, an overall analysis and proposed action plan should already have been developed. HR and Communications can be effective 'sparring partners' here – but bear in mind that, although they can help develop an action plan, the final responsibility for ownership and execution rests with line management. No plan will succeed if the organization, and especially its management, is not behind it. By contrast, enthusiastic sponsorship and support will bring the plan to life, and convey the message to employees that their feedback is being taken seriously and that something will happen as a result. This means mobilizing the organization at different levels so that real momentum occurs. As a starting point, top-level sponsorship is key for several reasons:

- Senior management support shows to everyone that the survey results (and follow-up action) really matter. This is especially important in smaller organizations, where the head of the organization (who may also be the owner) is seen as being key in setting priorities and overall organizational 'tone'.
- If middle management is busy on survey-related activity but there is silence from above, the process will lack credibility and the exercise may quickly run out of steam.
- Through the process of Connection, top-level management often has a direct effect on engagement levels – trust in the overall direction of an organization, quality of leadership, and the organization's vision, values and strategy can be key drivers of engagement.

It's important for leaders of organizations to involve their management team in this process so that they are fully briefed on the results, that they have had the chance to reflect on and debate the findings, and that everyone has had the chance to be heard. By this stage, the team is likely to be interested and ready to finalize action plans. If not, Chapter 7 discusses how to overcome potential resistance or inertia, especially at the top.

Cascading actions through the organization

In larger organizations there will be different levels of management, and each of them may well receive their own reports to analyse and work on. In such a case, careful planning is needed to make sure that adequate time is allowed for this work to be done, while ensuring that the follow-up exercise does not lose momentum and the eventual action plans are aligned down through the organization. HR can help here by:

- aiding management in creating an overall schedule for cascading results and action plans

- keeping engagement as a live topic for management
- advising managers on how to interpret and act on data
- helping keep employee representatives involved in the work on engagement.

However, HR should not be playing the lead role and employee engagement should not be relegated to being a 'Personnel topic'. At the middle management level, David MacLeod and Chris Brady (2007, p. 200) point to the untapped potential of harnessing the energy of leaders there and add that their research 'indicates a desire by managers to achieve outstanding results, engage their people and secure deep personal satisfaction, which is often frustrated by the mundane and other bureaucratic demands of their jobs.' Their advice is to seek to remove some of these roadblocks – otherwise, 'if middle management are not at the heart of your efforts to improve levels of engagement and hence performance, they will become an obstruction to it' (MacLeod and Brady, 2007, p. 201).

But aside from the management teams themselves, it can also be helpful to identify internal 'champions' (e.g. managers who are enthusiastic or high-potential individual contributors) who can be internal change agents in support of the survey process. While care is needed in making sure the demands of these roles are realistic and clearly defined so they don't get confused with the roles of line managers or HR, such champions can be useful in spreading best practices, coaching others, gathering employee feedback, etc. According to the UK Department for Business Innovation and Skills (2011), to be effective, they should ideally have:

- understanding of engagement – what it means and its benefits
- enthusiasm and energy for the subject
- knowledge of the business and the people in their area
- connections and credibility among the people in their area
- confidence to deal with others on the business's behalf
- confidence to handle feedback – positive or negative – on the business's behalf.

With some initial guidance and training to point them in the right direction, such champions can provide a valuable multiplier effect to overall engagement efforts.

Ensuring quality action plans

Finally, successful action depends on the quality of the action plan itself. Some suggested tips for setting an effective action plan are summarized in Box 6.1.

Some survey providers also offer online tools for setting up action plans that can then be monitored centrally to ensure quality and alignment, and to foster subsequent sharing of best practices. These can give a 'jump start' to planning and encourage some internal competition to get actions moving. However, these tools are not cheap and – aside from their cost – lower-level managers may

---

Box 6.1 Key tips for setting an effective action plan

- Set goals that are clear (i.e. specific and measurable), with accountability assigned to named individuals.
- Be clear about the timelines for the work. If all the actions will take quite some time to produce results, consider replacing some by a few that will yield earlier outcomes and show sooner the difference that is being made.
- Identify the critical dependencies for the action. If there are other stakeholders that are key to success (e.g. works councils), make sure they are involved too, as appropriate. Similarly, if there are significant resources needed, check the budget is there for them.
- Make sure that the action plan is seen as a central business activity – can the above metrics be included in organizational key performance indicators or balanced scorecards?
- Ensure that the action plan is a regular review topic with management teams.
- Identify how the action plan can be broken down into specific actions that can be taken by individual managers or employees so that they can be made aware of what they too can do in support.
- Be clear about the desired outcome of the action, such as better quality of supervision by increasing training on key aspects such as active listening or providing feedback. Then make sure that the subsequent survey can measure the change in desired outcome.

---

feel such tools are too rigid and burdensome, and that they smack too much of central interference and control. How action planning is done therefore depends on the organization's resources and management culture. But in all cases, the intent is not planning for its own sake, but to ensure that such plans get converted into actions that have meaningful and lasting effects.

Irrespective of whether an online tool is used, one challenge is striking the right balance in how extensive the planning process that occurs should be. The traditional approach is to encourage every recipient of a report to generate their own plan, and then (if desired) for these to be aggregated later. But the risk in bigger organizations is that there could be hundreds of plans as a result, leading to dissipation of energy and effort, and widespread 'reinventing of the wheel'. Quite often, many of the same themes and issues will appear across all the reports. A more efficient and effective way may be for a core action plan to be defined at the top level of the organization, with lower-level units working on this plan and only adding very limited supplementary actions if there are results that highlight other local topics that really deserve special attention.

Measuring and encouraging progress

If employee engagement is not to become simply a lot of unrealized good intentions, it has to be reinforced by measurement and follow-up. One organization that has increased their engagement levels significantly over recent years and won widespread recognition for their business results is **Campbell's Soup**. An important element in driving progress was that employee engagement was not treated as an afterthought but was turned into one of the company's key performance metrics. Increasingly, too, companies are making employee engagement a key metric that is reported externally – for example, the UK's Standard Chartered Bank includes the ratio of engaged to disengaged staff reported through the Gallup Q^{12} survey as one of its publicly communicated key performance indicators. The Dutch health, nutrition and materials company **DSM** goes further by not only reporting its employee engagement levels publicly, but also making this one of the metrics that drives the sustainability component of the short-term incentive plan applied to its managing board.

Progress with employee engagement can be encouraged in several different ways. Some suggested metrics to consider are shown in Table 6.1.

Table 6.1 Engagement survey follow-up metrics

Metric	Details	Benefits	Potential challenges
Action plan progress	Measures timeliness and comprehensiveness in completing the follow-up action plans	Ensures action plans are not overlooked	Tends to track activities rather than overall change in the organization
Employee perception of action plan follow-up	Questions used to ask employees how far they were aware of the results and follow-up to the survey. A battery of questions can even be used to create a 'Behaviour Change Index' (BCI) (Wiley, 2010b, pp. 120–24)	Reflects importance of communication and that employees that are aware of action tend to be more engaged than those that are unaware. BCI can foster comprehensive managerial accountability for action	Measures perception rather than actual change
Activity measures for managers	Measure how far managers are carrying out the behaviours required to drive engagement (e.g. if performance management matters, what percentage have held appraisals with their staff?)	Specific and output-related	Some activities may be less easy to track (e.g. frequency of coaching)
360-degree feedback	Measures manager behaviours that may in turn drive employee engagement	Collects candid feedback from subordinates, peers and boss. May collect specific written suggestions or comments	Survey instrument may not address all issues arising from a survey, and is unlikely to be feasible on a regular basis

Action plan outcomes	Measures how far the ultimate outcome of the action plan is realized (e.g. if the goal was to foster more regular performance management activity, what percentage of employees had their appraisals completed on time?)	More outcome-oriented. Can be tied to specific strategic goals of the organization	Need to ensure outcomes selected are meaningful and can be influenced by those held to account Important to anticipate any unintended consequences of a metric (e.g. a tight deadline for completing appraisals leads to them being done quickly, but at low quality)
Extrapolation of existing results	Sets future target based on what seems reasonable, taking into account what is statistically significant and what have been historic trends (if such data exists)	Underlines importance of achieving improvement in future surveys	May be difficult to set realistic goal (not all metrics may increase at same rate); potentially open to negotiation or 'gaming'
Internal benchmarking	Sets future target based on a comparison against other parts of the organization	As above	May be unfair to compare scores if they are affected by different cultural factors, etc. Risk of creating negative internal competition
External benchmarking	Sets future target by reference to an external yardstick (e.g. a current country or sector/industry norm). Note that if there is a significant gap, it may be necessary to set interim steps over a number of years to get there	As above, but should be more objective through using external comparison	Care needed in selecting right comparator

While tracking action plan progress is a 'must', adding further metrics can help to make sure that employee engagement is seen as an ongoing priority for management. This is especially the case if the metrics are treated as key performance indicators for the business (e.g. as a balanced scorecard metric) and so will be subject to periodic senior-level review. Alternatively, they can be turned into personal performance objectives. Whichever method is used, MacLeod and Brady (2007, p. 229) stress that:

> For the managerial level, you need to make sure that doing the things that lead to engagement pays – and that not doing them hurts. People-based issues in the form of engagement scores should form part of the metrics on which you judge an individual's performance.

Bearing in mind that improvement in engagement scores can take time – especially as there is a delay between the survey and action taking place – so challenging and meaningful goals should be set for what may in reality be a multi-year improvement journey rather than assuming overnight success. Where targets are set using survey results (e.g. future improvement in survey scores), bear in mind what is reasonable as improvement from a statistical significance viewpoint (see 'Step 1: Check' in Chapter 5). Survey specialists Macey et al. (2009, pp. 121–2) suggest an improvement of 5 per cent may be suitable for an individual survey question, as opposed to 3–4 per cent for a survey category/topic that comprises several questions, or 2–3 per cent for engagement itself (which is reliant on potentially multiple drivers of the score). However, targets also need to take into account scope for future improvement; for example, a topic that has had little attention, or an organization where previous management have not focused on engagement, may be able to advance much more, whereas a high-scoring unit that has already worked on many survey issues may be doing well to see a one per cent gain. Goal-setting, therefore, is situational. As noted by CRF (Lambert, 2010, p. 32):

> For the managerial level, you need to make sure that doing the things that lead to engagement pays – and that not doing them hurts.

Bear in mind that performance improvement is typically like being on an escalator. The aiming point is always moving – the context changes, competitors and comparators will not be standing still, and there will be new managers to inculcate with positive values.

Given the prevalence of pay-for-performance programmes, this use of metrics also raises the question of how far managers should be incentivized for achieving such goals (e.g.

> Appropriate care is needed to watch out for the danger of incentives driving the wrong outcomes.

through business performance indicators or personal performance ratings impacting pay increases and/or bonus payments). The advantage of this is that it provides an added reason to ensure targets are achieved, and that engagement-related objectives are not simply seen as 'nice to have' but elevated to the same importance as other goals. As always, appropriate care is needed to watch out for the danger of incentives driving the wrong outcomes – for example:

- Managers may be tempted to pressure staff to get improvements in future survey scores.
- If the target is part of metrics applied to staff more widely – such as a balanced scorecard – everyone may be tempted to give favourable survey responses next time, simply to impact positively the resulting payout.
- There may be insufficient 'line of sight' to make pursuing the target worthwhile. For example, a line manager may feel there is little they can do if the goal is to improve a company's global engagement level, or the action plan may be focused on activities that can mostly only be impacted by headquarters.
- Setting survey-related improvement targets can sometimes be difficult. In such cases, there is a risk of either exceeding the goal easily (creating windfall payments) or of the goal being too difficult (and so discouraging effort).

Setting improvement metrics can therefore drive change and is well worth considering. But it needs care and it is important that the metrics are not seen as an end in their own right. After all, the goal is to improve engagement and not just to 'make the numbers'.

Case study: Merck Serono

Merck Serono is the largest division of Merck KGaA, a leading German DAX 30 company operating in pharmaceuticals, chemicals and life science. Headquartered in Geneva, Switzerland, Merck Serono was established in January 2007, following Merck's acquisition of Serono. Although the integration was carried out within a year, it was clear that it would take longer to create a common culture, as it involved combining a start-up style biotech with the world's oldest pharma company. Although neither company had carried out global engagement surveys in the past, it was clear that gathering such data could help identify and overcome potential barriers to commitment. Moreover, the survey process itself could help employees feel they were heard and were valued, and so the first survey was held in March 2008 – just over a year after Merck Serono was created.

A challenging timetable was set to ensure rapid follow-up and avoid getting stuck in 'analysis paralysis'. Importantly, rather than encourage action plans at all levels, effort was focused on addressing key global engagement drivers first and getting everyone to put most of their efforts behind the global action plan that was developed. Key steps included helping employees understand the vision and values of the new business, developing talent and fostering a higher performance culture, and streamlining decision-making in areas such as R&D. To underline the importance of engagement, improvement targets were derived from external benchmarks and embedded into business balanced scorecards.

From lagging behind the pharma industry benchmark in the first survey, the results in the following one in 2009 saw Merck Serono's engagement score exceed the benchmark by 3 per cent, and increase by a further 3 per cent a year later. Although local units were of course free to address any major issues highlighted in their own results reports, this global and focused follow-up process enabled Merck Serono to address key engagement challenges quickly, and to align and maximize the effects of their action plans.

Step 4: Communicate

Chapter 4 discussed the communication steps needed when launching and running a survey, but the bulk of the communications effort actually should occur once the survey has closed. Even with a great analysis of a survey and strong action plan, the effect of both will be reduced considerably unless there is good communication of these to employees. While management teams may have discussed the results and actions at length, employees may hear little in comparison, in which case there is a risk that these efforts go unnoticed and – worse still – the survey is perceived as having been ignored by management, so fostering cynicism about the whole process.

Widespread and regular communication is key to making sure that employees are aware of the survey results, the associated action plan and the progress being made. The Centre for Performance-led HR even goes so far as to argue that 'for more and more organizations we suspect that engagement is an outcome of the internal communication strategy of an organization' (Balain and Sparrow, 2009, p. 36). While we would contend that there is more to engagement than this, clearly communication is a key plank of 'Voice' in the employee engagement model, and the greatest risk for most organizations is to under- rather than over-communicate what is going on.

Initial results communication

This is the first chance to share results and to take the opportunity to show appreciation for everyone who took part. For larger organizations, it's recommended that a message goes out from the top management to all employees to thank them for their feedback, to share highlights of the results and the response rate percentage, and some initial conclusions (e.g. where the results need addressing or further investigation). Highlighting strengths in the results and recognizing progress on any issues identified for follow-up from the last survey, or acknowledging those units that have seen particularly strong improvements in scores, are also important (Macey et al., 2009, pp. 112–13). This communication should also explain the next steps in the survey process, for example when employees will get to hear local results, when action plans will be announced and how they can contribute to the follow-up process. However, if communication is just one-way, it will lack impact, so it needs local follow-up by line managers using two-way communication.

It's important for all managers to use this opportunity to acknowledge the readiness of employees to respond to the survey and to thank them for their candour. Employees will be particularly interested to know their local results (and whether their own feedback was echoed in that given by their co-workers), which is why a face-to-face feedback session is important for them to ask questions, seek clarification, etc. Finally, if works councils are in place, it is advisable to hold a briefing session with them before the overall communications cascade so that they are aware of what came out of the survey, and can give early input with their views.

In all cases, it's important to share the data in a balanced way – employee audiences will be sensitive to possible bias, so avoid 'overselling', or being defensive or dismissive about scores that come out low. It's important to cover strengths and not just weaknesses, but be careful not to turn it into an exercise in blame ('the scores are low because of the poor leadership by X') or triumphalism ('we can be glad our scores are not as bad as at unit Y'). Be transparent with the results and be up-front if they are not clear and need more investigation. Explain, too, what happens next, so that employees know when to expect more to happen; otherwise an inexplicable delay in further news may generate suspicions about what is going on.

It's important that employees are given the chance to ask questions and give their views – this can be invaluable in understanding possible survey issues. After all, management's view of what is causing the problem might be quite different from how employees see things. Some simple questions to consider asking are in Box 6.2.

Generally, involving employees this way both builds confidence in the survey follow-up process and makes everyone feel shared ownership for the topic. The Centre for Performance-led HR contends that 'in general, engagement has become the new mechanism for trust and for employee voice' (Balain and Sparrow, 2009, p. 37), but the mistake then is to short-circuit this dialogue and instead have a situation where – to quote The Mind Gym – 'leaders do a big "mea culpa" and rush to respond to specific employee wishes. This promotes a culture of dependence that leads to ever-increasing expectations (and disappointment)' (The Mind Gym, 2011, p. 12).

Box 6.2 Questions for clarifying survey issues with employees

- Why do employees feel this way? What causes the opinion?
- Whom does the issue affect?
- When [or how often] does this occur?
- What's the impact on the performance of the group?
- What are ideas or recommendations for how the issue can be addressed, fixed, or improved?

Source: Wiley, 2010b, p. 110

How much to communicate

Given the considerable amount of data generated from a survey, an obvious issue is how much of the results should be communicated to participants. At a communication event such as an employee briefing or town hall meeting, it's advisable to share the highlights but not to dwell too long on any one topic: otherwise, employees will feel they are being overloaded with details, the communication will be too long and everyone will rapidly lose interest. Keeping back too much information will of course engender fears that management has something to hide, so one alternative is to provide fuller data online afterwards so employees can inspect the results in more detail if they want. For example, IDS (2009, p. 7) reports that at Sainsbury's supermarkets:

> All employees have access to a dynamic reporting tool, hosted on an external website. The tool includes a range of facilities that enable employees to view and interrogate the survey results. For example, they are able to see their division's scores in relation to other areas of the business. The tool also allows them to view engagement scores by age, gender, grade and ethnic origin.

By sharing more information this way but without bringing into question the confidentiality of the survey responses, such transparency can help build confidence in the overall survey process.

Communication channels

Each organization will have its usual communication channels, whether newsletters, intranet sites, videos, emails, podcasts, supervisor-team briefings or town hall meetings. All of these can help in different ways, but effective communications involve responding to how employees prefer to get information, and taking into account factors such as geographical dispersion of the workforce and the degree to which they are all at work at any one time (e.g. due to shift work or being 'on the road'). Using multiple means of communication will:

- address the variety of ways news travels internally
- allow a combination of 'push' and 'pull' in communication channels
- permit employee feedback and questions.

For remote-based staff, this may mean more reliance on tools like text messages or webinars rather than conventional means of communication.

Drawing mostly on respondents from North America, a recent report from the International Association of Business Communicators indicated that email was the commonest means of communication for engaging employees and was frequently used by 81 per cent of respondents, followed by the intranet (71 per cent), although less than half used communication in person as a channel (e.g. face-to-face meetings, town halls, etc). Additionally, 69 per cent of communications specialists reported that 46 per cent of top executives used social media to some degree in helping to engage their staff (IABC Research Foundation and Buck Consultants, 2011).

Yet despite the prevalence of electronic communication and the growth of social media, communication in person is important to add credibility to messages to employees, with this starting at the top of the organization. Positive, candid communications from senior management can signal strongly their sponsorship for follow-up actions from the engagement survey; conversely, lukewarm or ambiguous support must be avoided, as it can quickly undermine these efforts. According to the MacLeod Report, Towers Watson found in 2007 that only 31 per cent of UK employees thought their senior managers generally communicated openly and honestly, and – worse still – 60 per cent felt their senior managers treated them as just another organizational asset to be managed (MacLeod and Clarke, 2009, p. 32). Given the potential for mistrust, therefore, senior-level communications need to be well-crafted in order to be credible and convincing.

This in turn needs to be backed up by corresponding communication down the management chain, especially at the immediate supervisor level. Too often, supervisors can get circumvented by top-down electronic communications; in the process, organizations miss a valuable communications opportunity, because supervisors can play an important role in answering follow-up questions from employees and showing that engagement isn't just a HQ topic but is important at a local team level too. MacLeod and Brady also emphasize that front-line managers have much higher credibility when it comes to communication. They cite data from 2004 that 49 per cent of employees agreed that 'I receive more credible data from my supervisor than from my CEO', with only 25 per cent having a mixed view and 26 per cent disagreeing (MacLeod and Brady, 2007, p. 203). Furthermore, there is a good deal of evidence linking overall quality of supervision to employee engagement levels. In this sense, managers are key to 'walking the talk' about engagement by supporting survey follow-up initiatives and creating the environment for people to succeed through empowerment and delegation, listening and appreciation, and giving feedback and coaching. Notwithstanding the best intentions behind it, simply relying on an upbeat email from a CEO, crafted by internal communicators, will just not have the same effect.

CRF notes that trade unions can be another potential audience and communications channel, but caution that 'by definition, the "engagement" relationship must be with the

> Positive, candid communications from senior management can signal strongly their sponsorship for follow-up actions from the engagement survey; conversely, lukewarm or ambiguous support must be avoided, as it can quickly undermine these efforts.

organization and therefore its managers. This applies particularly in managing change... and when organizations' and trade unions' strategies differ, partnership becomes problematic' (Lambert, 2010, p. 46). If communications often involve trade unions, then it is important to leverage this, but recognizing that their agenda and management's may not always be wholly aligned.

As communications channels evolve, it's important also to recheck the effectiveness of those being used in case they are not highly valued by employees. For example, Aon Hewitt reported that in the US, employers thought their staff would rate company intranets as their second favourite place to find employee survey news, whereas employees in fact ranked it in sixth place; likewise, employers supposed town hall meetings would be employees' sixth choice when in fact it came in at fourteenth place (Aon Hewitt, 2010, p. 21).

Communicating actions and subsequent progress

A communications campaign around employee engagement also needs to take into account the fact that it may take some time before survey feedback is translated into visible action and noticeable change. Given this, it's important to create a sense of realism in the workforce: that acting on the survey feedback is a longer-term journey and that news will therefore be shared over time as progress is made. Follow-up communications can then report back on successful activity (such as 'you said – we did'), especially if there are some 'early wins' that can be achieved. (For a good example of this, see the RCT Homes case study in Chapter 8.) By including two-way communication as a part of this, it also allows employees to give feedback on how they feel that follow-up actions are progressing. This allows them the opportunity to give input on (for example) possible corrective steps to get a particular action plan back on track.

Giving progress updates every few months helps ensure that the action plans aren't forgotten and shows to employees that the commitment is there to responding to their feedback. This is important, since some research suggests that roughly two-thirds of employees recall having received information about survey results but less than half actually recall any action taking place (Wiley, 2010b, p. 123). As with any change activity, therefore, it's important not to underestimate the need for effective and continuous communication. As BlessingWhite Research (2011, p. 27) comments:

Executives need to weave 'engagement' into the daily workplace conversation. This requires managing employee expectations that engagement is not some-

thing that organizations do to employees or something that is a short-lived priority once a year.

Furthermore, over-promising and under-delivering can have very negative consequences; BlessingWhite found that, whereas 31 per cent of employees surveyed globally were engaged, this dropped to 26 per cent for organizations where staff experienced a survey and saw no follow-up, and fell even further to 21 per cent if employees saw 'a lot of talk, but no action' (BlessingWhite Research, 2011, p. 21).

Some tips for successful communications are summarized in Box 6.3.

Box 6.3 Questions for clarifying survey issues with employees

- Identify the various audience segments you'll be addressing – how far do messages need to differ e.g. by site/job level/function, etc.? If you are dealing with employees in different countries, how far do communications need translation into local language so they are really understood?
- Think about what expectations supervisors and employees have from the communications – make sure you will be addressing what is most of interest to them, rather than trying to cover every possible topic.
- Communications should speak to the audience in a way they'll easily understand, i.e. avoiding jargon, not overloading everyone with statistics, etc.
- Don't treat survey communications in isolation – coordinate plans with internal Communications staff to align overall messages to employees.
- If there are multiple survey recipients and action plan owners, make sure there is an aligned schedule for communication. Otherwise, the risk is that messages appear sporadically, creating confusion among employees about what some have heard before others, or where local information has appeared before organization-wide communications have occurred that can provide a bigger context for local messages.

- Think about how to create some 'buzz' around the survey follow-up. What you do depends on the organization's culture, but there may be ways to make communications more fun and interesting, and retain everyone's attention (e.g. linking it to the organization's overall brand or to a specific branding around employee engagement).
- Make sure that communications are clear and concise, and that everyone knows what to do next.
- Also ensure that communications are not just a one-way process – give people the chance to ask questions, offer feedback, etc., as this helps build shared ownership.
- Set realistic expectations about the survey. Improvements do take time, so although it helps to have some 'quick wins', it's important not to 'declare victory' too soon.
- Make sure everyone is kept up to date on progress, and that communications are honest. If actions are not on track, it's better to say so than to disguise this and lose credibility in the process.

Step 5: Conclude

Capturing lessons learnt so far – moving to continuous improvement

Having done so much in terms of analysis, planning, implementation and communication, it may be tempting to decide that this is enough and turn your attention to other challenges. But before doing so, it's worthwhile setting aside a little time towards the end of the action plan period and in advance of the next survey to draw lessons from what has gone on and gather insights into how to improve further for the future. It's helpful to bring together those most actively involved in the survey follow-up activities for this review, as well as the survey provider (if a third party source is used). A facilitator or organizational development advisor can help ensure the review is as productive as possible. Suggested topics for discussion are:

- How successful was the original survey exercise (e.g. response rate, clarity of understanding of the questions, generation of timely and reliable reports)? What could be improved next time and what questions could be added, changed or removed?
- What progress has been made with the follow-up actions identified? If progress has been less than expected, what have been the reasons for this?
- How effective has the support of management been? Has top-level management sponsorship been visible and sufficient? Have middle and first-line managers been actively involved? What could help them all further in these tasks?
- How have employees responded to the overall engagement activities? What has been their level of awareness and interest? What could be done to harness this better in the future?
- Has there been an improvement in people- and business-related metrics, and how far does this seem to be related to the activities undertaken?
- What emerging business issues might also be covered in the next survey?
- What topics arising from the survey analysis did not get addressed so far that might need a higher priority in future?
- What best practices have there been around the organization that could be extended to other locations or units?

By following this process systematically, an organization can become more mature in how it handles employee engagement. Instead of responding reactively to the survey, a continuous improvement exercise comes into place and momentum is created: engagement is not seen as an exceptional activity or an 'add-on' to daily business, but as a key contributor to future success. As Andrew Lambert (2010, p. 5) concludes in his review of best practices for CRF:

Organizations learn over time that chasing engagement survey scores is not what it's about – it's everyday managerial behaviour, from the front line to the top. Mature organizations discuss engagement measures and actions as part of regular business agendas and metrics, not as an extrinsic initiative, and examine how engagement correlates with financial and operational results.

Ultimately, then, the survey stops just being a one-off trigger for action but instead becomes one of a variety of different inputs in driving longer-term strategy and achieving sustainable improvement in organizational performance. It also represents a risk management tool that top management should use to monitor as a leading indicator for the business. As noted by CRF, employee engagement then moves from 'Measure, Understand, Act', to 'Understand, Act, Measure' (Lambert, 2010, pp. 30–31). Thus the survey becomes evidence of progress against pre-defined goals, and not merely a prompt to respond to after the results have been received.

Conclusion

Committing to follow-up plans makes sure that engagement issues get addressed, analysis turns into action and progress begins to be made. After this, accountability and follow-up are necessary to make sure that the plans deliver real benefits and are not simply expressions of good intentions. Integrating engagement follow-up with other business metrics and processes is especially useful in ensuring that it is taken seriously; furthermore, by getting into a rhythm of follow-up and continuous improvement, engagement changes from being a response triggered by a survey to an ongoing strategic process towards key business and people-related goals. While it matters before and during an engagement survey, communication is especially important afterwards, so that employees feel that their original feedback was not ignored and they can see that their concerns are being actively addressed. And while it's valuable to harness the energy of all levels of the organization to do this, sponsorship from the top is an essential precondition for success. The degree to which senior managers talk about and are seen to follow up on engagement results will inevitably provide the cue for how the rest of the organization will behave.

Checklist

- Is there genuine senior-level sponsorship for the action plan and readiness for follow-up through the rest of the organization to make it happen?
- Is there a timely schedule for cascading results and action plans so that there is not an undue delay in informing everyone of the survey outcomes?
- Do communications take account of the different audiences being addressed?
- Are communications balanced, open, and credible? Do they set realistic expectations as to when – and how – follow-up will occur?
- Do leaders take responsibility for communication, rather than leaving it to Communications or HR? Is engagement something they regularly talk about with staff?
- Is the role of supervisors clear in the communication process? Do they feel able and empowered to handle face-to-face communications?
- Have challenging but realistic improvement targets been set for future engagement levels? Are they treated as a business KPI?
- Are action plans tracked to ensure completion? Are they a regular management review topic?
- Are managers encouraged to take follow-up seriously through having engagement-related individual objectives, and even linking part of their rewards to this?
- Has a 'lessons learnt' exercise been conducted before all the follow-up efforts have been completed to identify potential improvements for the next survey and action planning exercise?

CHAPTER 7

In Chapters 5 and 6 we've looked at how to use survey results as the basis for taking follow-up measures that can foster employee engagement. The five-step process of check, calibrate, commit, communicate and conclude can help focus time and effort while involving employees to make sure activities are well-directed and appreciated. Yet despite the best intentions, it may not always be as easy as this. Moving from analysis to action can turn out to be more difficult than expected. Progress can be slowed down, for instance by resistance from supervisors or top management inertia; employees and their representatives may be suspicious rather than enthusiastic; and the whole exercise can eventually run the risk of simply fizzling out altogether. To avoid engagement follow-up being marginalized – or even killed off – by internal opposition, this chapter discusses some typical roadblocks that may be encountered and how to overcome them.

Addressing managerial resistance

As mentioned several times already, management sponsorship is important for the success of survey follow-up, so the most immediate roadblock may simply be that the issue is not taken seriously by the organization's leaders. Some may feel it is a nuisance or a distraction ('I've got a business to run and no time for this' or 'why are we spending all this time on keeping everyone happy?'), or may trivialize the exercise, for example by making results communication more of a 'selling exercise' than an opportunity to act on issues identified from the results. In such cases, it's important to remind everyone that employee engagement is *not* the same as employee satisfaction *nor* is it some sort of 'me too' exercise in corporate social responsibility. On the contrary, everyone needs to remember the bottom-line benefits it can deliver, which are therefore in management's interests to pursue. Furthermore, this is not an issue that top management can hand over to someone else ('Keeping employees committed is what we pay supervisors to do'). Since there is a good deal of evidence that it is organization-wide actions that make the most difference – for example, a clear direction for the organization, supporting people programs, etc. – progress can therefore only be driven from the senior leadership level (Gebauer and Lowman, 2008, p. 235).

Other managers lower down in the organization may be uncomfortable with the outcomes of the survey and feel threatened by the poor scores they have received. In such cases, there may be attempts to:

- discredit the survey process, e.g. 'who knows what the truth is – this whole thing is just a "black box"' or 'people are just getting their own back because it's an anonymous survey'
- deny the validity of the results, e.g. 'you just can't please some people, can you?' or 'the results are just down because of how the business is doing – there's nothing that can be done about that'.

While these are more difficult responses to address, it can be helpful to remind everyone of the robustness of the survey process, and that, however unwelcome it is, there is no denying the reality of the feedback. Moreover, given such negative sentiment has been latent in the organization already, the survey can be viewed as a chance at last to turn the situation around by acknowledging the problem(s) that exist, and then starting to take steps to resolve them. 'Coming clean' on such issues will likely gain a positive employee reaction that issues are finally being addressed head on, but then it is important afterwards to turn words quickly into action.

Paradoxically, good survey scores can sometimes also present problems. The risk then is that managers may become complacent as a result ('given these scores are pretty good, I need to spend my time on other more urgent problems'). In these circumstances, it may be helpful to get beyond the absolute scores achieved and ask if there are deeper issues to address, or to check how the scores compare to other internal and external benchmarks. While there may be limits to how high the scores can go, the risk is that 'declaring victory' can mean that engagement-related topics get little attention thereafter, new issues get overlooked and scores retreat again in future. The key message that needs to be conveyed to managers here is that engagement is not a one-off issue that can be 'fixed' and then everyone can move on to other topics. On the contrary, employee engagement will always be changing as the business and the organizational environment evolve: it is not a one-time activity but a journey of continuous improvement that needs to be worked on consistently over time.

> It may be helpful to get beyond the absolute scores achieved and ask if there are deeper issues to address, or to check how the scores compare to other internal and external benchmarks.

Sometimes, resistance to taking action may be a cover for managers' concerns about not having the right 'soft skills' to support the survey follow-up (such as knowing how to respond to challenging employee questions, handling a more participative way of working with staff, etc.), and may require some targeted training and coaching to overcome this. Here, internal champions (as mentioned in Chapter 6) can be helpful in coaching and supporting managers who feel less comfortable in handling survey follow-up. But if resistance is particularly strong, it's important to assess if this isn't a reflection of deeper cultural issues in the organization (such as a tradition of only communicating information on a 'need-to-know' basis, or a reluctance to involve employees in decision-making) that may need to be addressed in parallel if the engagement follow-up is not to be thwarted.

The wrong sorts of management sponsorship

A different challenge is presented when managers give apparent endorsement to employee engagement as an issue but in reality don't practise what they preach. For example, engagement may be initially announced as being a priority for the management team, but then little action is taken, it is rarely (if at all) mentioned by executives or supervisors later on, and it never gets beyond slogans or posters. Or commitment may be given to addressing certain issues from the survey (e.g. equal opportunities or improved internal communication) when in reality everyone knows the prevailing culture continues to run counter to this.

Such pseudo-commitment is a particularly serious problem because it risks not only discrediting the survey but also undermining trust in management as a whole, and so it needs to be confronted quickly by senior management. This is where the top-level sponsors for the survey need to be called in to tackle those managers not 'walking the talk', making it clear that their behaviour needs to change. Measuring employee perceptions of what has happened after the survey can help here (especially if a Behavioral Change Index is used – see Chapter 6). But ultimately it is a test of how strong an accountability culture exists in management.

A related risk is when managers treat engagement more as a competition – that the goal is just to get a higher score or to outdo other units in some sort of in-house contest. The problem here is that the message to employees becomes that management action is no longer really triggered by concern for the issues raised but purely because engagement is simply another target or goal to be reached. Such an approach risks focusing improvement attention just on examples of 'low-hanging fruit' that are quick to address, rather than grappling with more complex (but potentially more important) issues from the survey. Also, a spirit of internal competition may be a false contest – for example, cultural differences may impact the scores between different units, or there may be exceptional factors affecting scores – so that such 'underperformers' may find it difficult to do well and be discouraged from trying hard in future. Worst of all, such an approach risks creating all-round disenchantment among employees, who will quickly realize that they are not really being taken seriously and that engagement has deteriorated into some sort of management 'numbers game'.

If there are signs of this taking place, it's vital for senior management sponsoring the survey to make it clear that this is not a question of 'winners' and 'losers', that everyone will have to address their own scores and challenges in their own way, and that the point of the exercise is not the score achieved but how seriously the response is taken on board and action pursued afterwards.

Opposition from employee representatives

Aside from challenges from management, another potential source of resistance may be opposition from employee representatives. Whether direct members of the workforce or their union representatives, these are key stakeholders in employee engagement who need to be involved early on – otherwise they may have suspicions about the whole process and will seek to block or undermine it. Underlying this may be a fear on their part that the survey has a hidden purpose and/or that the engagement process could circumvent their role as employee advocates – possibly spurred by awareness that general employee surveys originated in the US partly to help prevent workforces becoming unionized (Wiley, 2010b, pp. 25–33).

If this is so, it is important to provide the necessary reassurance that such surveys are a complementary way of getting feedback and not a replacement of their role. By making them aware in advance of what's going on, and by involving them through allowing them to review the proposed survey questions, and later by providing early previews of the survey results that they can comment on (before they are widely communicated), they can be properly included and allowed to make a valuable contribution.

Obvious concerns from employee representatives will be (a) how confidentiality of feedback will be ensured and (b) whether employees are able to give negative feedback without fear of retribution. To do this, it is important to clarify how the security of the survey is set up – for example:

- the use of personal passwords or codes to access the survey
- how replies are kept anonymous
- what is done to ensure only aggregated data is seen by management and not individual replies

- what steps are being taken to meet data protection legislation
- what the minimum organizational size is at which data can be reported (for example, that a minimum of (say) ten respondents are needed before a report can be generated).

Aside from making it clear that data is aggregated and anonymous, and cannot be traced back to individual respondents, it is important to provide reassurance that engagement surveys are not some sort of 'loyalty test' and are a genuine effort to get honest feedback as the basis for future improvement. Clearly, the history of employee relations in an organization will affect how hard or easy it is to create this trust and acceptance. But once a survey is being run, it is important too that managers are prevented from pressuring their staff to give favourable responses.

Overcoming 'survey fatigue'

For organizations that have conducted engagement surveys for some time, one challenge can be that of 'survey fatigue' – when employees are less ready to take part, or the topic appears overdone or a fad whose time has passed. In such circumstances, careful investigation is needed to discover why employee engagement has 'run out of steam' as a topic. Possible causes could be:

- a feeling that levels are satisfactory and – as a result – engagement has become less urgent as a topic
- lack of belief that action gets taken in response to the survey feedback
- concern that the survey issues are too difficult to tackle
- a sense that prior announcements about survey follow-up have overprom-ised and under-delivered
- the existence of other pressing business issues (e.g. the risk of restructur-ing) that may overshadow everything else.

In such cases, further investigation is key to finding out why there is a loss of momentum and to define steps to remove these roadblocks. Below are some possible reasons for energy about engagement dropping.

Complacency about current levels of engagement

It may be that engagement has simply become a 'me too' activity for the organization; in other words, the original reasons for it being championed have been forgotten and the organization is seen as talking about engagement simply because others are as well, and because it is necessary to keep up appearances on the corporate social responsibility front. If this is the case, it's important to reframe communications about employee engagement to stress that it is a means to improve business performance and is not 'window-dressing' or something that is just a 'nice to have'. It may also help to show everyone again how survey questions can be used to measure progress towards key business- and HR-related goals – such as encouraging a quality mindset, compliance with company values, becoming a 'best place to work', fostering a more diverse workplace, etc. – and, if needed, updating the questions accordingly.

Another problem may be that the engagement survey itself is no longer seen as being relevant to business success. If the survey has been running for some time, it may no longer be wholly anchored in the current and future priorities of the business. In this case, take the time to recheck the survey questions and topics to see if they really reflect the strategic goals of the business. Examine, too, whether there are more ways that the survey data can be linked to business outcomes (e.g. profitability, reducing scrap rates) and so become a more integral part of driving the business.

A third possible cause of complacency is that the organization has become too focused on getting to a targeted level of engagement and – having got there – no longer feels the topic is important. The danger is that a lack of attention may lead to engagement levels declining again in future, so it is crucial to reinforce the message that employee engagement is a journey and not a destination to be reached. Moreover, it needs to be made clear that the ultimate goal is not a given survey score but the associated action that is taken to improve the organization's effectiveness.

However, it may be worthwhile in such a situation to re-examine those areas of weakness in the last survey to see if there really are no areas for action, and to check if there might be more appropriate external benchmarks that could be used – high-performing companies, for example, rather than just industry peers – that could reset the bar for the organization and so encourage further effort. Alternatively, a fuller examination of past results may yield data that can shed light on potential problems in the organization, or produce correlations between survey topics or questions and key organizational metrics (such as revenue growth or customer satisfaction) that can be used to drive overall business improvement. Finally, it can be worth reconsidering if expectations cannot be raised anyway; for example, Sainsbury's supermarkets in the UK used to ask staff to rate the statement 'I would tell people that Sainsbury's is a good place to work', but having achieved high scores here the question was altered in their 2008/09 survey to read 'I *tell* people that Sainsbury's is a *great* place to work' (IDS, 2009, p. 5).

Lack of confidence in follow-up action being taken

Loss of momentum may also occur because there is a feeling that follow-up from the engagement survey is not worth the effort. One potential cause of this may be insufficient management support for these action plans. Here, top-level management needs to play a more active sponsorship role to make sure that actions are taken throughout the organization so that everyone sees this really matters. To reinforce this, it can be useful – as described in Chapter 4 – to identify internal survey 'champions' who can help overcome such a lack of self-confidence by spreading successful techniques and helping others to adopt them by training and coaching. Senior management can also help this by showcasing and recognizing best practice cases to demonstrate what can be done and so spur others to action. Finally, if failure to take action has no consequence for managers, it is important to make raising engagement levels (or applying follow-up action plans) an objective for them that becomes a regular topic for business reviews, and is also reinforced through personal objectives.

> Even if managers are convinced of the importance of taking action, they may not be able to do so if they have inadequate resources to support them.

Of course, even if managers are convinced of the importance of taking action, they may not be able to do so if they have inadequate resources to support them. If this is an issue, and it is not possible to increase the means to back up these efforts, consider focusing survey follow-up actions so that there is no risk of spreading resources too thinly, and see if employees can be involved more actively as volunteers in prioritized activities. But it's important also not to assume that follow-up work depends on new policies or investments of money. On the contrary, as Professor John Purcell commented on UK research by the CIPD (Aitken et al., 2006, p. 3) in 2006:

> *What emerges from this survey of 2000 workers of all levels and trades is that what turns them on, makes them more engaged and intending to stay working for their organization is effective relationships and behaviours, rather than just their experience of HR practices. We need to think and act harder to build better organizations and develop a sense of community.*

In many cases, then, it's the human interactions that need to change in order to boost engagement – and this can be addressed regardless of budget size.

Finally, people may question the point of taking action if they are unaware of what has been achieved so far (and so what might be possible in future). In this case, it may be necessary to reinforce internal communications about employee engagement, such as by using branding for engagement efforts to help link actions back to the survey so that people see the connection. (Several of the case studies in later chapters use branding to good effect.) It might also be worth revisiting communication channels used for engagement to see if they are still effective: would RSS (really simple syndication) feeds or blogs appeal more to employees than printed newsletters, for example?

Difficulty of how to address the survey issues identified

Sometimes the roadblock may be uncertainty about how to act on survey findings. If the problem is one of understanding the data, the survey provider should be called in to help tackle this and shed light on the meaning of the results. But it may be that, although the data is clear, the resulting survey issue is so broad that it is difficult to know where to begin. If so, it may be worthwhile carrying out a further analysis using Total Quality Management tools such as a fishbone analysis or 'five whys' to break down the issues identified into more manageable topics for action. Employee feedback can also help 'size' the problems more realistically and identify what matters the most. Because this may be quite an onerous task that a management team lacks the time to work on fully, it may be worthwhile to consider assigning a high-potential manager to explore the issues as a learning opportunity and to come back with recommendations for the management team.

Past failure to deliver

The problem may otherwise be that, despite the fact that there have been plenty of survey actions, these have missed what really matters. One critique of follow-up actions (The Mind Gym, 2011, p. 12) points to a reliance on:

> A few grand gestures rather than a thousand little changes. Big announcements about child care, free Starbucks, flexible benefits, a cutting-edge intranet site, but no action to address the tough stuff – the conversations, decisions and behaviour that shape our lives at work.

Some focus group work can help here to identify what is going awry. But if this is the case, a frank discussion is needed at the top team level about what are the real issues on employees' minds and getting clear on management's readiness to take action. A more meaningful action plan will then be needed – one that will likely require more grassroots involvement, greater responsibility for immediate supervisors and a strong communications plan that explains that this time the plan will have substance – rather than simply style.

> It may also help to create one common plan for the whole organization to work on rather than letting everyone create their own actions and so dissipating efforts.

Worse still, actions may have been promised but not delivered. The problem here may be a lack of adequate planning, in which case it is important to ensure for the future that there is a solid action plan in place and that someone is assigned to provide project management to make sure that plans don't go 'off-track' again. Another risk is that of creating over-ambitious plans. If this is the case, it is important to ensure that future plans are kept to fewer actions – other goals can always be added later once the first ones are reached. As mentioned in the previous chapter, it may also help to create one common plan for the whole organization to work on rather than letting everyone create their own actions and so dissipating efforts. It's worth checking the resourcing of the plans – even if the timelines for delivery look realistic, they may not be if there is insufficient capacity to make them happen. Lastly, if plans underperform, one cause may be the failure to involve key stakeholders sufficiently. If so, try and identify up-front whose support is key to the actions and make sure they are involved and committed before continuing the plan.

Competition from other business issues

The Mind Gym warn that a common cause of engagement efforts failing is 'easily distracted leaders', adding that 'the leadership start out enthusiastic and full of bold promises about how they will lead the change but the momentum peters out when something more urgent, glamorous or susceptible to quick wins, comes along' (The Mind Gym, 2011, p. 12).

This may be a somewhat cynical view, yet serious and urgent business issues may start to take precedence over employee engagement – such as when an acquisition is underway, or an organization needs to go through restructuring. While such challenges are obviously a key priority, they are not incompatible with employee engagement because the latter can be critical to the success of reaching the planned business goal (such as keeping people committed during a restructuring). Survey data can in fact contribute to the success of the change, like measuring how far employees understand the future direction of the business after a takeover. If the issue is one of management 'bandwidth', it may be worth considering extending the time between surveys and/or scaling back follow-up actions to a more manageable size until the business is better able to support engagement activities. But, as mentioned earlier, care needs to be taken to avoid reducing engagement levels by making employees feel they are being listened to less.

However, if the business situation is less critical and there is still a sense that the survey output seems less relevant to business needs, this may be a sign that the survey itself needs an overhaul. If so, it is worth revisiting the structure of the survey and seeing whether the topics in it are addressing all the issues that matter to the organization.

Decline of employee interest

Even if management is committed to engagement as a topic, it may be that employees themselves become disenchanted. Sometimes – as discussed above – it can be due to lack of awareness of what follow-up work has been done, or a feeling that the actions were not targeting what really matters. But another possible problem may be if internal communications about the engagement activities lack credibility. If employees feel that messages sound too much like 'spin', they will 'tune out' and lose interest. In such a case, it's essential to ensure future communications are repackaged (so there is a clean break with the past) and that they are balanced and do not gloss over key survey issues that may be keenly felt by some or all employees. As part of this, communication needs to take care that credit for success is appropriately shared (including with employees for having given the original feedback), rather than coming across as a top-down success story. Most of all, the style of future communications needs to be built on reality, not rhetoric.

When engagement improves but doesn't feed through to improved organizational performance

Sometimes, organizations might have high engagement levels that nevertheless do not translate into higher performance overall. While there can be a time lag between increased engagement and business performance, the lack of flow-through may point to obstacles holding things back.

One such barrier may be a lack of self-belief. Jessica Pryce-Jones, in her research on happiness at work, contends that, while people may feel like they fit in at work, are motivated and committed, and ready to make an effort, this will not materialize in the absence of 'confidence' or a real sense of belief in oneself and one's job. As she observes, 'with it, today's hopes turn into tomorrow's reality; without it, motivation is never converted into action' (Pryce-Jones, 2010, p. 126). In this sense, managers can help by providing an

environment that is challenging but encouraging. As discussed in Chapter 3, Support
is a key engagement driver.
Through this, employees de-

> Managers can help by providing an
> environment that is challenging but
> encouraging.

velop necessary self-confidence and can perform to their fullest. This means
offering trust and encouragement beforehand, and acknowledgement and
praise afterwards.

Another related barrier is raised by the Hay Group, who suggest that
engagement makes the biggest difference when staff are also enabled – i.e.
that they possess the skills, tools and autonomy to contribute at their highest
potential. Its survey data indicates that, although nine-tenths of employees
say they are committed to success, less than two-thirds believe they are as
productive as they could be. Its linkage research suggests revenue growth
is two-and-a-half times greater for organizations with high engagement but
four-and-a-half times more when there is both high engagement *and* high
enablement (Hay Group, 2010, pp. 6–7). In their detailed study of four different employers in the UK (Gifford et al., 2010, p. 93), researchers at Roffey
Park Institute reported:

> *We came across a number of examples of employees who were highly engaged*
> *with their work and had a strong desire to deliver the best service they could,*
> *but felt inhibited by their employer from doing so. Examples included call cen-*
> *tre workers who felt unable to take the time to establish a good rapport with*
> *individual customers; and caretakers who understood they were not allowed*
> *to undertake certain essential tasks for elderly tenants who needed their help.*
> *Essentially, these employees embodied an attitude of 'Don't talk to me about*
> *going the extra mile! I want to go the extra mile; it's management who are*
> *stopping me!*

Jim Haudan argues that too often employees are so overwhelmed by complex
work environments that they are pushed onto the back foot and so 'reacting
stops engagement'. In contrast, by eliminating needless tasks and promoting simplification, managers help increase that engagement: 'when companies stop any processes, actions, or behaviours, they inevitably provide their

employees with greater clarity and simplicity of purpose. Not only do they help their people connect the dots again, but the people have fewer dots to connect' (Haudan, 2008, p. 34). Line managers therefore need to recheck if they are creating the right environment for people to perform or if they are simply frustrating those who are at heart engaged and just desperately want to do a better job.

Macey et al. argue that some managers may mistake organizational commitment for engagement. For them, engagement is represented by 'enthusiasm, urgency and intensity', whereas organizational commitment is a more passive condition, characterized by a sense of general understanding of what needs to be done combined with a strong sense of attachment to the organization (Macey et al., 2009, p. 36). For them, commitment only moves into engagement when employees are aligned to organizational goals that they then internalize and act on.

MacLeod and Brady (2007, p. 27) take a slightly different view; for them, alignment is about ensuring employees know what to do and engagement is about them wanting to do it. But they contend that lack of alignment is even more detrimental, because:

> An organization with high levels of engagement but low levels of alignment will simply become chaotic. Vast amounts of discretionary energy applied by everyone with no overarching goal will result in mayhem as various impulses collide and conflict. The people within it will be like headless chickens. True engagement, without alignment, is unsustainable in a coherent organization since it will become dissipated, and ultimately unsuccessful.

If this is the case it's vital to spend more time in making clear to people what is expected of them, both in terms of business goals and the values that they are expected to demonstrate. If this has been done already, check if employees understand what it means for them personally. It may be that they realize what the strategy is but they're not clear how they fit in, or how they can contribute fully. Briefing sessions and town hall meetings can help create this sense of connection and allow for clarifying questions and dialogue. Supervisors play an especially important 'translation' role here, while the performance management process can reinforce this by clarifying what is expected at the individual level. Jim Haudan (2008, p. 44) argues that leaders are pivotal in translating strategies into actions for their staff:

> *The essential task of a leader as translator is to literally and figuratively draw out and illustrate for employees all of the drama of the business. This includes the current business environment, the specifics of the marketplace, its customers, its competition, and its main strategies.*

If managers aren't doing this effectively, then it may be that they need help in developing the right skills to set goals, provide coaching and feedback and enabling employees to feel connected to the bigger picture. Alignment is therefore critical, so a key engagement driver here – as the subsequent MacLeod Report (MacLeod and Clarke, 2009, p. 33) argued – is:

> *Leadership which ensures a strong, transparent and explicit organizational culture which gives employees a line of sight between their job and the vision and aims of the organization.*

When engagement goes too far

The potential for enhanced business performance does of course leave the topic of employee engagement open to misuse. The MacLeod Report (MacLeod and Clarke, 2009, p. 9) cautions that:

> *Although improved performance and productivity is at the heart of engagement, it cannot be achieved by a mechanistic approach which tries to extract discretionary effort by manipulating employees' commitment and emotions. Employees see through such attempts very quickly; they lead instead to cynicism and disillusionment. By contrast, engaged employees freely and willingly give discretionary effort, not as an 'add-on', but as an integral part of their daily activity at work.*

But what happens if managers try to do this all the same? The potential barrier to engagement here can be that if the drive for such employee commitment goes too far, it eventually becomes self-defeating by pushing the organization too much. Macey et al. (2009, p. 137) go so far as to warn that:

> ... too much of an engagement culture can also have bad consequences, including burnout, disengagement, and other negative psychological and behavioural outcomes (e.g. not adapting to the changes required for the company to succeed).

These risks may not be immediately apparent, but over time various symptoms may appear as warning signs – as shown in Table 7.1.

The IPA contends that 'the strong focus on sustainable performance and productivity mitigates against engagement becoming simply a matter of making employees work harder. Rather, engagement describes the process of enabling and encouraging employees to become more effective' (Jameson, 2009, p. 3). But managers at all levels nevertheless need to watch out for when engagement means 'working too much' rather than 'working smarter'. Such pressure means that the effort expended by employees is no longer discretionary and this can run two potential risks: creating undue stress and undermining the organization's culture.

Table 7.1 When engagement goes too far

Positive engagement	Symptoms of going too far
Commitment to goals and values	Blindness to potential issues Reluctance to highlight problems or issues for fear of not appearing to be supportive of the organization
Pride in the organization	Increasing internal focus 'Groupthink' and excessive 'cheerleading' Absence of disagreement or diversity of opinions
Sense of personal commitment	Employees feel overwhelmed by challenges Absence of work-life balance
'Going the extra mile'	Excessive hours seen as the norm Exhaustion and stress-related illness Presenteeism

The signs of stress may appear slowly. But as work challenges become increasingly overwhelming, information-sharing, collaboration and teamwork can disappear as each person looks after themselves in order to survive the pressure. Work will provide less and less personal meaning when it becomes instead an ever-faster race to stay on top of a job that seems

Managers at all levels nevertheless need to watch out for when engagement means 'working too much' rather than 'working smarter'. Such pressure means that the effort expended by employees is no longer discretionary and this can run two potential risks: creating undue stress and undermining the organization's culture.

increasingly out of control. Csikszentmihalyi's studies on 'flow' argue that this optimal state of work occurs when high challenges are matched by corresponding high skills, but that if the former outweighs the latter, the employee shifts into a state of anxiety. Judith Bardwick (2008, p. 38) further comments that:

> The crux of excessive anxiety is the feeling that you have no control over what is happening to you. You cannot even influence what's happening. At work, it's as though the playing field is no longer level. You no longer have a manageable deal. You've lost the sense that if you do your part, you can make it okay. You've lost the feeling that you know the rules. Anxiety makes people feel like victims.

In this situation, enthusiasm and drive get replaced by exhaustion and disengagement. As we discussed in Chapter 3, Maslach et al.'s research (2001) suggests that engagement and burnout are opposite poles of the same dimensions. Macey et al. (2009, p. 148) also point to the paradoxical situation that often 'those who are most engaged are most at risk to suffer from burnout'. In the fullest sense of the term, burnout is often also characterized by cynicism and withdrawal, which may in turn have a corrosive effect on co-workers who are otherwise well. Managers therefore need to pay attention to this and make sure that they:

- set objectives that are stretching but not unrealistic and avoid a situation where goals get changed frequently
- take care to review progress periodically in case goals need adjusting or if resources need increasing
- check teams function effectively and that tasks are fairly (and clearly) allocated
- monitor job design to ensure accountabilities are clear and that the jobholders are empowered to do their assigned tasks
- make sure employees have the right training so they can master their work
- create a climate of trust where employees can say how they feel and that it is acceptable to raise concerns over workload
- discourage presenteeism and make it clear that work-life balance is important too
- make time for socializing to help understand how employees feel, rather than simply talking about the business or the task at hand.

The risks of escalation of commitment

The second risk is to the organization's culture. A healthy workplace depends on trust and openness – but undue focus on engagement may tip over into creating an environment where there becomes only one accepted way of doing things. Ultimately, this can lead to an 'escalation of commitment' where people become so fixated on one approach – such as a set company vision or way of doing work – that they become progressively unwilling to let go because they have invested so much of themselves in it emotionally. This may lead to an excessive emphasis on organizational pride, a demand for unquestioning loyalty or a reluctance to confront the challenges facing the organization. In any case, the culture will have been dangerously undermined and the business may become blind to external risks or operate in an atmosphere of denial about what is going wrong. When finally the time comes to change, the greatest resisters to change may then prove to be those who are most engaged (Macey et al., 2009, p. 159).

Case study: Innocent Drinks

Founded in 1998, Innocent Drinks is a UK-based fast-growing producer of healthy food and drinks, particularly fruit smoothies. From a fledgling start-up, in just over a decade it has grown from three founders to 250 staff, and sells two million smoothies a week across the UK and a growing share of Europe. Now 58 per cent-owned by Coca-Cola, its ambitious 30-year goal is to establish Innocent as 'the Earth's favourite little healthy food and drinks company'.

Dynamic, entrepreneurial but often frenetic, staff show the extraordinary commitment often found in small start-ups. But Richard Reed, one of Innocent's co-founders, warns that 'if anything, we have such high levels of engagement that we need to make sure people aren't taking on too much. Our best people will half-kill themselves in doing a top-notch job, so it's important they manage their energy levels, too, and don't burn out. As a board, we try to set the standard by continually refocusing the business on a small set of priorities every month, and actively managing workload hotspots around the company.' Innocent also tries to avoid complexity and remove barriers to effectiveness; Karen Callaghan, Innocent's people director, says that 'whenever people ask me about being innovative, I just say we do the simple things, better. Simplicity in objectives; if your people don't know what success looks like, how can they be successful? And simplicity in conversation: we always say why wouldn't we tell the truth? If it's important to people, we will share it! It's very simple.'

Employees share in the success of Innocent Drinks through a profit-related pay scheme, and staff wellbeing is helped through free breakfasts; private healthcare; on-site massage, yoga and gym; and (of course) free smoothies. But the company also takes time out through an all-employee annual nature weekend (in, say, Italy or Switzerland), votes quarterly on which co-workers should receive scholarships to develop new skills or interests, and offers foundation scholarships for employees to go for two weeks to help with projects in developing countries.

Source: Walker, 2011, pp. 18–23.

Here, managers need to think about:

- making sure the organization doesn't lose touch with reality by keeping abreast of what is happening in the external environment
- encouraging employees to speak up – such as at town hall meetings
- being open about setbacks and using failures as an opportunity to learn
- ensuring internal communication is balanced and not propagandist
- being clear about what is constant in the organization (e.g. certain key values) and also being clear that other aspects are open to change (e.g. strategies, organizational set-ups)
- avoiding recruiting wholly from within but bringing in external hires as well to provide new knowledge and perspectives.

Conclusion

Although running an engagement survey and establishing some follow-up actions might seem relatively straightforward, the reality can be quite different. Aside from the competing challenges of attending to other business issues, fostering engagement in an organization does require commitment and effort from managers to overcome the sorts of barriers described above. But at the same time, engagement is not something that can mandated as a short-cut to better results. As Macey et al. (2009, p. 161) rightly conclude:

> Our experience is that managers and executives who approach engagement just need to get a reality check on what they are thinking. If they are thinking this is a good way to get more for less, they are due for an unpleasant surprise. If they are thinking we can simply continue to raise the bar once we get them engaged, stress and disengagement and perhaps burnout will be the result.

Engagement, then, is not a one-way, purely top-down exercise, nor a cookie-cutter approach that ignores individuals' separate personal needs. Rather – as already mentioned – it's an art that needs to reflect individuals' separate needs and how they are affected by the different elements of engagement described in Chapter 3 – in other words, Connection, Support, Voice and Scope. In the remaining chapters, we'll take you through these four elements of engagement and suggest how you can address these in your organization.

Checklist

- How far does there seem to be resistance to tackling engagement issues? Are the reasons for this clear – and possible to resolve using the above advice?
- Is lip service paid to engagement or is it misrepresented? (For example, is it confused with employee satisfaction or treated as a 'numbers game'?)
- Are employee representatives supportive of the engagement steps being taken or do they have concerns that need addressing?
- Do surveys fail to ignite interest or enthusiasm, and is there a plan to overcome this and reinvigorate activities?
- Has action planning become too remote from staff, failing to catch their attention and mobilize their energy and ideas?
- Do action plans come across as relevant ... or just rhetoric?
- Do managers tend to succumb too quickly to 'quick fixes' and/or move on hastily to other business issues?
- If there are challenging business issues to address, can engagement activity be refocused instead as a key contributor to effective change management?
- Are actions too focused on one or two of the key engagement drivers and lack impact by failing to take a holistic approach and addressing other ones?
- Are expectations of engagement improvements realistic? Or do action plans risk driving pressure too high and causing excessive stress and burnout, or corroding the culture by demanding commitment without question?

CHAPTER 8

Over the last few chapters we've looked at how surveys – together with more informal 'soft' data – can provide invaluable insight into what is driving engagement in an organization, and at how organizations can take focused, effective steps in response. These insights can be used to create a culture in which more people, more of the time, are likely to be committed and high-performing.

But what does such a culture look like, and can you really build one? We believe that building a culture of engagement starts with managers making engagement central to how things are done, as well as showing leadership so that all staff are pulling in the same direction. As Cris Beswick – entrepreneur and CEO of several companies – points out, genuine commitment from the top is essential:

> Is the quest for engagement really a journey only Indiana Jones should attempt? I don't think so! From my perspective it's just about very hard work and being sincere. If as a CEO, senior exec or manager, you really care about your people and I mean really care, then topics like engagement should be a fundamental and clearly visible part of your organization's strategy. If it isn't, you're paying lip-service to it and it's just another buzzword or short-term initiative!

So in this chapter, we focus on how some leaders are building cultures of engagement; and how they create **Connection** by:

- developing a clear vision and powerful sense of shared purpose
- providing a strong strategic narrative about the organization – where it's come from and where it's going
- focusing people and structuring the organization and its tasks so that people can get on with what matters
- managing culture change
- demonstrating values-based leadership
- building leadership at all levels.

First let's consider the challenges facing leaders as they seek to create a culture of engagement.

Creating Connection – the leadership challenge

Creating Connection in today's context of continuous change and 'more from less' can be challenging. There are widespread engagement (and trust) deficits with respect to leaders and institutions, calls for better governance, and increasing emphasis on risk management and compliance. With work increasingly carried out across time zones and organizational boundaries, managers and leaders can find themselves managing people they do not employ, but for whose output they are accountable. They are required to respond to the changing expectations of today's increasingly diverse and multigenerational workforces, especially with respect to involvement. They have to manage individualized employee relations and collective industrial relations, and navigate the growing tensions implicit in leading through a chronic economic downturn. They also need to grow future leaders who can respond to changing requirements, given that, as Beer (1994, p. 15) notes:

> The old world was characterized by the need to manage things. ... The new world is characterized by the need to manage complexity.

At the same time, leaders need to engage and motivate their workforces. After all, leadership is about 'capturing attention and motivating people to follow your way – your vision and your dreams' (Augier and Teece, 2005, p. 116), as well as 'influencing others to accomplish organizational goals' (Tubbs and Schulz, 2006, p. 30). Yet according to several commentators, and in spite of the plethora of studies, we still seem to know little about the defining characteristics of effective leadership (Dulewicz et al., 2005). Indeed, 'as a scientific concept, leadership is a mess' (Augier and Teece, 2005, p. 116). So, if there is no blueprint for engaging leadership, this prompts the question: what do employees want from their leaders? What do they find engaging?

What do employees want from their leaders?

In research carried out by one of us (Holbeche, 2009), more than 2000 UK employees were asked what they wanted from their leaders. The top three things mentioned were about leaders who:

- can create and effectively communicate a vision
- inspire, engage and motivate others
- are brave, and not afraid to face challenges and take risks.

Typical comments included:

- 'Can create a vision that stands up to political change, and communicate that effectively and convincingly to politicians, stakeholders and staff.'
- 'Are effective through being able to deliver in the present, and are visionaries about the future, and bring their people with them.'
- 'Can inspire and enthuse as well as manage and enjoy change.'
- 'Can implement the changes necessary to face a challenging future by engaging staff throughout the organization.'
- 'Brave enough to step into the unknown and do something different.'
- 'Are not afraid of change and making tough decisions.'
- 'Look beyond old, established ways of working and face up to the challenges of the real world.'

If leaders behave in these ways, employees are more likely to experience fulfilment of the three categories of engagement elements we discussed in Chapter 3:

- **Intellectual** – do I have chance for achievement, responsibility and growth? Am I trusted; do I have some autonomy?
- **Affective/emotional** – am I proud of what I do and feel my work serves a worthwhile purpose? Can I see the impact of my work on others?
- **Social** – is this a community I want to belong to? Do I trust leaders and my colleagues? Am I valued and do I value others? Is the organization doing 'good work' for the community?

Employees also want to be fairly treated and to have their voice heard. When these conditions are satisfied, it is likely that employees will be motivated and willing to 'go the extra mile'. We conclude that leaders who can lead in the way that employees want are best equipped to build engaging organizational cultures, since they are able to:

- bring out the best in people and take them further than they would go on their own
- inspire and engage others through a strong sense of shared purpose
- provide clarity in uncertainty
- exercise stewardship and 'walk the talk' on values
- see organization development as their responsibility
- deliberately build changeable cultures – that are agile, adaptable, and conducive to learning, innovation and sustainable high performance (Holbeche, 2005)
- build collaborative communities and develop leadership, not just leaders.

Heading in the right direction

Part of creating Connection is being able to articulate an overall vision. Being clear about what an organization stands for, what it wants to achieve and where it's heading not only helps guide actions but motivates employees by the appeal to a higher purpose. The MacLeod Report concurred, arguing that what they called 'a strong strategic narrative' was a key contributor to employee engagement since it helped people see where the organization was going and how they fitted in. Of course most organizations do have mission statements, but too often they are forgettable and could easily apply to any number of other organizations. Engaging managers set out a vision that is more of a catalysing challenge for everyone – what Collins and Porras (1994) termed a Big Hairy Audacious Goal ('BHAG'). While not a substitute for cascading business goals, setting appropriate budgets and aligning personal objectives, the benefit of a compelling vision is that it provides a line of sight that reminds everyone what they're aiming for and helps them to check if what they're doing is adding to (or detracting from) this end goal.

The 'soft' skills are the 'hard' skills

But setting out a vision on its own is not enough. Inspiring others and bringing out the best in them calls for a specific set of leadership skills, often referred to as the 'softer' skills of good people management. These include listening, delegation and the ability to engage teams. Yet traditionally senior managers have reached the top not through demonstrating 'soft' skills, but scientific, technical or business know-how. This is a problem given that nowadays, as Peter Cheese (2011), Chairman of the Institute of Leadership and Management, points out:

> These soft skills are the real determinants of good versus average, or great versus good. And they are also the harder things to measure and the harder things to train and develop.

So what do these soft skills involve? Rob Goffee and Gareth Jones (2005) argue that inspirational leaders stand out by their ability to come across authentically. To do this, they know how to display enough of their own weaknesses that they appeal to others by appearing more open and personable. They use their strong sense of intuition in assessing organizational timing and judging how to interact with others. They motivate others through a combination of being very supportive *and* practising 'tough love'. And while conforming enough with their organization, they use what's different about themselves to stand out and motivate others (Goffee and Jones, 2006).

Engaging managers realize the importance of this. Krista Baetens – whom we met in Chapter 2 – is Managing Director in Asia for the Dutch bank ING.

She leads a team of 32 lending professionals across Asia, heads up the Singapore office with 450 staff and manages the south-east Asia network, encompassing Singapore, Indonesia, Malaysia, Vietnam and Thailand. Krista is considered by her teams and peers to be a highly engaging manager and, as she points out, employee engagement is neither a 'bolt-on' extra, nor is it 'soft':

> *Employee engagement is very close to my heart and to the business I run and how I run it. People used to think that engagement is 'soft stuff' which I do not agree with. I like to tell the cynics that 'engagement is just another business driver and if you get it (i.e. engagement) right it's a very powerful tool to run the business in an even more efficient way with people who like what they do, more than if they don't'. Of course you need to use techniques or skills which are slightly different from just purely setting objectives. The outcome is definitely not soft, and you can measure the tangible results, for example profitability or staff turnover.*

For leaders to whom these skills do not come naturally, it's a question of being willing to accept and work on their own limitations – creating an environment in which the leader is also a learner.

Case study: Nampak Plastics Europe Ltd

Nampak Plastics Europe Ltd, a subsidiary of Africa's largest packaging group, is a leader in the production of HDPE (high density polyethylene) bottles for the food and drink industry and employs more than 600 people in the UK and Ireland. Eric Collins, who became Managing Director in 2007, passionately believes that ordinary employees have the potential to transform the performance of the business. He had a vision about how business performance and employee wellbeing could be transformed through employee engagement, which, for him, was not an HR but a management initiative.

A staff survey in 2008 showed his challenge – only 6 per cent of staff were strongly engaged – so Eric himself ran a series of four-hour long workforce focus groups held at different times of night and day, so that people working on different shifts would have an equal chance to be heard. The more these took place, the more the discussions moved from local matters ('why are there no coffee machines?') to more challenging questions about the business. Key customers were asked what the company could do better and a series of follow-up measures were introduced, such as:

- all new starters having a buddy
- awards for staff excellence
- a suggestion scheme that offers a financial reward for the best ideas
- working groups for any major new projects
- a general strategy to involve staff more in setting goals and the future direction of the business.

The staff magazine *Message in a Bottle* encompasses this integrated culture, with many articles written by employees. Managers' leadership skills are developed and they are incentivized on their behavioural skills, as reflected in 360-degree feedback. Assessment centres make sure that future managers have good people skills, as well as technical expertise.

The collapse of one of the firm's main clients left debts of £1.5m and the need to lay off 90 staff, close the final salary pension scheme and impose a salary freeze. Nevertheless, people felt treated with dignity – and, as Eric insists, it is crucial that management leads by example and commitment.

In 2006, 80 per cent of employees responded that they wouldn't have recommended working for the company to their friends; in a survey three years later, 80 per cent of employees said that they would. By 2010, the staff engagement survey findings reflected a positive shift in attitudes, with 11 per cent of employees now strongly engaged, 67 per cent in the moderately engaged camp and only 18 per cent in the 'fence-sitter' category. Employees are enthused, proud to share their successes and actively volunteering to get involved in initiatives. Over the period 2007–11, key performance indicators such as bottle reject rates reduced by 27 per cent; other staff indicators such as absence levels, reportable accidents and labour turnover rates all showed significant improvements.

Employee engagement has shown clear benefits in terms of improved customer relationships and business results. As Eric points out, 'engagement does not cost pounds. The only price is consistent commitment from the very top of the organization.' Not surprisingly, Nampak was the overall winner of the 2010 CIPD People Management Awards.

Leaders and culture-building

Edgar Schein (2004, p. 1) argues that leadership and culture are two sides of the same coin, since leaders exert an extraordinary influence on culture and vice versa. Organizational culture – or a shared system of beliefs, values, and assumptions among an organization's inhabitants (Davis, 1984; Schein, 1999, 2004; Sergiovanni and Corbally, 1984) – guides the activities of an organization and its members (Sims, 1994). It provides organizational members with a common understanding that unites them, helps them to understand how they fit in, what is valued, appropriate, and inappropriate (Whitt, 1997; Allen and Cherrey, 2000). Standard elements of culture (Schein, 2004; Kuh and Whitt, 1988; Kuh, 1991) include:

- artefacts (e.g., traditions, rituals, myths, stories, ceremonies, customs, language, physical, and social environment)
- values
- basic assumptions (e.g. thoughts, unconscious perceptions).

Of course, cultures are complex; they can have a positive, neutral or negative impact on employee engagement and performance. So what makes up a high engagement culture?

High engagement cultures

Empowerment is a key characteristic of high engagement cultures. Organizational values and purpose become principles that guide people's actions and are reflected in the stories, legends and myths that are shared. Structures tend to be flat and decision-making processes are transparent. Communications are effective and two-way, and individuals have interesting roles with line of sight to their organization's purpose. They are supported and enabled to achieve challenging and worthwhile goals. People know what is required and how to do things because they have the right skills, opportunities and mobility within the structure. People are clear about their own roles and responsibilities and those of others. They feel trusted, valued, involved and fairly treated.

> Empowerment is a key characteristic of high engagement cultures.

Change also tends to be the norm, and people at all levels can initiate change to make improvements. People know what's happening, when and why. Good intentions are quickly translated into practical realities, such as using a dashboard against objectives, or systems where people can find out the information they need. As a result, people are confident enough to 'go for it' and be innovative.

Culture change

Sometimes, however, it becomes clear that the business strategy needs to change, and with it existing business practices and behaviours. Generally this is top-down, CEO-initiated change. Schein (2004) argues that top leaders can influence the nature of the resulting culture through primary mechanisms (what leaders pay attention to, rewards, recruitment and communication) and secondary mechanisms (organization design, structure, systems and procedures, and design of physical space). The CEO therefore becomes the commissioner of organization development to improve the effectiveness and health of the organization.

However, bringing about 'top-down' culture change is never easy – and in larger organizations, with many levels of management, it may be harder to engage staff. Senior managers may find themselves working with teams and business units who do not 'buy in' to the new direction, especially if the pressured environment includes potentially adversarial employee relations. They may find themselves negotiating with clever yet disaffected or intransigent staff, and managing politicized relationships with peers, boards and other stakeholders. Such scenarios can test the confidence, resilience and interpersonal dexterity of even the strongest. In such cases, a simplistic top-down 'recipe book' approach to change is unlikely to work and may only create disengagement instead. Before embarking on such an initiative, it's important to assess how change-ready the organization is, how fast the change can (and needs to) be progressed, and how far employee participation can occur so as to help foster ownership for the change and instil longer-term organizational learning (Kerber and Buono, 2005).

> Bringing about 'top-down' culture change is never easy – and in larger organizations, with many levels of management, it may be harder to engage staff.

As we'll explore further in Chapter 10, change management can be successfully achieved while maintaining organizational health. But especially in the case of culture change, it requires strong leadership from the CEO, together with clarity of focus, frequent communication and role modelling of the required 'new' behaviours. Indeed, Robert Marshak argues that the very expression 'culture change' is unhelpful, since change is not a project with a set end point but is rather an ongoing process. Instead, he argues, top management should embrace the notion of 'morphing' to describe whole system change and develop 'morphing mindsets' that reflect the concepts of continuous change and flexible organizational forms (Marshak, 2004).

Co-creation

In Chapter 3 we talked about 'active partnership with employees' as a key enabler of both engagement and performance. Joe Raelin (2005) describes the resulting culture as 'leaderful', where leadership is exercised at all levels concurrently and communities are compassionate and act for the collective good. Emmanuel Gobillot (2007) argues that sustainable organizational change should essentially be constructed or negotiated *with*, rather than *for* organizational members, thereby reflecting the plurality of stakeholder interests. Similarly, Dick Axelrod (2011) argues that culture change is really about generating a social movement through:

- widening the circle of involvement
- connecting people to each other
- creating communities for action
- promoting fairness.

Thus leadership becomes an interactive process, with leaders bringing together different groups of people and systems and creating synergy between them. This involves rethinking change in terms of dialogue or open conversations. If organizations are viewed as conversations, what changes? What leadership skills and attitudes are needed for real dialogue?

Empowerment by design: from 'I' to 'we'
Traditional organizations are based on control, checking and hierarchy. But in the co-created organization, fluidity, involvement and 'boundarylessness' are key. Management's role changes: its task is to create the conditions for high learning in the individual and in the team, improved quality of thinking, reflection, and the ability to develop shared visions and understanding of complex business issues and opportunities. With the shift to self-organization, leaders need to be 'change-able', with the learning agility to respond to new situations and to:

- recognize and accept some degree of chaos, and work with it as a source of creative energy
- identify, clarify and communicate the 'givens' or boundaries accurately
- create limited organizational structures and principles such that there is both enough form and also fluidity for rapid, organized action
- create resource flexibility in terms of availability and application
- remove barriers
- focus, grow and cultivate the shared values and purpose of the organization

- ensure organizational learning to quickly develop and deploy new competencies
- bridge from the present to the future using clear transition processes while avoiding focusing on the future to the detriment of the present
- let go of control.

Such a shift in their role can be very scary for some managers, but outstanding leaders work through their anxieties and seek to create conditions of trust as a foundation of greater self-management. As Will Hutton (2011a) points out, the best managers are those who can create Connection:

> *The best managers and leaders eschew tricks and tactics for the steady path of being consistent and authentic. They have a knack for bringing meaning to a task and making connections for people. Wherever possible they give power away so as to transmit responsibility. And they know that, to a knowledge-intensive workforce, the value that matters more than anything else is respect. Of course, saying that makes it sound easy, but it's anything but.*

It's about being psychologically adaptable and able to challenge existing mindsets and mental models about how the world works and about the nature of their own power and influence. When leaders adopt a learning approach to managing others, typically, micro-management is banished, employees can exercise greater autonomy and excellence is possible. This is the recipe for 'empowerment', a vital ingredient of an effective knowledge economy firm.

> When leaders adopt a learning approach to managing others, typically, micro-management is banished, employees can exercise greater autonomy and excellence is possible.

For instance, **Effectory**, the international employee survey provider, recognizes that employees are smart enough to think for themselves and want to ensure that their contribution leads to something worthwhile. The decision was taken to completely de-layer the organization of 170 employees: apart from two owner-directors and a small corporate team to ensure brand consistency and positioning, the workforce now works within a flat structure. Each team appoints its own 'captain' whose task is to deliver client satisfaction, growth, profitability and employee satisfaction. Teams appraise their captain on how well he or she is fulfilling this role.

> Leaders need to be clear about what they expect the outcomes to be, but they should give individuals the freedom to decide how best to get there.

Leaders need to be clear about what they expect the outcomes to be, but they should give individuals the freedom to decide how bestto get there. In **Cougar Automation**, a control and industrial management systems supplier that has been a UK *Sunday Times* Top 100 Best Companies Award winner for three years running, people are free to play to their strengths. Everyone is clear about what they are there to achieve and they are encouraged to find ways to achieve these outcomes by doing the things they love. This simple philosophy makes the company work and allows most of the normal management superstructure to be dismantled. Stripping away rules and bureaucracy makes everyone happier and more productive. People are trusted to pick their own leaders and control when and where they work, as well as to choose what they work on. They can take holidays when they think it is reasonable without asking permission and even wear what they think is appropriate. Leaders are there to provide encouragement and support, and to help improve the systems so that people find their jobs easier; they recognize that there is always need for improvement but they still believe they have created a trust-based, high-performance workplace.

Similarly, at **Blue Focus**, the leading PR consulting company in China, authority and responsibility are delegated as far down the organization as possible. As CEO Oscar Zhao comments:

> We believe that if people are given the responsibility and accountability they will not only produce a better result for the company but they will also achieve a much higher level of job satisfaction.

Tips for managers relating to empowerment are given in Box 8.1.

Box 8.1 Tips for managers: empowerment

- Consider what this leadership emphasis means for you. How do you see your job changing, if at all? How do you see accountability, responsibility, and authority?
- As a leader, what do you think needs to be done to assist the organization to become healthy, based on your own perception of health? Draw from any ideas or experience that you already have about achieving an optimum state of health in an organization.
- What other kinds of changes would need to take place in the organization to provide resources and remove barriers, such as a different performance review focus? How would technology assist?
- Storytelling is a powerful way to build community in the organization. Hold a storytelling event the evening before a change team meeting, in which stories – of accomplishment, of struggle – are told to honour the past and present. This is critical before moving to the future. What do you see as the potential challenges and pitfalls of this approach? What do you see as the benefits that will emerge?
- Remove barriers caused by:
  - insufficient skill training
  - unnecessary regulations
  - poor equipment
  - poor workspace
  - bad information systems.
- How far are employees encouraged to follow the new behaviours in terms of how they are evaluated, rewarded and recognized?
- Does the existing structure allow the organization to take advantage of new opportunities, creativity or ideas?
- How will communication take place so that the organization as a whole can become aware of activities as they take place?

- As a leader, become a commissioner of organization development (OD), working closely with trusted and skilled OD experts to develop the appropriate structure and communications, ensuring these are appropriate to support the dynamic purpose and potential of the organization.

Values as the basis of empowerment

Strong shared values can act as a firm basis for empowerment, because they provide the parameters within which employees can 'release their discretionary effort' to the benefit of the organization. As Andrew Lycett, CEO of **RCT Homes**, whose case study features in this chapter, points out:

So much of what we needed to do was change. Really laying down the foundations of strong values from the outset enables people to have greater freedoms. The way I used to describe it to people in the early days was: 'I'm telling you where the field boundaries are, but I'm not telling you how to cross the field. You'll know by just looking at the values if you're doing something that would take you out the field – because it'll feel wrong to you.'

Bringing values to life and embedding them in everyday practice is key to employees having the freedom to perform at their best. For instance, if you want innovation as a leader, you cannot allow fear into an organization. When you are trying something new, success and failure are finely balanced. If you fail to recognize success, and readily punish failure, you will create an institutionally risk-averse culture.

Luminus Group, a socially responsible business providing homes and building sustainable communities in eastern England, has a unique, strengths-focused culture and a high level of trust. The atmosphere and culture of Luminus Group is one of support, encouragement and learning from mistakes. Employees are not blamed for mistakes but encouraged to use them as opportunities to examine procedures and working styles, and put systems in place to prevent them recurring. This culture means that the workplace remains positive and productive. A special induction programme, 'Understanding Luminus – The Way We Do Things Around Here', is attended by all new hires so that everyone knows exactly what is expected of them to achieve the company's aims. This starts at the top with the senior management team, who set an example for managers, who in turn set an example for employees.

To play their part in making organizations relevant to customers, employees need to be aware what's happening outside the organization. At **Instant**, a market leader in all key global serviced office markets, 'The Lime Green Standard' is Instant's behaviour benchmark – the DNA of what it means to be Instant. It is a set of aspirational behaviours for all staff at team member, manager and board level, grouped under the three headings of business, customer and people. Lime Green behaviours such as 'Actively bring the outside world in' allow everyone to focus on doing something extraordinary every day to make Instant the best company for clients to deal with and to develop people's skills. It is now so much part of their culture and language that to say 'You are so Lime Green!' is the greatest compliment.

Organizing for empowerment
Of course organizational complexity is a major barrier to empowerment. Multiple management hierarchies, unclear roles and byzantine governance processes all serve to inject organizational ambiguity, reduced accountability and

Case study: Sika AG

Sika AG is a global company headquartered in Baar, Switzerland, and is a world-leading specialty chemicals business. With 13,482 employees Sika achieved annual sales of CHF4.4 billion in 2010, which in the mid-term they aim to double. The company places high value on the 'Sika Spirit', a culture of employee empowerment and responsibility, a strong sense of belonging and feeling valued and respected, and a passionate drive for achieving ambitious business targets. Although the company measures engagement selectively via surveys, it sees that, first and foremost, management is responsible for fostering this empowerment culture in order to have committed people that can outpace the competition.

To foster this, Sika has used organization design as a key enabler of empowerment. It has deliberately kept to a lean company structure so as to drive decision-making to the lowest reasonable level and – according to Head of Corporate HR Peter Ziswiler – 'decisions here are often taken one to two levels lower than would be the case in other companies'. To do this, the company has only five to six organizational levels (including the CEO); spans of control for managers are generally wide. The company has a lean corporate HQ and avoids appointing staff officers or other assistants, forcing managers to delegate decisions instead. New managers are given coaching and training to foster the right approach, which means trusting their staff, pushing authority down the organization and operating more as a coach to other staff.

Reflecting the importance of empowerment, there are no managers who spend all their time just managing or coordinating others; all of them are expected to be responsible for a particular task or activity in its own right. Sika's 'principle of maximum delegation of responsibility' is supported by a strong Management by Objectives (MbO) approach, where employees are kept as informed as possible, participate in processes and decision-making, and are given room for initiative and creativity. The result is that employees at all levels feel they can make a real impact; that they are empowered, and can decide without seeking endless approvals. The company is dynamic and fast-growing: even if this freedom does sometimes leads to things being a bit chaotic, the benefit is speed and any issues that arise are ones that people are encouraged to resolve in a pragmatic and open way.

Underpinning this, Sika seeks to foster a culture of respect, dignity, listening, approachability and appreciation. Specifically, senior management encourage staff to speak up about problems and challenges and to create a more open culture, regardless of hierarchy. People are on first-name terms and address internal communications as 'Dear Friends'. Likewise, the company is single-status in terms of most benefits – there are no executive dining rooms, limos, etc., because the aim is to create a collaborative environment where anyone can freely approach anyone else. In this way, by combining organization design with strong commitment to clear cultural values, Sika enables employees to be engaged, empowered and high performing, even during challenging times.

restrict room for individuals to do their job. So as well as fostering a culture of empowerment, smart companies 'hard-wire' it into their set-up, constantly monitoring their organization to ensure that bureaucracy is curbed and delegation and engagement are optimized.

Purpose

As we discussed in Chapter 3, a key aspect of Connection is a strong shared purpose. **Marriott Hotels International**, for instance, has a clear people-centric culture based on the belief that 'if you take care of your associates, they will take care of the customer and the customer will keep coming back'. Its corporate culture and management style is founded on a concern for all employees, hands-on management and a commitment to meeting customer needs through excellence in quality, service and hospitality. This culture gives employees meaning, purpose and guidance, and empowers them to do whatever it takes to take care of the customer, pay extraordinary attention to detail, take pride in their physical surroundings and use their creativity to find new ways to meet the needs of customers. The culture is expressed through the 'Marriott's Associate Appreciation Week': a global initiative held every year at all hotels and offices worldwide, where managers say 'thank you' to their teams by hosting a week-long calendar of events, many of which are linked to community and charity partners.

Customer purpose

Tesco, the international supermarket chain, has built its business strategy around an intensely customer-focused purpose. The strategy is about creating benefit for customers and building lifetime loyalty. The company values were developed with employees who were asked what they would like Tesco to stand for. Its promises to customers are on display in all Tesco stores. Customers' lives change quickly – their fashions, pressures and concerns. Tesco believes it is vital to keep closer to the customer than its competitors, so as to be in the best position to respond quickly.

> Tesco believes it is vital to keep closer to the customer than its competitors, so as to be in the best position to respond quickly.

Tesco uses its customer data to pinpoint what is needed, and the customer purpose is made real to staff through communications, meetings, working practices and staff rewards. As a result of Tesco's success being values–driven, staff surveys suggest that employees have confidence and trust in the firm.

At PR firm **Blue Focus**, customers are asked for feedback on employees as part of the bonus scheme. As Oscar Zhao puts it:

> *Experience has taught us that feedback from our customers is a great indicator about how our people feel about Blue Focus. We see direct correlation between motivated and happy people and satisfied customers and vice versa.*

Social responsibility

A truly invigorating purpose conveys something distinctive that is both uplifting and deliverable, and also appeals to a person's altruism (Bains et al., 2007). The eighteenth century philosopher Adam Smith noted that within each person there is a better angel. In Smith's words, there is a 'stronger power' than self-love, and this is 'reason, principle, conscience. ... It is he who shows us the propriety of generosity and the deformity of injustice.' CIPD's 2009 survey of 3000 UK employees bore this out, and found that social purpose elicited the highest levels of shared purpose (CIPD Research, 2009).

Consequently, purposes with a strong social motive and a clear line of sight to the customer and/or society are likely to be most engaging for employees. For instance, half the graduates applying to work for **Standard Chartered Bank** cite the bank's ethical approach as a reason for wanting to join. Employees are given two days' additional leave each year to volunteer for community initiatives, and this really enhances employee engagement. Employees have been involved in helping to teach blind students interview techniques and to develop their careers. Other projects include the Global Fund to Fight Aids, Tuberculosis and Malaria in Gambia.

Igniting purpose

In her book *Hot Spots*, Lynda Gratton argues that a mindset of cooperation, boundary-spanning and an igniting purpose enhances the possibility of a 'hot spot' or intense flow emerging. She argues that latent energy can be propelled by an igniting question that sparks activity and reflection. It can further generate an igniting vision that creates a future state so vivid that energy and action are directed toward it and energized by an igniting task that is meaningful, ambiguous and developmental. At the heart of these three forms of igniting purposes are conversations between peers. Insightful data, an emphasis on values and being given the space for reflection all help to support and shape these conversations (Gratton, 2007).

Leading US medical technology company **Medtronic**'s mission is 'to alleviate pain, restore health, and extend life'. New employees receive a Medtronic Medallion reminding them of this mission and hold an annual holiday party where employees meet patients whose lives have been changed by the company's products, which include defibrillators and pacemakers. In this way, employees are connected to – and engaged by – the igniting purpose of the company.

The following case study illustrates how one company's strong social purpose has been the mainspring of a significant business turnaround and continuing innovation.

Case study: RCT Homes

RCT Homes, based in South Wales, is a social enterprise that was the first Community Mutual Housing Organization in UK. Created in 2007 and charged with taking over the housing stock of three local authorities in Rhondda Cynon Taff, RCT Homes is probably the largest tenant-represented organization in the UK since 5500 tenants have exercised their right to become shareholders. At the outset, the 250 staff that transferred to it from the council brought their traditional mindset with them: tenants were rarely regarded as customers, and bureaucracy rather than flexibility held sway.

Authentic leadership was a key ingredient of the turnaround. Keen to foster thriving communities as well as a successful organization, CEO Andrew Lycett was determined to shift the culture, and engaged tenants in the process. At the outset, tenants were given 86 promises about what RCT Homes would do, and these promises were built on by a follow-up vision and values workshop between tenants and employees. This helped staff to understand why services needed to improve, enabling them to explore together how RCT Homes could be (as they later called it) 'more than a landlord', and add value. Here, the mutuality of interest and commitment came about by bringing staff and tenants together, involving them all in co-creating what success would look like in future.

The workshop clarified the organization's values and plans for the future. Language and action were welded together around the shared purpose of being 'More than a Landlord'. The overall culture change was branded as 'We're Better, Working Together' to reflect the organizational ambition to become high-performing. Reinforcing the values of trust and continuous improvement, the brand was designed to change the kind of thinking that restricts innovation and customer service. Corporate communication vehicles were used to signal change and action: for instance, the house magazine regularly features 'You Said ... We Did ...' reports, which highlight how staff feedback has been acted on. The language used is intentionally very straightforward and avoids corporate-speak.

A combination of training, job enrichment, bringing in new talent and moving in a single day from multiple sites to one site with an open plan layout helped foster a positive and 'can do' attitude in the workforce. Another key aspect of the shift was improving the quality of management and leadership at all levels through the 'Leading Better Together' programme, which combined feedback, development, coaching, volunteering and practical tools to help managers deal with the paradoxes and ambiguities of managing people. Simple and straightforward performance management processes ('Performing Better') were introduced, along with user-friendly toolkits for managers and staff. Progress was reported on internally and the change process was brought to life by storytelling and innovative forms of recognition.

Alongside customer focus and staff empowerment, passion became another key feature of the new culture. Inspired by the vision that RCT Homes be 'More than a Landlord', staff took on new challenges such as the finance team developing a new information pack for tenants called 'Sound as a Pound', which helped them to manage their own money better and so be more dependable tenants. Others volunteered for community regeneration projects through a charity they created called Meadow Prospect as well as a social enterprise, Grow Enterprise Wales (GrEW), and another social enterprise acquired in 2011, Young Wales. Projects included training the young unemployed (e.g. to provide gardening services) and providing education for children excluded or at risk of exclusion from school. Across the Group, the RCT Homes approach to training and development has resulted in more than 1000 new jobs or work-based training opportunities being created by the Group in just three years.

RCT Homes' engaging culture has created real dynamic shifts in people's attitudes about what they come to work for, with the proportion of staff reporting 'my job has meaning' soaring from 41 per cent in 2008 to 80 per cent in 2010. In just a few years, RCT Homes has gained several awards for its housing and social enterprise work, while key performance indices have dramatically improved. Urgent (as opposed to emergency) repairs completed within seven days have risen from 70 to 95 per cent, with 98 per cent of tenants satisfied with repair work. Moreover, the level of vacant properties and tenant turnovers has dropped – a major contribution to the bottom line.

Embedding a culture of engagement

But how can we ensure that today's engagement focus does not become yesterday's forgotten initiative? Perhaps the best 'guarantee' is by developing future leaders who can make **Connection**, bring out the best in people and build agile organizational cultures.

Growing tomorrow's leaders

Leaders are born but we believe they can also be 'made'. We argue that most managers can learn to bring out the best in other people. While some managers may be naturally predisposed to do this, others can improve their potential to be good managers through training in people management and strategic visioning skills. Generally, middle managers need to be able to understand the corporate purpose, vision, values and strategy, and be able to communicate these to employees. They must know how to develop and motivate their staff, and understand for instance younger employees and their search for a work/life balance and meaning. They must know how to inform and consult, manage stress and conflict, and coach and mentor others. They need to create a positive working environment, show appreciation of good performance, and hold difficult conversations. They may need training and, following training, all managers should receive feedback from their team (360-degree feedback) to make sure that their new skills are being used effectively.

Unless managers can do these things well, we argue that they should not be in roles where they have responsibility for managing other people. Conversely, managers who are able to engage their teams should be recognized and rewarded for this. For instance, **Cadbury's**, winner of the 'Best Places to Work' award, launched a 'Purple Hearts' award to recognize great people managers, based on the employee survey results.

HR is the function with responsibility for ensuring that line managers are appropriately selected for people management roles. The UK's **Nationwide Building Society** takes employee engagement very seriously. Its rules of thumb for developing an engaging workplace highlight the crucial importance of both the getting the 'fit' right, and of developing engaging managers:

- recruit staff for their attitude and work hard to keep them
- flexible reward packages fairly and transparently delivered
- develop frontline managers to deliver the emotional as well as the task element of their job
- coach and mentor managers.

HR must ensure that managers are equipped and supported to do their jobs of managing people effectively. Coaching managers can also be helpful. Sometimes providing managers with user-friendly guidance can help to make them feel more confident and become more effective at people management. For instance, managers at **RCT Homes** are supplied with practical tools to help them communicate effectively. For instance, when delivering bad news, managers are advised:

Even if you don't have all the answers, honest and frank discussion with teams can allay many fears. Any sense among your team that you are holding back or, of course, providing misleading information, could lead to the situation worsening.

As the guidance notes point out, turning the tide on challenging issues is a marathon, not a sprint. Effective communication is a matter of discipline – the day-in, day-out conversations that address questions and issues candidly.

The approach to developing people managers at lifestyle retailer **White Stuff** is branded 'Living and Leading White Stuff'. New hires attend 'Living White Stuff', which is all about learning to be the best version of yourself: the idea being that without being in the best shape possible, you cannot lead yourself at work and your life in general. Following on from this, all White Stuff managers attend 'Leading White Stuff' and learn what followers expect from a leader, together with a 'Leader as Coach' programme for all those managing people. The focus is on developing and stretching people rather than just giving them the answers. These initial programmes are reinforced by ongoing development through quarterly 90-minute workshops and monthly podcasts that address more specific leadership issues such as conducting effective one-to-ones and managing change. Managers get feedback on their progress with these new skills through 'upward' feedback and 360-degree reviews.

Taking the long view

There are enormous pressures on organizations to let short-term thinking dominate business practice and decision-making. Business reporting cycles and funding regimes all emphasize very time-limited horizons. To truly embed a new approach, however, can take time. Having the courage to take the longer view when others are frenetically grasping the present moment can be difficult, but we believe it is essential for sustainable success.

Given the context we outlined in Chapter 2, the balance of power in the employment relationship appears to have tipped very firmly in favour of employers in recent years. Rebuilding a more mutual 'deal' is likely to be a more meaningful and enduring basis for employee engagement. Executives must also lead the way in making sure that their organization is fair to its own internal stakeholders (that is, its employees). This is about rebalancing the scales, challenging the 'givens' of the marketplace, taking a longer-term perspective and creating a shared stake in building successful organizations.

Case study: Farrer and Co.

In a legal world characterized by raging corporatism, Farrer and Co. stands out as a successful law firm that does the small things in a modest but entirely self-assured way, with a strong grip on its history. Whereas many other big name solicitors have responded to the financial crisis by desperately trying to reinvent themselves, former senior partner James Furber and his colleagues have insisted on staying true to their heritage. As Furber states, 'I'm committed to thinking about the long-term future of the firm and that means not the next six months, but about the next ten years. Although work slackened off during the crisis we sacked nobody because these are the people we will need for the future. The idea of real service to the client is no longer core to what many solicitors do.'

So rather than being focused on transactions, Furber's commitment is to long-term relationships with the clients. He identifies with their interests and understands their perspective.

When it comes to the culture within the firm itself, it is again a service approach that comes through: 'We have a stewardship approach. Our role is to pass the firm on to the next generation in better shape than we found it.' What this produces is a sense of camaraderie, not just among the partners but throughout the firm and between generations.

As senior partner, Furber went out of his way to get to know all the trainees and associates and to socialize with them regularly: 'That is the way to transmit the culture and values of the firm to embed it among new recruits.' One priority is to discourage any sense of rivalry between departments and their respective profitability levels.

> 'We are very fortunate here – and it reflects the sense of a common purpose – that we don't have backbiting. It would frankly be unthinkable. Farrer's is a middle-ground firm but we are not middle of the road. Because of our values and the way we do things, we are confident that there will continue to be a demand for what we offer. As a firm we engage heart as well as head, and I believe that engenders the loyalty we attract from clients and staff alike.'
>
> Source: Fennell, 2011
> Reprinted with kind permission from News International

In this professional services firm, this combination of longer-term perspective, client focus, values-based leadership, talent management and an employment relationship based on mutual commitment creates a powerful foundation for sustainable success.

Interestingly, it seems that enduring commitment between employees and employers is also a characteristic of family-owned firms. A study by Stanley Siebert (2011) found that family-owned firms produce more worker loyalty than any other type of privately owned, publicly listed or public sector workplace. Perhaps surprisingly, employee loyalty to family companies comes despite employees appearing to enjoy no better benefits than other workers; the real difference comes from the way that the closer relationship between bosses and staff makes people feel included. As Professor Siebert explains:

Family businesses tend to treat employees much more transparently and consistently than other employers. In particular, family businesses encourage (but do not guarantee) long- term employment.

For the third generation owner of one family firm that created a sports car brand, the secret to a happy workforce is not so much that they work for a family company but that there is a long-term plan and a product that they can be proud of. Again, being part of something worthwhile, feeling valued and being able to take a longer-term perspective are powerful factors in creating employee engagement.

Conclusion

So these case studies demonstrate what a culture of engagement is all about. That's when more people, more of the time, are willing and able to give of their best and have passion for what they do. Cultures of engagement are underpinned by strong vision and values, and a purpose focused on both customer and society. As a result, short-term actions are informed by what is needed longer term. There is authentic leadership, a genuine belief in the value of helping people to help themselves and great partnering between executives, customers, OD/HR and staff to deliver the big vision.

Top leaders provide focus and inject pace, follow through on commitments and 'walk the talk' on values. They have the grace to apologize when they get things wrong. Leadership communication – so critical to earning and keeping workforce trust – is frequent, open, high quality and with consistency of messaging. It's also two-way; there is genuine involvement of staff and of customers in co-creating the 'how' if not the 'what' and 'why' of strategy.

People work in structures where they have the authority, autonomy and the resources they need. In other words, they feel 'empowered'. They have roles in which they can grow, have scope for initiative and a clear line of sight to how their job delivers the purpose. The task of top leadership is to enable and unblock the organization, removing the bureaucracy and other barriers that clutter the sight line.

Leadership is not just top-down, but dispersed. There is a genuine sense of community, with many people at all levels taking personal responsibility for business as usual, innovation and proactively driving things forward. People enjoy and value their work, feel recognized and valued for what they contribute, and experience meaning from what they do.

Reaching milestones towards the vision allows progress to be celebrated and aspirations to expand. This provides the rationale for ongoing change that employees too can initiate, and is the spur to innovation. Employees are up for the next challenge: after all, an engaging purpose is a journey, not a destination. In their own way these various case studies provide evidence that employee engagement is the key to sustainable employee performance, organizational agility and great business results. In addition, they show that what works for the business also works for its key stakeholders – customers and staff – and directly benefits the community.

In today's challenging times, creating **Connection** is no longer an optional extra but essential if organizations are to be nimble, aligned and – above all – engaged.

Checklist

- Be explicit about what the organization stands for and is trying to do.
- Are people rewarded for collaboration and doing the right thing? Do rewards drive short-term thinking or ensure everyone shares success in progressing towards the organization's vision?
- Try to make change normal, so that people have no reason to fear change.
- 'Walk the talk' on values.
- Work out how to make today's tough working life a little easier for employees.
- Let people take risks so that they become agile.
- Take short-term decisions with the longer term in mind.

CHAPTER 9

So far we've looked at what employee engagement is about and why it's important to employers and to employees themselves. We've looked at some of the main drivers and barriers to engagement, and at how you can get a fix on these in your organization through surveys. We've emphasized the importance of acting on what you learn from surveys, but we've also acknowledged just how difficult that can be sometimes. In the last chapter we considered some of the key features of organizational cultures conducive to engagement. We looked at how engaging leadership creates a shared sense of purpose and direction that provides meaning for an organization's employees and creates value for all its stakeholders, while enabling the organization to adapt to its changing environment.

In this chapter, the focus shifts more specifically to the **Support** quadrant of our model and the key role managers play in engagement. Whether they are first-level supervisors, front-line managers or senior leaders, managers are at the heart of the employee engagement challenge (The Work Foundation, 2010). The defining contribution of great managers is that they boost the engagement levels of the people who work for them (Michaelman, 2004) by helping people have interesting and worthwhile jobs through which they can develop and grow, and hence deliver results that matter.

So we're going to focus in more detail on what 'engaging managers' actually do that enables employee engagement; that is, how they:

- get to know their people as individuals
- create an open and positive work environment
- build teams
- deliver on the employer brand
- care for employees
- provide a 'fair deal'.

Let's first consider the role of managers in engaging their teams.

What do engaging leaders and managers actually do?

Middle managers act as bridge between top management and their teams. They are often described as 'the squeezed middle', since they are usually under pressure from all sides. Yet a lengthy study of links between people management practices and performance (Purcell et al., 2003) suggests that the quality of line management clearly impacts on nearly all aspects of organizational life, including employee engagement and performance. It is typically the line manager who has the day-to-day job of ensuring that the 'right' people are in the 'right' jobs, and that these are interesting and satisfying.

Line managers carry out many roles in the campaign for employees' hearts and minds. They are a motivator, team builder, performance coach, company ambassador, resilience builder and deliverer of the employer brand. The ways in which managers implement, enact, enable and control have a significant effect on employee commitment, motivation and job satisfaction, which in turn affects how willingly employees release their discretionary effort and produce high-performance outcomes.

So how do engaging managers go about these tasks?

They get to know people as individuals

Engaging managers get to know their team as individuals and treat people with empathy, fairness and a concern for employee wellbeing. They are aware of different personalities and styles of team working, and notice when a team member behaves out of character. But in large organizations, especially when senior managers are responsible for large numbers of staff, how do managers get to 'know' their teams as individuals? Here Krista Baetens, Managing Director in Asia for Dutch bank **ING**, describes how she gets to know individuals in her various teams:

When I go to the locations once or twice a year I try to spend quality time with everyone. I try to spend more time than what is strictly necessary from a pure business perspective to sense the energy in the office and observe people closely. Is the team having fun, or are there tensions? Is the team at the centre of the office and activity or are they not? Do they interact with other teams? If I make appointments with people and sit with them for half an hour or an hour, there's only so much that can come up, but if you are just there and available, and you listen and observe carefully, it can make a difference, at least for me.

Another way for me is that I have always taken time out from my regular job – even at very junior level – to find someone in the office I don't know. Fifteen or 20 minutes a week may not sound like a lot, but it builds up over the years. I would typically walk around and, if I see a face of someone I don't know, I'll go to that person and say, 'Hi, I'm Krista, I don't know you – I've been working here for a while, are you new?' (In a friendly way, of course!) And over so many years and working in so many offices, I have built up quite a network. And then I've always been involved in staff clubs, corporate responsibility activities, office-wide projects, you name it. That also helps me to be a bit closer to what's happening.

So I find myself relying on different things. I find walking over a floor very telling because you can sense the electricity in the air and in some areas you can hear laughter, where people are having fun; in other offices people won't even look up from their desks – they'll almost hide. It says a lot about the management style. You can't achieve that overnight with one action. It takes maybe years, just building that up. Because people won't trust you if you just walk the floor once. But it's not always easy – if you have a busy schedule, it's very easy to have it removed from your calendar because there's no immediate deliverable attached to that. But if you consistently set aside 15 minutes or half an hour to do that, it is a long-term investment which in my view is definitely worth it.

And as Krista points out, getting to know your team as individuals is all a question of priorities. Her approach is one of MBWA (Management by Wandering Around) – which not only helps managers to spot issues, but also makes it easier for people to relate to senior managers:

> *An activity we started a few years back with the management team is 'speed meeting'. This is a one and a half hour informal face-to-face session between senior management and staff. Each pair of participants will spend ten minutes conversing before they move onto another participant, until all of them have made connections with one another. The main objectives of the speed meeting sessions are to increase visibility of senior management with staff, and to put a face to a name, especially in today's virtual world. This has quickly become one of the most popular activities in our organization, for senior management and staff alike.*

So the point is, making the effort to get to know people as individuals pays off.

If it's only done once or twice MBWA will backfire, because it can seem like unnecessary checking up or management snooping, and employees may be reluctant to raise real concerns. But if done regularly and well, as in this example, it can be a valuable early warning system for managers, as well as making leaders accessible to help employees resolve problems. (See Box 9.1 for more tips.) Together with an 'Open Door' policy, MBWA has been one of the cornerstones of the 'HP Way'. Dave Packard (1995, pp. 156–7), Hewlett-Packard's co-founder, advised that:

> So the point is, making the effort to get to know people as individuals pays off.

> *Straightforward as it sounds, there are some subtleties and requirements that go with MBWA. For one thing, not every manager finds it easy or natural to do. And if it's done reluctantly or infrequently, it just won't work. It needs to be frequent, friendly, unfocused, and unscheduled – but far from pointless. And since its principal aim is to seek out people's thoughts and opinions, it requires good listening.*

Box 9.1 Tips for managers: getting to know people

- Take some time to get to know your people more fully – not just what they do at work but what else is important in their lives.
- Don't try to 'steer' the conversation – use open questions and let the discussion go where the energy is.
- Show you are open to feedback about individuals' jobs and the workplace – ask what are the things they like most or least.
- Help employees to generate ideas about how to improve their engagement. When employees identify ways, they are more likely to take ownership and create positive change.
- Make yourself accessible – keep the door open and spend time in MBWA to feel the pulse of the organization and to get input and troubleshoot issues. Make it clear that employees are free to raise any subject and there are no negative consequences if they do so.

They create a climate of open communication

Creating a climate of open communication is the single most important thing that line managers can do to improve levels of employee engagement, according to 60 per cent of those surveyed by Melcrum Publishing (2005). As a result, employees feel able to voice their concerns, a key engagement factor (CIPD Research, 2011b). Similarly, CIPD research found that the main drivers of engagement were having opportunities to feed your views upwards, feeling well-informed about what is happening in the organization and believing that your manager is committed to the organization (Truss et al., 2006). Managers who are able to do this are described as open, honest and clear, and also able to give and receive feedback and invite opinions. Similar feedback has been found among US workers too – a study by Accenture found that employees were four times more likely to want to stay and five times more likely to be highly engaged if they worked in a trusting and respectful environment in which employees could safely raise issues without fear of punishment. Box 9.2 includes some tips for managers on open communication.

Box 9.2 Tips for managers: open communication

- Be open and honest with all communication.
- Keep people informed of progress and change.
- Take time for listening as opposed to telling.
- Treat people fairly and with respect.
- Be sensitive to language and how it may be misconstrued, especially in a cross-cultural setting.
- Show empathy and understanding of team/individual pressures.
- Encourage open and honest communication within the team.

While face-to-face communication is vital, new technologies allow this to be supplemented in many powerful ways. Indian global consulting and IT services company **Infosys** is ranked 15th in Forbes' list of the world's most innovative companies. With more than 140,000 employees, the challenge is how to ensure they are engaged and can provide the creative force to sustain their rapid business growth. With an average age of 27 and more than three-quarters being engineering graduates, Infosys uses technology to connect and involve its staff. Aside from emails and intranets, it also operates in-house TV and radio channels. To foster two-way exchange, input is collected through online instant polls (usually there are three a month) as well as via internal online chat rooms and discussion forums ('Infy WaterCooler'). Their CEO, S. Gopalakrishnan (popularly known as Kris), posts blogs and gets more than 300 queries a month through an 'Ask Kris' channel. More recently, Infosys updated its business strategy and ran more than 65 technology-based

> While face-to-face communication is vital, new technologies allow this to be supplemented in many powerful ways.

events worldwide to run chat sessions, knowledge cafés and so on to get 'grass-roots' input on its future strategy. More than 46,000 employees took part and generated 20,000+ ideas that helped shape their latest strategy.

They build engaged teams

It is in the creation of a strong team culture that engaging managers stand out from others. In each of the studies, engaging managers are described as positive, even when the going gets tough. In the IES study, they are able to select and keep a good team (Robinson et al., 2004, p. 43). For Michelman (2004), what distinguishes great managers from others is that, in leading engagement, they will seek the right fit for a person's talent; they work to see that employees are rewarded for their performance and endeavour to ensure that talent is developed through progressively more challenging and meaningful assignments. Research by Yarker et al. (2008, p. 2) suggests that effective line managers help their teams manage workload and resources by:

- monitoring team workload
- bringing in additional resource to handle extra pressures
- dealing rationally with problems
- reviewing processes to see if work can be process improved
- prioritizing future workloads
- Working proactively rather than reactively.

Engaging managers work hard on team spirit and build a strong bond within teams. They value their teams, involve them, care about their achievements and show mutual respect. Engaging managers listen to employees and help them come up with new ideas and ways to do their work. They welcome the suggestions of staff and encourage shared decision-making and collaborative working. They show appreciation of the contributions of individuals and actively promote their team within the organization and with senior management. They help their team understand its role in the wider organizational context. Consequently, compared with others, their teams show greater feelings of being valued.

Engaging managers use every communication vehicle to connect with and support their teams. Team meetings are positive experiences because managers:

- facilitate the meeting in a way that is positive, constructive, open and honest
- start and end on time
- agree outcomes for each agenda item
- share news, giving team members some time to report on progress made on their areas of responsibility
- teach something, such as inviting a guest to give a ten-minute presentation on some information, skills or technology that benefits the team
- share learning, creating team learning activities that teach skills – for example, asking members of the team to bring an activity that reviews or teaches a valuable skill
- solve problems, giving each group member a minute to describe a challenge that hinders work on a current project and letting everyone propose solutions (a process that requires a positive and supportive environment to be successful)
- invite another team to come and share what they do and their role in the business
- celebrate team successes – introducing some fun!

But real communication is about more than mere words. Here Krista Baetens describes how she created **Connection** and shared understanding within her multicultural team about the value of their work:

I was once part of a team meeting where the focus of the discussion was on what we couldn't do, rather than on what we could achieve as a team. I don't think that as a leader you can be complacent or be pessimistic, since your people would be looking at you to feel inspired and confident about the business. In that meeting, I asked everyone to close their eyes and they did (except one team member) and I asked them to put their fingers on their pulse and feel what it is to be at the heart of things, the core of things – it gives you energy, it reconnects to what 'core' really means. It was maybe a bit crazy but quite powerful and the tone of the meeting changed. The team became more forward-looking. It's about trying to find something that speaks to people.

Another way to create connection and shared understanding was by agreeing on shared values translated into three objects. The three objects represented the way we would deal with each other, and what the team would stand for, at all times. The pictures of the objects placed on the desks of the team members are a constant reminder of what our shared values are.

They show empathy: keep finger on the morale pulse

Sometimes, even a high-performing team can lose its edge. Many things can cause this, not least external factors such as difficult trading conditions or damage to company reputation. The key thing is for managers to notice when this is happening, and to do something to help improve staff's morale. This isn't a 'nice to have' – on the contrary, research by the Center for Creative Leadership indicates that managerial empathy is positively related to employee performance, and that simple steps such as active listening, watching out for non-verbal communication, taking the time to show a genuine interest in staff and putting oneself in the other person's shoes all help increase awareness of employees' needs. The research also shows that a more empathic response increases leadership effectiveness as a result (Gentry et al., 2010).

They create a positive work climate

When people enjoy what they do, they tend to work hard and play hard. Creating a positive work climate is about developing a sense of community while engaged in meaningful work. It's about being sensitive to timing, telling the 'story' of the vision, values and behaviours for the next phase, and celebrating achievements. Managers should see the employee as a 'whole' person outside of the work role and aim to create work communities that people want to belong to and feel proud of. They should encourage more social activities and get their organizations seriously involved in charitable and socially responsible work. Social interactions between leaders and staff can help break down barriers but should not be forced. This may involve team-building events, using gatherings and social media for cathartic and collective learning purposes.

Highly engaged teams in the IES study score more highly than others on all aspects of working life, such as satisfaction with immediate management, team working, performance management and appraisals, and training and development (Robinson et al., 2004). For instance, in one fast food restaurant chain, employees are typically aged between 18 and 35 and are generally strong advocates of the company. When asked why they choose to work for the firm, here is a typical response:

It's an incredible company to work for, it really is. When I think of my friends and the conversations I've had with them and how they feel de-motivated about their jobs, how they don't want to go to work in the morning, there's not a morning that I wake up and feel that I can't be bothered to work today. It's continually challenging, rewarding, the people that work for the company are amazing and such a wide range of characters. It's not a boring place to be. And the guests you come in contact with as well challenge you, and it's nice to see the satisfaction they get from you doing your job well, and creating an experience and a memory for them that they won't forget.

Happy workers have a knock-on effect on customer service, which in turn helps an organization to retain business in a challenging economy. An observation from another employee of the same fast food firm illustrates the connection:

We have fun, but it's a serious business. We give fantastic service to our guests. Sometimes you go into good restaurants, they give you good service but they're not happy and you can actually see that. It's infectious.

This example suggests that 'the main role of the place of work may, in future, lie in its ability to support contact, congeniality, emotional engagement and sharing of tacit knowledge, not the delivery of routine tasks' (Totterdill, 2010).

They focus people and set them up for success

Engaging managers are performance-driven and intent on creating the conditions for success. They lead with passion and energy. They have strong interpersonal skills, are emotionally intelligent, inspiring and enabling. These managers are well organized, and trust and delegate well. Instead of micro-managing, they take a personal interest and are supportive, helpful and encouraging. Andrew Lycett, CEO of **RCT Homes**, argues that leaders should be passionate – people have to believe that you mean what you're saying. For engaging managers this is not simply a passion for results but also a deep-rooted desire to help others to develop. Engaging managers help individuals improve their performance, seeing themselves as coaches or mentors. They demonstrate understanding of the jobs that people do, identify any gaps in knowledge or skills and provide coaching if needed. As performance advisors, engaging managers offer advice and guidance, serving as a sounding board for difficult challenges, helping direct reports understand unintended consequences, and providing feedback on their greatest strengths (Corporate Leadership Council, 2004).

Engaging managers challenge their teams to step outside their comfort zone and keep them focused on the customer, using positive, measurable, stretching goals. Work deadlines are realistic and the job does not interfere with employees' responsibilities at home. They set high standards, are clear about the outcomes and behaviours they expect, and encourage employees to take responsibility for their performance. This allows employees freedom to do the job the way they want. They use performance management to motivate teams to achieve, monitor work to improve its quality and give guidance when required. They make effective use of appraisals or one-to-ones, and have regular, energizing, dynamic performance conversations with frequent feedback.

Case study: Boots Opticians

Boots Opticians – a member of Alliance Boots – operates around 630 optical practices in the UK (including franchises) and has the ambition to be the world's leading health and beauty-led opticians. Boots Opticians merged with Dollond & Aitchison in 2009 to form the second largest optical chain in the UK. Notwithstanding the significant changes this merger entailed, just two years later Boots Opticians topped the *Sunday Times* 2011 list of the Best Companies to Work For in the 'Big Companies' category.

With more than 5300 employees, the company seeks to offer great career opportunities in a positive team environment. Employees are motivated by close customer contact and the chance to improve people's quality of life through better sight. In 2011, 78 per cent of employees reported that, as a result, they feel they can make a difference. But what is also remarkable about Boots Opticians is the top marks they get for having such supportive managers. Over 80 per cent of staff in 2011 reported their managers as being honest and open, and as seeing employees as individuals. Supervisors are seen as treating staff fairly and being appreciative. Employees doing a good job can also be recognized by their manager with gift vouchers from an instant recognition programme.

Learning and development are also important for Boots Opticians – it runs education and training courses for more than 1000 clinicians and is the biggest provider of National Vocational Qualifications in optical retailing. In 2011, 81 per cent of employees saw their job as good for their personal growth and 65 per cent felt all their skills were being used. As part of this supportive environment, more than three-quarters of employees reported that they knew exactly what was expected of them and found their work stimulating.

Additionally, employees are able to maintain good work-life balance – for example, the company offers paid time off for employees that are school governors. Almost half of Boots Opticians' employees have worked there for five or more years and more than a quarter for ten or more years, demonstrating the loyalty and commitment the company and its management culture have generated.

Having fair and just management processes for dealing with problems is important in driving up levels of performance. Engaging managers bring poor performers to account, typically by going through a performance improvement plan with them. They are able to manage 'difficult' people by coaching, using their interpersonal skills and taking quick action to prevent problems escalating. IES research (Robinson et al., 2004) found that engaging managers rarely appear to have 'difficult people' in their team – perhaps because they have instilled the right behaviour in them. They check and challenge progress, celebrate achievement and provide a role model of values-based behaviour.

Wise managers realize that this is not being honest with poor performers and also lets down the rest of the team, who may well end up picking up the slack.

Some managers find it difficult to talk to staff about behaviour. As a result, performance issues may be left unchallenged or treated overly harshly as disciplinary matters. But wise managers realize that this is not being honest with poor performers and also lets down the rest of the team, who may well end up picking up the slack. Timeliness and sensitivity are key to handling these discussions effectively. If you find tackling these discussions difficult, the HR team should be able to support and coach you in how to handle the situation. Box 9.3 provides a number of tips.

Box 9.3 Tips for managers: setting people up for success

- Communicate your priorities. Ensure that you reinforce the organization's priorities and values through regular, ongoing communication using whatever methods are appropriate. Check that people understand the bigger picture and current priorities, in particular those most important to your team. Listen to employees' views and encourage feedback and ideas from everyone.
- Ask your team for their objectives or the actions that need to be taken to contribute to the strategic themes.
- Clarify the link between individual performance objectives and actions within the organizational plan.
- Agree SMART (specific, measurable, achievable, relevant and timely) objectives and any behaviours that need improving.
- Discuss and agree *what* needs to be done to achieve that objective but empower individuals as to *how* they achieve it.

- Ensure that work is evenly distributed and that people are clear about who needs to work with whom; discover what support and resources your people need to carry out their tasks.
- Review and reflect on your own current knowledge, skills and ability to conduct an effective performance review conversation.
- Provide feedback that is positive, descriptive and factual, not judgemental.
- Don't side-step issues about poor work performance; be clear about organizational expectations and deal promptly with misunderstandings.
- Recognize good performance and celebrate individual and team success.
- Support team members with any learning and development, and ensure you discuss the impact of learning.
- Compare work practices in your department with how other teams operate to get the best out of people.

They deliver on the employer brand

The employer brand represents a promise made by the employer to the employee about the kind of employment relationship they can expect. This brand promise is usually referred to (or implied) in recruitment advertising and represents the 'employee value proposition' (EVP) that outlines what the organization stands for and its reward philosophy. It defines the explicit and implicit 'deal' between employer and employee, and hence defines in many respects the psychological contract.

Reward and recognition

Feedback, praise and recognition are crucial competencies of engaging line managers according to Roffey Park research (Gifford et al., 2010). Engaging managers are typically fair and consistent in the way they differentiate between and reward people. For talented individuals, a fair deal means rewards that are competitive and commensurate with contribution. Importantly, this requires taking a holistic 'total reward' approach that capitalizes on how these different elements – pay, bonuses, benefits, training, career development and so on – can best motivate someone. Then, when putting these into practice, it means taking the time to explain decisions and to manage expectations accordingly.

While much attention is paid to pay rises and bonuses as a way to encourage performance, their effect on engagement is limited, whereas motivation expert Chester Elton has demonstrated from a ten-year study of 200,000 managers and employees the significant impact that recognition can have on employee engagement – and in turn on company profitability (Gostick and Elton, 2007). This is especially important in a tough economic climate, when there may not be much you can do to increase financial reward for individuals. Recognition, then, becomes crucial, and when done regularly and genuinely – such as through praise, appreciation and feedback – can be a way of making individuals feel more valued and can help keep the best staff onside. After all, saying 'thank you' costs nothing – but too often is overlooked.

And if the business situation is uncertain, most staff will appreciate knowing first and foremost that their jobs are secure. Reassurance here , if based on fact, can avoid employees being defocused by fears that can easily be fuelled by the organization's rumour mill.

> Saying 'thank you' costs nothing – but too often is overlooked.

Delivering the reality of the brand is crucial to engagement and retention. If the reality is far from what is promised, employees soon become disgruntled and leave. An EVP reinforced by an effective employer brand is one that embodies what the organization stands for, attracts the right people and can deliver what employees want and need. Most importantly, the daily reality of the employer brand is delivered through the relationship between employees and line managers. As we have discussed, policies mean nothing if people don't have the chance to use them.

Policies tailored to employee needs

With a more and more diverse workforce, the EVP can no longer be a case of 'one size fits all'. Employees will have different needs depending on their age, career stage, lifestyle choices and so on, so providing choice and flexibility in what is delivered can make a real difference in attracting, retaining and motivating staff.

The EVP at **Orchid Group**, the pub and restaurant chain, reflects this and is both practical and innovative. Orchid recognizes that working in this fast-paced and demanding industry means that staff struggle to achieve work-life balance, so they go the extra mile to help employees achieve this. The extra support at Orchid includes a concierge service scheme that gives employees the opportunity to take care of all the little things that people usually don't have time to sort out, such as arranging a party or looking for a plumber. Everyone can work flexibly, with options such as job-sharing, home-working, term-time-only contracts, staggered hours, sabbaticals and career breaks. Other benefits include access to the Orchid Health care scheme and a cash plan provider that enables staff to meet the increasing costs of private healthcare. Many other benefits are available, including childcare vouchers, subsidized sports club memberships, and dental and life insurance policies. The personal touch is a key feature. Everyone's birthday is remembered with a card and a free drinks voucher, and prizes in the monthly Orchid lottery include hot air ballooning, a fashion makeover, etc.

Case study: Blue Focus

In China, the concept of private businesses and employer responsibilities for the welfare of employees is relatively new. Traditionally people were employed in state-owned enterprises that were also responsible for their social welfare. Blue Focus PR Consulting is the leading PR firm in China and in 2010 became the first such firm to be publicly listed. Founded in 1996, it now has more than 1000 staff across China. Its CEO, Oscar Zhao, states 'Our people and their wellbeing is our number one core value. Our view is that it is the responsibility of the company to look after our people wherever possible.'

Oscar points out the strong business and social imperative for attending to employees' wellbeing:

China and Chinese society is changing very quickly, economically and socially, and this affects our people. For example, at our main office in Beijing, in the past two years the average journey time for people coming to work has increased by 50 per cent. If we do not find some way to help our people with this we may lose them as they look for work nearer their home. There is a similar situation with housing as young people find it increasingly difficult to buy even a small apartment and we must find some way to help them. (Our banks do not give loans to young people for housing as is normal in some countries.)

Consequently, Blue Focus gives loans to employees to help them purchase cars or apartments. They have health schemes and educational opportunities outside of normal business training and development. It is in Blue Focus's interests to do so since, as Oscar Zhao points out:

The shortage of talent will only increase as China's economy grows and develops. Every company will have to face up to this situation and the competition to attract and retain good people will be as fierce as the competition to attract and retain customers. As a services company we depend 100 per cent on our people. If Blue Focus cannot attract and retain great people we will not have a business and therefore we do whatever we realistically can to make Blue Focus an employer of choice.

While it may be difficult in tough economic times for employers to enhance the benefits that they offer their staff, there are other no- or low-cost ways of motivating employees that are worth considering. These include discount schemes or voluntary benefits (which leverage the employer's purchasing power to help employees), career breaks, flexible working hours, job sharing, and part-time or term-time work (which give the opportunity to work more flexibly and achieve a better work-life balance).

Tips for managers relating to the employer brand are listed in Box 9.4.

> **Box 9.4 Tips for managers: the employer brand**
>
> - Take ownership for delivering the reality of the employer brand.
> - Make sure that new staff members are clear about their terms and conditions.
> - Ensure information about policies and practices is easy for employees (including part-timers) to find out about.
> - Non-cash benefits such as recognition count for a great deal, so recognize individuals and teams spontaneously – both tangibly and visibly – in ways that matter most to individuals.
> - Just remembering to say 'thank you' and 'well done' can make a difference.
> - For many people career development opportunities are the best sort of reward, so give people the chance to grow in roles that have some 'stretch'.
> - Make sure that bonuses, other rewards and forms of recognition link back to the organization's values.

Caring for employees

There is no stronger illustration of Connection and Support than when an employer demonstrates a caring approach to employees when they are experiencing difficulties. Challenging work-life situations highlight the need for resilience, or the ability to bounce back from adversity. One of the fundamental characteristics of resilience is people's ability to use difficult experiences in their lives as opportunities to learn. Thus, with the right support, the tough experiences that employees face can make them stronger. More generally, engaging managers help build employee resilience by setting tough but achievable goals with a clear line of sight to shared purpose. They communicate well and provide regular feedback. They also spend time coaching and developing the people who work for them, and are aware of the important things happening in individuals' private lives.

Employee wellbeing

Of course employers are legally responsible for ensuring that staff are not made ill by their work, though the specific Health and Safety legislation will vary according to context. And of course there should be no occupations that are regarded as intrinsically dangerous to mental health. Stress assessments usually look at whether harm to a particular employee was reasonably foreseeable: that is to say that an employer is entitled to assume that the employee can withstand the normal pressure of the job unless it knows of some particular problem or vulnerability.

> One of the fundamental characteristics of resilience is people's ability to use difficult experiences in their lives as opportunities to learn.

Because stress is such a personal matter, recognizing the symptoms in someone else can be difficult. Some people may have a history of erratic work behaviour and failure to deliver on time. Others may have a high level of absence for minor ailments. These may or may not be symptoms of stress. Robertson and Cooper (2011) argue that while it is not a line manager's job to diagnose whether an employee is suffering from stress, it is their duty to pay careful attention to the psychological wellbeing (PWB) of employees and spot changes in behaviour. Vigilance is therefore important. In today's tough climate, the PWB of many employees is likely to be under threat. In organizational terms, stress may show up in:

- high staff turnover
- high levels of overtime
- high levels of absenteeism
- high levels of grievance
- poor industrial/employee relationships
- increased customer complaints, supplier problems or accidents.

PWB has two important aspects. The first refers to the extent to which we feel positive emotions such as happiness; the second is the feeling that what we do has some meaning and purpose. Robertson and Cooper (2011) have found a link between whether employees feel their organization shows concern for their welfare and its level of productivity. In service organizations, levels of customer satisfaction and service quality are shown to be strongly linked with PWB. For instance, the UK's **University of Chester** found among its staff a significant positive correlation between survey scores for 'happiness and psychological wellbeing' and those for 'total quality of working' scale and 'total sense of purpose and engagement'. At the **University of Leeds**, a programme of individual executive coaching for a number of academic and non-academic middle managers to help staff build resilience generated statistically significant shifts, not only in resilience but also in self-rated productivity.

PWB is therefore impacted significantly by work, and it's important to realise the psychological needs that are met through one's own job. A good line manager will be sensitive to this, and know their staff well enough to be aware of those who may be vulnerable. Line managers can play a key role in mitigating this threat by:

- showing genuine care and concern for employees, making clear that it is not a taboo for employees to raise concerns about stress, workload, etc.
- making themselves available
- holding regular one-to-one meetings so that potential stress situations can be recognized and dealt with.

If managers are unable to help the individual, they should work with HR to connect the person with the right kind of advice and support. By providing help when employees need it, managers can show them that they are valued (see Box 9.5).

Work-life balance

Work-life balance is increasingly recognized as the number one driver of wellbeing (and – when absent – source of frustration) for many employees. This is about getting and keeping a reasonable balance between time available and outputs required – so that we can do our jobs effectively but also have enough time for the other things in our lives. Balance is not a minority issue but affects most employees. In today's fast-paced environments, people often find themselves working long additional hours and under severe work pressure. Job insecurity may also increase the tendency towards 'presenteeism'. In such circumstances,

---

Box 9.5 Tips for managers: caring for employees

- Take a proactive approach to managing stress. To prevent or reduce stress, the CIPD recommends an open door policy, setting aside time to talk with employees (CIPD, 2011a).
- Ensure you communicate often and effectively with staff, not just about major changes but about day-to-day progress and other activities, changes to the team, etc., so they do not find out first from other sources.
- Watch out for early warning signs of stress among staff, especially during periods of change and uncertainty.
- Investigate further if an employee starts to behave uncharacteristically.
- Where personal problems are intruding on work, take appropriate action to help the employee, such as referring them to Occupational Health, an Employee Assistance Program (EAP) or welfare agencies.
- Find mentors and role models to encourage and support individuals through periods of transition.
- When there are disputes, listen to both sides of the conflict, deal with the conflict head on and follow up after resolution.
- Be aware of your own stress responses and act calmly under pressure, walking away if you feel unable to control your emotions.
- Recognize and apologize if your behaviour is poor.
- Act with integrity; keep employee issues private and confidential.
- Find out who to refer people to for further help, if they need it.
- Actively promote work-life balance and employee wellbeing.

---

good managers make it clear that it's the results achieved, not the visible hours put in, that show commitment. Where employees are under pressure, engaging managers take steps to ease the situation perhaps by reducing people's workload, arranging extra resources, redistributing workload or offering time off in lieu. They pitch in to help during busy periods. They recognize when people are 'going the extra mile', thank them and make sure there is sufficient opportunity for respite – and that people can actually take a breather.

Managers should encourage a culture where everyone takes responsibility for work-life balance. This is about involving people at all levels in developing new, more effective working methods and encouraging shared ownership through two-way communication, working together to find productive solutions. At a practical level, it means involving team members in decision-making about work flow and planning. Employees are the 'experts' on their jobs and work-life needs. This stakeholder approach can enhance organizational commitment and lead to mutual flexibility. Sometimes just small changes to ways of working can make a big difference.

Perhaps the single most important ingredient in developing and sustaining a culture conducive to work-life balance is support from the top of the organization – the chief executive and senior management. While the behaviour of one's immediate manager does play an important role in setting the tone of what is expected from an employee, the role modelling behaviour of the most senior executives within the organization has a far more powerful impact on creating a culture where work-life balance needs are acknowledged and respected. Flexible working is fine in theory, but an environment where staff are reluctant to walk in front of the CEO's occupied office when they leave work for the day before a certain hour, or where managers are penalized for experimenting with new ways of working, is clearly not one that is fully supportive of work-life balance.

Conversely, the voiced opinions of senior managers in favour of work-life balance, if they are perceived to be sincere, carry a great deal of weight and empower more junior managers to support work-life balance for their reports. Verbal support does, however, need to be backed up with evidence and action. Where there are examples of senior executives who balance work and life, and yet have still reached high levels within the organization, the employee receives a strong message that progress is possible within the organization even when one opts for balance. This is especially vital in encouraging a more diverse workforce, where employees are juggling their job and their duties either to children or elderly dependents. Moreover, as we have seen, balance is even more important in the eyes of Generation Y employees and so will grow as a priority as generational shifts occur in the workplace. Tips for managers relating to work-life balance are listed in Box 9.6.

Box 9.6 Tips for managers: work-life balance

- Set an example by trying to improve your own work-life balance.
- Make sure you are up to date with employer's obligations on issues such as working hours, part-time workers and people with caring responsibilities.
- Break a culture of continuous long working hours by encouraging people to work smarter, not harder, and show leadership yourself.
- Value people for the quality of their output, not the hours they put in.
- Look for innovative ways to organize work to enhance productivity and work-life balance. Use pilots to test out new ways of working and gain acceptance.
- Manage schedules and meetings so that they do not usually impinge on other dimensions of people's lives. Take your team into consideration when managing your own work schedule.
- Do you have a consistent and fair approach to dealing with requests to change working hours or take leave?
- Encourage staff to think as a team when it comes to scheduling work hours and allocating tasks, and be open to proposals for part-time work or job-sharing.
- Ensure that your team's flexible working hours meet the needs of customers and other stakeholders, as well as those of employees.
- Set your own targets against which you can review and report on progress to your team and to senior management.
- Plan ways of keeping in touch with those who work flexibly and make sure they feel included whenever possible at team briefings and social events. Likewise, make sure other team members know their availability.

Sika AG (profiled in Chapter 8) shows a strong concern for its staff. Employees are encouraged to use up their vacation and the company is very flexible about allowing staff time to sort out personal problems or illness – it recognizes that ignoring these simply means that the employee is back at work, but is likely to be operating at less than 100 per cent. Managers too are expected to value and like their staff. The relationship is not transactional or task-based but built on the importance of fostering a positive workplace climate.

Conclusion

The 'soft stuff' of management – good people management – is in fact the most potent way of stimulating innovation and building competitive advantage through employee engagement. Managers and leaders at all levels have important roles to play in this regard. Engaging managers are key to delivering the employee value proposition or 'deal' through good people management practices – managing performance fairly, and innovative approaches to reward and recognition. They are also responsible for designing interesting and stretching roles, and for developing people's skills through training and coaching, as we shall discuss in more detail in the final chapter.

When employees feel fairly treated – that they are listened to and are able to satisfy their intellectual, social and emotional needs – they are more likely to be engaged. When employees feel involved, equipped to do their jobs and appropriately rewarded, and when they can learn and develop, progress their career, and balance their home and work life, then the deal feels fair. And when the deal feels right, employee engagement becomes the fuel that drives the engine of individual and collective success in good times and in bad. In the next chapter we shall look more specifically at how to maintain engagement in today's tough times.

Checklist

- Do you balance care and performance?
- Do you treat colleagues as customers? Do you know what your colleagues need from you and do you deliver it?
- Do you clarify direction, goals and responsibilities? Does your team know what is expected of them?
- Do you agree stretch goals, give your employees space to do their jobs and 'hold people to account'?
- Do you focus on delivery, set high standards and find new ways of helping people to work smart rather than hard?
- Do you delegate effectively?
- Do you provide coaching and training if required?
- Do you involve people in decisions that affect them?
- Do you have meaningful conversations with people about pay, performance and careers?
- Do you strive to align individual aspirations with future organizational needs?
- Do you practice performance management as an ongoing dialogue – rather than an event – and include encouragement and development rather than just feedback on what's not working?
- Do you turn your attention to things that fit the 'important though not urgent' category, such as staff development? These are the things that will make a difference to your business and to your own effectiveness in the long term.

CHAPTER 10

If employee engagement can be a challenge even in good times, it is all the more at risk in today's tough economic climate. As Ben Willmott, senior policy advisor at the CIPD, says:

> In the current environment, there is evidence that people are under increasing pressure in the workplace, that there's a growing trust deficit between people at the bottom and the top of organizations. You've also got the squeeze on incomes, with people either having their pay frozen or receiving pay rises that are less than the rate of inflation. Against that backdrop, it's difficult to build engagement. (CIPD Employee Outlook, June 2009)

For downsizing 'survivors', working life can be tough. It's not just a question of adjusting to one change, but rather to multiple waves of change as businesses struggle to survive and thrive in these turbulent times. With no early end in sight to the economic downturn, many organizations are experiencing considerable difficulty keeping or finding new customers. Consequently their employees are working much harder to keep clients happy, although they may not receive commensurate financial reward for their efforts. 'More for less' has become the mantra. In many cases, employees are expected to pick up the workloads of people whose jobs have been made redundant – and in some cases as much as 50 per cent of the workforce may have disappeared.

Yet we believe it is possible to maintain and even grow employee engagement in these circumstances. That's because we have found evidence of workplaces where this is happening. We're drawing on findings from an ongoing enquiry, initiated by one of us in 2007, into what is happening to engagement in challenging times. This has involved focus groups and interviews with UK managers, Human Resource professionals and representatives of employer bodies, trades unions and conciliation services. In this chapter we'll look at what we have learned about what we're calling 'engaging employer' approaches.

What do 'engaging employers' do?

We've found that all the good practice we have already discussed about creating a context conducive to engagement still applies – only more so in challenging times. Effective managers remain focused on employee engagement and lead from the front. In particular, they place heavy emphasis on communication with employees. That's why, in this chapter we place a special focus on the **Voice** quadrant of our model:

- how employee voice operates throughout the organization for reinforcing and challenging views
- how employees are seen as central to the solution (MacLeod and Clarke, 2009)
- how employers involve people in decisions that affect them – and more besides.

We have also found that the key **Connection** practices must be strengthened in tough times:

- how organizational integrity is demonstrated
- 'walking the talk' when it comes to company values
- finding a way to keep faith with employees.

These practices distinguish organizations that maintain employee engagement from those that do not. **Support** too is vital, and we look at how engaging employers successfully manage change by putting the people first, not last. And if downsizing is inevitable, they handle this sensitively.

Why do these things matter so much in tough times? That's because people need to be 'bought in' to the future, not simply have it imposed on them. If employers want to retain and motivate people, keeping them onboard and connected with the organization, they need to remain focused on engagement. Leaders should be visible, accessible and approachable – and willing to listen and act on what they hear. HR must keep a finger on the pulse of how people are feeling and help to ensure that executives proactively respond to the most important issues. This is the time, above all, where the 'values on the wall' need to be put into practice.

They keep faith with employees

Tough times are when organizations face the greatest challenge in living up to what they say they stand for. It's tempting to cut corners under pressure and to put aside 'living the values' until better days come. But from our focus group research it is clear that some organizations are remaining true to their values, and in these cases employees are well aware of the broader context issues and are generally working together with management to find win-win solutions to the current challenges. As one focus group participant put it, 'there is very much the mentality of "we must all fight the common enemy of unemployment together"'. Another commented that 'ownership of the problem seems quite a lot broader than one would expect – it's not just management's problem. It feels like everyone's problem and everyone seems to be trying to help each other, rather than "dog eat dog", as has happened previously.'

> Tough times are when organizations face the greatest challenge in living up to what they say they stand for.

Looking for alternatives to redundancy

Many employers recognize that talented people are crucial to current and future business success, and are keen to retain talent even though revenues may be down. Many have managed cost-cutting without automatically resorting to laying off staff, taking actions such as:

- laying off contractors first
- pay freezes
- recruitment freezes or slowdowns
- deferred graduate employment
- flexible working
- sabbaticals (unpaid)
- cutting overtime
- taking holidays rather than pay in lieu.

One example of a company that has found an innovative solution to retain and utilize the skills of its staff is the luxury car maker **Bentley**. Faced with a slump in sales following the onset of the recession in 2008, Bentley's 140 skilled woodworkers turned their hand to furniture making in an effort to stave off redundancies at its Crewe factory (Millward, *Daily Telegraph*, 3 March 2009). Employees subsequently agreed to respond to the reduced demand by staying at home on paid leave but offsetting this by putting in unpaid overtime when the business recovered (Ashton, 6 June 2010).

Another common solution has been to reduce working hours temporarily in place of cutting jobs. For instance, one medium-sized manufacturing firm lost some key customers and work demand dropped significantly. Management gave employees the choice: would they rather have redundancies or reduce hours to a four-day week? Managers explained up front to the employees that they would lose money but staff nevertheless opted for the pay cuts. Managers were very hands-on and supportive, showing respect for employees and continuing to look positively to the future. Within just three months, all the employees were back to working five days a week.

Honouring commitments

Another aspect of keeping faith with employees involves employers having the courage to remain true to their values, despite many short-term pressures to save costs. Employers continue to attempt to differentiate themselves in the recruitment market by building strong employer brands – typically implying a fair 'deal', strong values that people can relate to and opportunities for growth, etc. Yet how are employers remaining true to their employer branding promise? We've found that many former 'great employers' have quietly jettisoned much of the employee value proposition they had previously offered, and in some cases industrial action has arisen as a result. So which organizations are maintaining their determination to live their values, building their talent base and improving the quality of management and leadership, rather than letting short-term expediency push these out of the frame?

Case study: John Lewis Partnership

One company that remains very true to its values and principles is the UK's John Lewis Partnership and its supermarket chain Waitrose. It is usually at, or near, the top of 'favourite retailer' categories of consumer polls. Owned by its permanent employees, or 'partners', this co-ownership means there is a strong sense of '**Voice**' internally.

The partnership's 'spirit' is based on four principles:

- ensuring the happiness of partners is at the centre of everything we do
- building a sustainable business through profit and growth
- serving our customers to the very best of our ability
- caring about our communities and our environment.

Even before the First World War the company offered shortened working days, the setting up of a staff committee and a third week's paid holiday – all revolutionary for the time. But most striking was the introduction of profit-sharing and, in 1950, the transfer of ownership to its employees.

Profits are distributed through bonuses and since the start of the economic downturn the John Lewis Partnership has continued to pay its 76,000 staff their annual bonus, despite the challenging trading conditions. Added to that, the bonus pot has decreased by a third, from £180 million in 2007 to £125.5 million in 2008, due to the effects of the recession on profits. Employees receive the same percentage bonus, which fosters a 'we're all in it together' mentality, and following a stronger 2010, they shared in a bigger bonus pot of £194.5 million – equivalent to more than nine weeks' pay for Waitrose and John Lewis department store employees. By being true to its principles, the John Lewis Partnership is likely to maintain employee trust and commitment.

Voice

In tough times, people's uncertainty and anxieties about the future multiply. Lack of clarity about strategy and poor internal communication are two very important factors when it comes to disengagement. Of course, when faced with rapid change it can be impossible to know what will happen next – which can be very difficult for leaders who don't want to be seen as being on the back foot or who have always seen risks or deviations from plans as undesirable. Yet unless top managers provide clarity and a sense of direction, employees will soon lose faith in them and avoid taking risks. So a lack of direction from the top, at the very time when employee proactivity, customer focus and empowerment are most needed, can be very damaging.

Good communication is therefore vital in creating a climate for change. When staff understand the bigger picture, know what's going on, and have opportunities to be heard, they become more empowered. Effective leaders are able to encourage others to come with them through change, even if they are unsure about the future outcome. High visibility and consistent messages from leaders and managers help to reduce uncertainty and mean that people cope better with change. So leaders and managers must communicate a lot (and with considerable depth) about the bigger picture, strategy and direction. In doing so, they must be authentic, values-driven and consistent, as Andrew Lycett, CEO of **RCT Homes**, advises:

> Lack of clarity about strategy and poor internal communication are two very important factors when it comes to disengagement.

> *Be considered, because everything that you do, especially in the early days, is very highly scrutinized and talked about, and one wrong step can have a disproportionately adverse impact, so consider what you do and be consistent.*

This is not just about top-down communication, but also about fostering honest and genuine dialogue at the team level, which in turn builds trust. Staff will respond very positively if they believe their immediate line manager is listening to their concerns and communicating as openly as possible about any prospective changes. During the first wave of change, people need to understand *why* change is needed. Being collaborative and bringing people along, giving employees maximum involvement in decision-making, increases their sense of ownership. So when employees are involved in thinking through the *how* if not the *what* of change, they are more likely to feel valued and regain a sense of control over their destiny. Plus, they will have some good ideas to contribute!

Box 10.1 features tips for managers relating to Voice.

Box 10.1 Tips for managers: Voice

- Place customers, and understanding their needs, at the forefront of all decisions.
- Keep employees informed and involved in changes.
- Don't overlook employee representatives or trade unions. Involve them so that they feel they're part of the solution.
- Encourage innovative solutions to problems.
- Show energy and enthusiasm for new ideas and challenges.
- Follow up with individual responsibilities in one-to-ones.

Communication mechanisms

Transparency, the basis of trust, is vital. When tough decisions are being made, people need to feel confident that the right decisions have been taken and that all concerned have been treated fairly. As change starts to happen, communication should concentrate on the positives achieved in the first wave of change, to influence and motivate people for the next wave.

Of course different communication mechanisms work for different people, so a variety of methods should be used, both formal and informal. Conventional 'sounding' mechanisms – such as staff surveys, suggestions schemes and focus groups – should be maintained and even stepped up. After all, how can employers take specific action to improve things if the organization appears to stop listening to employees?

> Of course different communication mechanisms work for different people, so a variety of methods should be used, both formal and informal.

Visible leadership communications from the CEO and top management are important. Many organizations hold management road-shows and 'Town Hall' sessions every six months to keep people up to date with what's happening. 'Normal' briefing mechanisms – such as team meetings, site-based briefings and short daily updates – should be used consistently and regularly, with the emphasis on high quality two-way communication.

Opportunities for involvement and participation should be embedded in employee relations approaches. Some organizations have internal People Champions – not line managers, but people working specifically on organizational purpose and strategy. Others work with both trade unions and staff consultative committees. Increasingly, organizations are involving all staff in the business planning process. A variety of Organization Development (OD) technologies are typically used, such as open space meetings, real-time strategic change, Future Space and so on. The UK's **British Broadcasting Corporation (BBC)**, at a time of great pressure on the organization to save costs, used live TV links to allow all its employees in different locations to simultaneously discuss the changes that were being introduced by the then Director-General, Greg Dyke. Employees were encouraged to give their ideas and there was real dialogue. As a result, people of all ages were willing to learn, try out new things and contribute to implementing the changes.

Technology, especially social media, now enables interactivity and communication immediacy on a scale not possible in the past, as shown in the case of Infosys in the previous chapter. CEO blogs and online messages, company Facebook and Twitter accounts, instant messaging, discussion boards, YouTube, TV rooms, 'communications zones', WebEx, and video conferencing ensure that there can be more frequent and timely dialogue between employees and management. The use of such methods transcends hierarchy and creates a seemingly personal connection between top leaders and employees. This interactive connection is all the more important in organizations where staff work remotely and in different time zones. This is not just about information exchange but also about stimulating dialogue, reinforcing the feeling of community.

Training managers to communicate

Training line managers how to communicate can be crucial to success. For instance, **British Gas**'s 'Make a Difference' business engagement events brought together managers and leaders from across the business. The focus of these events was to develop managers' communication capabilities and enable them to cascade key messages to their people. Each event featured five key messages, which were brought to life by real-life business examples. Each message was presented by an 'influencer', someone from each business unit who could really communicate a message. In addition, the event included marketplace-style displays that communicated major business projects. The events were followed up with a manager's toolkit to reinforce the 'Make a Difference' messages and give practical support to managers in cascading the messages and engaging directly with their teams, such as best practice advice, sample exercises and a library of stories and video footage to facilitate team discussions.

Box 10.2 features tips for managers relating to how to communicate.

Box 10.2 Tips for managers: how to communicate

- Make sure communication is not treated as a last-minute after-thought but a key management activity to make sure that your people are 'all on the same page'.
- Think about the different elements of communication – not just the words used, but tone and setting, visual messages, etc.
- Recognize that repeated communication may be needed to get the word across, so find different ways to follow up and reinforce key messages.
- Adopt a positive 'can do' attitude, encouraging people to look at change constructively.
- Share news – good or bad – and be ready to acknowledge where answers are still lacking.
- Take time to explain and clarify and dispel any potential misunderstandings.
- Champion the vision and values, and clarify individual and team contributions.
- Communicate corporate messages in a way that motivates.
- Use every available means of communication, such as 'open spaces', social media, bulletin boards, graffiti boards, table notes, focus groups or Q&A services.
- Use internal Communications staff (if available), but remember that you own the message.
- If you are a head of service or a member of a senior management team, meet with other senior managers to identify areas of integration and collaboration with other teams.

Managing change

Change is not something that managers always relish. Aside from the complexity and uncertainty involved, it presents considerable personal and emotional challenges, and countless studies highlight the difficulties and the high risk of failure of change initiatives to produce the desired results. Too often, the key cause of failure is when the human aspects are poorly managed, in particular neglecting to help people to navigate through change. Change is situational, such as when roles are reorganized or made redundant – and in the current economic context, there is a lot of organizational change going on! Yet even if these changes have taken place, it doesn't mean that employees have coped with them or internalized what they mean.

Leading expert William Bridges differentiates between *change*, which happens around us, and *transition*, which is our psychological reorientation in response to change and can be a longer and more complex process than the change itself (Bridges, 2003). While some people appear to thrive on change, many find it threatening, especially when it is externally driven and they have had little or no involvement in deciding how it will happen. Some of the psychological reactions to change are predictable: they include anxiety, a sense of loss of control and personal stress. Even if they keep their jobs, 'survivors' may experience loss of status, role ambiguity and feelings of guilt about the past. Typical reactions include people coming to believe the worst-case scenarios, responding with inertia, risk aversion and a sense of paralysis. There may be lack of follow-through on key projects and increased political behaviour as people protect their backs. Employees may demonstrate change-weariness, cynicism and loss of trust. As Hamel points out, 'mistrust demoralizes and fear paralyses, so they must be wrung out of tomorrow's management systems' (Hamel, 2009).

These reactions are symptomatic of damage to psychological contracts. When these are violated – for example, by not being honest about the challenges faced by the business or being uneven in sharing out cutbacks – employees tend to withdraw their goodwill, so discretionary effort is suspended and engagement undermined. The employment relationship then tends to become more transactional. So, thinking about your organization, identify the critical success factors for making your change work:

> While some people appear to thrive on change, many find it threatening, especially when it is externally driven and they have had little or no involvement in deciding how it will happen.

- What are you asking people to do differently?
- How will they be affected?
- How will their part of the organization change?
- What reactions can you expect?
- What can you learn from past experiences?
- Do staff have the right skills for the change? If not, do they have access to training that will develop those skills?
- What practical and other support will they need to make the changes required of them?

Leaders and managers – who may themselves be experiencing challenging personal transitions – have a key role to play in supporting other people going through transitions, so they have to manage their own change journey and help their teams through theirs. However, many managers find managing the 'people side' of change a daunting prospect. Understanding something of the emotional journey of change can be helpful, then, in gauging what support people need. Since some of the reactions to change can be anticipated, actions can be taken to help reduce the negative impact on people.

The emotional journey of change – the transition curve

It is not for nothing that Elisabeth Kübler-Ross's grief cycle model (1969), originally used to describe an individual's bereavement change journey, is also widely used to explain the emotional transitions that people experience during organizational change. During the first phase of change, when people typically experience shock, denial, anger and other negative emotions, they are typically focused inwards on how they are feeling, 'holding on' to what they know, fighting disintegration. During this phase, leaders should be visible and accessible to interact with those affected. It's about giving clear information and communicating fully, even if people may not be taking in the implications for them. Managers should anticipate and acknowledge issues. They can help by listening, guiding and simply 'being there' for people. They should set short-term targets and expect some confusion. They should clarify what stays the same and treat the past with respect.

The 'holding on' phase gradually gives way to a phase of 'letting go', in which testing and experimenting are taking place. As people move towards 'letting go', managers should monitor the situation, offering people support, encouraging and coaching them as well as helping them to develop new goals. In due course this leads on to the 'moving on' phase, where energy becomes more externally focused and where people experience new discovery and learning, and feelings of optimism, hope and renewed energy. Managers should communicate what people need to know, create new experiences, encourage experimentation and learning, let others take ownership, open up new opportunities and career development for the 'survivors'. As people move on emotionally, and discover new energy and momentum, managers should redefine performance measures, ensure some quick successes, build commitment and enthusiasm, celebrate with people, and help them reflect on their experience.

In his model describing the emotional journey of change, William Bridges (2003) identifies three phases of transition: 'endings' (when people accept that change has happened and say good-bye to the past); the 'neutral zone' (when they are as yet unsure what the future holds); and 'beginnings' (where they are starting to learn and try out new things).

However, research into the people aspects of mergers and acquisitions carried out by one of us with colleagues at Roffey Park identified that, in any

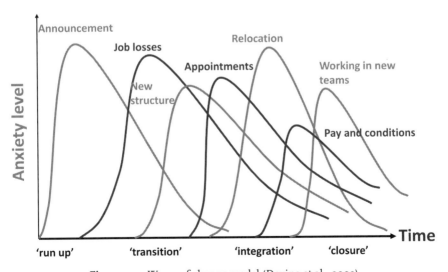

Figure 10.1 Waves of change model (Devine et al., 2002)

organizational change process, people typically experience not just one but multiple waves of change (Figure 10.1). This can lead to people becoming 'stuck' in the more internally focused phases of change in which they experience anxiety, personal stress, loss of control, political behaviour, risk aversion, etc., undermining their capacity to perform and their willingness to embrace yet more change. It's important to also remember that, as a manager, you may well have been aware of the change for quite some time before it was announced and have had time to digest it and begin to move through the phases of change described above. In contrast, for employees it may well be fresh news. So if they take time to get onboard with the change, it doesn't necessarily mean there's resistance – simply that people are further behind in their transitions and will need some time and support.

Handling redundancies

Making employees redundant is one of the toughest challenges of all. Managers may themselves be affected emotionally. They may be losing team members and colleagues they have worked with for many years. Yet managers must focus on how other people are feeling.

At a psychological level, redundancies represent a strong threat to social identity and arouse people's concerns for each other, and for themselves. Research by Applebaum and Donia (2001) suggests that the three key issues that determine the nature of the organization's relationship with surviving employees, and whether it will recover successfully from downsizing, are:

- employees' understanding of the reasons for the downsizing throughout the process
- the duration and frequency of the downsizing
- assistance provided to the terminated employees.

Therefore, the redundancy process must be transparent, equitable and sensitively handled. Managers need to be able to take ownership for communicating the bad news of redundancy. Both employees who are leaving and those who 'survive' must be treated with respect. Managers must also help everyone to move on and look to the future of the organization, and not get stuck in a short-term perspective. It's about being patient, discussing the implications as people become aware of them. Let people grieve and deal with repressed feelings. If people are still in shock and in

> At a psychological level, redundancies represent a strong threat to social identity and arouse people's concerns for each other, and for themselves.

the 'blame' phase, pay attention to small details, listen and empathize. There's a need for honesty, humility and an open mind without assumptions.

Case study: Agilent Technologies

Spun off from HP in 1999, Agilent is the world's leading measurement products company. Its turnover in 2011 was $6.6 billion and it employed around 18,700 people worldwide. This California-based company has faced multiple business challenges since it was publicly floated, not least the effects of the dotcom bubble bursting in 2000, the further effect of 9/11 and – most recently – the global recession since 2008. While the company reduced its workforce by nearly 15,000 during 2001–2003, and subsequently spun off parts of the business (and acquired others) so as to refocus its activities, the company has shown tremendous resilience and has bounced back to acquire one of its biggest competitors, Varian, and become one of the highest-performing companies in its sector for total shareholder return. Jean Halloran, Senior Vice President of Human Resources, says:

> *Our aim is to make Agilent a great place to work. This means winning business strategies in which each employee sees their role. This means engaged employees who feel that they are treated with dignity and respect.*

Clearly a key element in Agilent's ability to withstand tough times is the engagement of its employees. This commitment has been fostered in several ways. First, the company has stuck to its core values. As well as the values inherited from Dave Packard and Bill Hewlett – dedication to innovation; trust, respect and teamwork; and uncompromising integrity – Agilent has added speed, focus and accountability to meet customer needs. When facing tough times, the company has lived by these values. For example, teamwork is shown by involving employees in finding ways to reduce costs and – when needed – by collectively accepting temporary pay reductions. Although these are difficult measures, the company has fostered a 'we're all in it together' mentality that has also enabled them to trim expenses quickly when needed.

Where layoffs have been necessary, employees also understand that it is a last resort. Such steps have been communicated in an open way that encourages employees to dialogue with their managers. Those leaving are supported through a temporary income replacement scheme and help with external job searches. By treating employees with dignity and respect, Agilent has sustained workforce morale: after its major downsizing, a 2004 survey showed that 62 per cent of employees would nevertheless recommend Agilent as a good place to work.

In fact, such employee feedback is key to Agilent, which has continued to run periodic employee engagement surveys, supplemented since 2005 by regular leadership audits to measure and reinforce the critical leadership behaviours that drive employee engagement. By 2010, these audit scores showed that on average, Agilent had reached its goal of matching external 75th percentile performance. Intensive talent management and leadership development have helped retain and motivate staff while enabling scientists and engineers to grow into general managers that show decisiveness and risk-taking. Agilent has also progressed key people-related initiatives, such as fostering diversity and work-life balance. As a result, more than 15 per cent of staff take advantage of flexible work arrangements, and the 'Reinventing Work' programme enables managers to agree with employees how to revise work processes to meet job demands and work-pressure issues.

In 2009, Agilent also launched 'Working at Agilent', an innovative development programme for all individual contributors to empower, encourage and inspire employees to use their initiative, think creatively, push beyond conventional limits and innovate as individual leaders in collaboration with their manager and colleagues. Currently in the process of being rolled out globally, it is designed to help managers engage their employees and work together to improve business performance.

Agilent has also taken major steps to reduce the environmental impact of its business, and has been regularly listed in the Dow Jones Sustainability Index and as one of the Global 100 Most Sustainable Companies by the World Economic Forum at Davos. So as to be a 'good neighbour' locally, employees can use up to four hours a month of company-paid time for Agilent-supported or sponsored activities – 20 per cent of employees contribute more than 50,000 hours annually to such local community activities. As a result, Agilent has won employee commitment by showing it does not simply focus on the bottom line and, not surprisingly, has regularly won 'best employer' awards – even in the toughest of times.

Mergers and acquisitions

Corporate transactions, restructuring and business transformations, common during an economic downturn, exacerbate employee engagement challenges, since they most clearly cause employees' psychological contracts to be 'rewritten'. From an extensive study of the people aspects of mergers and acquisitions one of us carried out with colleagues at the UK's Roffey Park Institute (Devine et al., 1997), it is clear that mergers and acquisitions (M&A) involve change management writ large. They represent radical changes for staff, producing a wide variety of 'unknowns' that employees must navigate. As we have seen, employees may experience not just one transition but many waves of change as the merger process unfolds:

- corporate brands that employees have identified with may disappear
- people's career development and job security may be undermined
- they may find themselves competing with new and unfamiliar colleagues for scarce opportunities
- the workplace culture changes, or is replaced by a new one, in a way that can be confusing and disorienting.

Research by Aon Hewitt (2010, p. 10) finds that mergers, more than other forms of restructuring, typically have a significant (negative) impact on engagement, whether employees work for the acquiring or the acquired companies.

> Despite what we know about the good sense in involving staff in change, planning for M&A is usually shrouded in secrecy for commercial and legal reasons until the deal has been done.

It's clear that the way the people aspects of a merger process are handled, and people's experience of this, is what makes the vital difference to success or failure of integration. It not only affects employee engagement but also shapes the emerging culture, climate and brand personality of the new organization. Despite what we know about the good sense in involving staff in change, planning for M&A is usually shrouded in secrecy for commercial and legal reasons until the deal has been done. Lack of communication often means that staff find it hard to understand why some jobs have to go, if more people are being acquired. Other problems may arise if employees remain on different terms and conditions. So while we recognize the constraints, we argue that within the bounds of commercial sensitivity you cannot over-communicate in mergers.

Two other dangers with M&A are:

- the tendency to see deal 'closure' as the key goal, and so underestimate the crucial work afterwards when workforces get integrated
- given the pressure from investors, to see M&A primarily as a 'numbers game'.

Yet in a study of 167 mergers, Furbini et al. (2007) found that 'CEOs and senior executives who are skilled at integration are keenly aware that synergy targets and a few other publicly announced integration project goals do not give a full picture of the outcome of a merger'. In other words, they tended to keep working at securing the deeper potential of the integration, and in particular building a successful common culture, rather than be satisfied with merely achieving the headline goals of a transaction.

Box 10.3 features tips for managers relating to M&A.

Box 10.3 Tips for managers: M&A

- Consciously manage the merger process by identifying and planning for key people issues from the earliest point. Assemble an integration team that coordinates activities not just within the first six months but throughout the transition and integration period.
- Because differences here can derail M&A activity, make sure that workplace cultures are investigated as part of due diligence and are monitored and managed during and after the integration.
- Be clear if it is a merger or an acquisition – don't pretend it's the former if it's really a takeover.
- Parcel the merger or acquisition into a number of simple and easily understood stages, and communicate key milestones to everyone. Celebrate their achievement.
- Set short-term goals for the business at each stage to help everyone retain their focus on performance and the customer.
- Try to map out and plan for the various emotional waves of change that will sweep through the organization as different groups are affected by change. Fully anticipate key issues and create a communications plan designed to rebuild trust and engagement. Build in feedback mechanisms to inform executives how people are feeling at grass roots level.
- Communicate at every step, way beyond a 'need to know' basis – even when there is no news. You cannot over-communicate in mergers.
- Get people on board as quickly as possible, identifying who the key people are, and be willing to build flexible arrangements to retain them.
- 'Ring fence' the core business and provide additional management support while line managers are coping with the transitional period.

- Adopt a phased and professional approach to HR issues, identifying key and sensitive issues as early as possible. Design fair selection processes to rebuild trust in the workforce. Consciously phase the redesign of major personnel processes (pay, grading, appraisals, etc.) so that HR does not sink into a bureaucratic quagmire.
- Highlight crucial values from early on so that local teams can build them into the way they work.
- Don't try to 'paint the culture on' afterwards – remember that how the merger process is managed moulds the values and behaviour codes of the emerging organization.

Source: based on Devine et al., 1997

Although acquiring companies in M&A often appear to follow an assimilation strategy, in practice, you cannot 'do' change to people – as the following case study illustrates.

Case study: M&A and China

In 2011, China overtook Japan to become the world's second biggest economy and, even in the midst of the current economic crisis, is still seeing high single digit GDP growth. One of the signs of China's growing economic strength has been its increasing outbound M&A activity. Big name acquisitions, such as Lenovo's purchase of IBM's PC business, and Geely's of Volvo cars, belie a multitude of other takeovers or purchases of stakes in businesses around the world. But the usual risks for such transactions and employee engagement are heightened for Chinese companies expanding globally. Graham Valentine, co-founder of Choy Valentine, works extensively with Chinese companies and points to several issues they face. He notes that 'The first of these is lack of experience of business internationally and of acquiring other companies. Many leaders of Chinese business may have had little experience working abroad and so face a steep learning curve in getting to grips with a newly-acquired foreign business.' Another potential risk is that the acquiring company is little known internationally and the absence of a strong reputation may prevent the development of Connection between the acquired foreign workforce and their Chinese parent. Worse still, attempts to retain newly-gained staff through bonuses, etc., risk creating a rift in the workforce by increasing internal pay disparities at a time when everyone should be pulling together.

As more employees get to interact during post-merger integration, differences may become even more prominent. Graham Valentine comments:

> *Chinese companies typically have a strong sense of hierarchy and deference to leaders, as opposed to Western businesses where people may expect to be able to speak up. Another challenge is that business is highly relationship-based – which also means that Western companies acquiring in China need to pay attention to this or they may find that the business they bought there evaporates due to lack of attention to key customers and stakeholders.*

Yet as Chinese businesses expand abroad, there are some key lessons emerging for the future.

The pace of integration needs careful managing. A rapid process runs high risks and a better approach may be to manage the new business on a more arms-length basis. Lenovo, for example, left former IBM management running their business discretely, and they moved their chairman to the US, underlining their commitment to the former IBM business. Similarly, Geely has kept the day-to-day management of Volvo in Gothenburg, Sweden.

Building a strong sense of Connection is key. While Chinese staff may have a strong sense of intrinsic pride in their business, the newly-acquired non-Chinese employees may feel they have joined an unknown company with no international experience. This means a lot of effort will be needed to develop a stronger employee value proposition, to make staff aware of the potential offered by the acquiring company, and to develop a shared sense of engagement and passion. Commitment is not, therefore, something that can be taken for granted as Chinese companies expand from East to West.

Developing a stronger sense of cross-cultural awareness is essential. Western employees need to understand more clearly concepts such as 'loss of face', while Chinese managers may need to understand more fully the importance of Voice for their new staff. Additional manager training – such as in performance management and feedback – may be important too.

Make employee engagement a priority for the future. While this is important to help retain and motivate acquired international staff, Chinese companies increasingly need to work on this as a growing shortage of skilled managers and employees locally means their loyalty cannot be taken for granted. Training and management development are important here to retain and motivate, so managers need to focus on the dimensions of Support and Scope for their staff – wherever they are located. Importantly, by measuring employee engagement, companies can identify follow up steps to identify potential roadblocks and so help foster integration success.

Graham Valentine coaches several Chinese managers and sees a growing awareness of these issues: *"Employee engagement is not just a priority for American or European companies. Talent shortages combined with globalization of their enterprises means this is something Chinese business leaders are taking really seriously and will focus on more and more for the future."*

Thus a strategy of change through engagement is more likely to produce the hoped-for benefits (i.e. $1 + 1 = 3$) than the more usual acquisition strategy, which ignores the people aspects of change and results in $1 + 1 = 1$.

Leaders as a point of contact to rebuild trust

All too often, despite the best of intentions, trust becomes a casualty of change. The consequences of such a loss can be serious because, as we discussed in

Chapter 3, trust and fairness are preconditions for engagement. When trust is lost, it becomes very difficult to work in active partnership, and employer-employee relations can become fraught and cynical.

So what can you do as a leader, if you become aware that there is a trust issue?

- Recognize there is a problem of trust. This may not be entirely obvious, because trust problems are not often explicitly labelled as such. Problems of low trust are more likely in a 'command and control' environment, where leaders often ignore problems. In relationship-based organizations, people will tend to learn from mistakes and avoid a breakdown in trust.
- Have a conversation with people, clarifying expectations, assessing whether there is a willingness to rebuild the loss of trust or not, and creating a shared vision and agreement up front.
- Confront reality and diagnose the issue that has caused the loss of trust and the extent to which it has spread in the organization. Listening is very important to genuinely understand another person's thoughts and feelings.
- Communications between the parties must be two-way by including the voice of the employee. Listen first before you speak and genuinely understand the other person's thoughts and feelings before trying to diagnose or advise. Both parties need to be prepared to show empathy and humility.
- The quality and quantity of the communications is important. The organization and its representatives must deliver a direct message, including the good with the bad. Particular care must be taken in the way that words are used to avoid conveying the wrong message.
- Demonstrate respect and create transparency. You can establish trust more quickly by being open and authentic, erring on the side of disclosure and not having hidden agendas.
- Practise accountability. The dominant party, usually the organization or its leaders in this context, need to make visible concessions. These concessions should be prominent to show that real action is intended. Be clear on how you'll communicate progress.
- The values espoused need to be built into the culture of the organization. The culture of trust must be bolstered at all levels, including through performance appraisal, induction programmes and training courses.

- Ensure that the right leaders are in place. The way to rebuild trust is through instilling the correct values of integrity, honesty and openness throughout the organization. The leaders need to appreciate the need for these values and espouse them, and this includes living the values by role modelling.
- Ensure you follow up (by way of focus groups and surveys) to see if trust is restored.

Public sector engagement challenges

So while change can and does affect employee engagement in organizations in every sector, there are a number of reasons why change in public sector organizations can be harder to manage and may dent employee engagement more extensively than in other sectors. At the time of writing the public sector in many countries is under considerable pressure to cut costs, including jobs, and improve efficiencies. For instance, the UK's National Health Service (NHS) is facing a real terms cut of around £20 billion by 2014. Public sector pension arrangements are being transformed, with employees now required to contribute more to their own pensions and retire later. In many countries staff protests have been coordinated into cross-public sector strikes. These issues are unlikely to disappear any time soon.

> The public sector in many countries is under considerable pressure to cut costs, including jobs, and improve efficiencies.

One of the main reasons why downsizings and other restructurings are so problematic in the public sector is that such changes represent a highly visible re-ordering of a collective psychological contract that has been so widely shared that it is, in effect, a social contract. Conventional public sector terms and conditions have, until recently, most obviously reflected the 'old' bureaucratic or paternalistic psychological contract of white collar workers: job security and generally lower pay than the private sector on the basis that public sector pensions are generous. When these terms and conditions are unilaterally altered by employers, it is hardly surprising that public sector employees feel let down and that staff morale is reportedly low.

Another (stereotypical) reason why public sector employee engagement may be under threat during restructurings is that many employees originally may have been attracted to working in the public sector for vocational reasons. Any restructuring that reduces the possibility of employees fulfilling that vocation is likely to have an adverse effect on their morale and motivation. A third reason why employee engagement can be badly undermined in the public sector is that, compared to private sector organisations that are often quicker to react to downturns in their market by laying off staff, public sector reorganizations have in the past been slower-moving and usually linked to the political cycle. The relative speed and scale of 'cuts' now proposed is producing shockwaves of protest among public sector workers in several countries.

> Particular care should be given to handling downsizing sensitively and avoiding the common 'traps' such as lack of care over redundant staff, failure to convince staff that job reductions are necessary or changes that leave survivors unclear about what is expected of them, or how they will acquire the new skills they will need.

Of course there are no easy answers to this. That is why we believe that it is all the more important to keep focused on applying the messages of this book. Particular care should be given to handling downsizing sensitively and avoiding the common 'traps' such as lack of care over redundant staff, failure to convince staff that job reductions are necessary or changes that leave survivors unclear about what is expected of them, or how they will acquire the new skills they will need. Senior public sector managers need to spend time and effort reconnecting with the people they lead, making themselves as visible and accessible as possible. High quality two-way communication will go some way towards rebuilding trust. Employees need to really understand and come to terms with the reasons for such painful shifts and communication must be honest in dealing with the negative feelings and concerns of employees.

The challenge to policy makers is to avoid using targets or funding mechanisms to micro-manage services. Line managers should have the authority to set realistic and appropriate localized targets to reflect what is feasible in terms of reduced staff resource. Teams need to be empowered to deliver on their new tasks and be given the skills and motivation to deliver. There is a real need to ensure that line managers have the skills and confidence to address engagement and performance issues in their teams, and that they will be supported by their own managers in doing this. It can be useful for managers to share their concerns with their peers and discuss how to deal with staff issues, so regular forums for this purpose can avoid managers feeling isolated. Reward strategies may also need to be realigned.

It will be crucial to keep a focus on developing talent at all levels, especially if cuts result in a lack of career development options and promotion becomes unlikely. This will send the right message to employees who are crucial to delivering high-quality public services. People who understand at least part of the business, who have good internal networks and who have a vested interest in the success of their teams and their organization should be identified and helped to develop the skills and model the behaviours needed to ensure future success. Talent management tactics that focus on in-house development (perhaps shared between institutions) are appropriate to contexts of tighter budgets.

So it's a question of building strong foundations for the future. Make sure human capital activities are aligned to key organizational objectives. Put in place simple and effective systems that identify key roles and future leaders. Ensure clarity on responsibilities for managing people between senior managers, line managers and HR. Board-level directors should take personal responsibility for championing a strategic approach to talent management and line managers should be the owners of such initiatives, since they are the key talent-spotters, developers, motivators and retainers of talent. In a climate of tight budgets, line managers will have to rely more on 'on the job' development, and less on support from HR. This in turn requires

> It will be crucial to keep a focus on developing talent at all levels, especially if cuts result in a lack of career development options and promotion becomes unlikely.

public sector managers to 'raise their game' in terms of their management capabilities. In such an environment, competence in areas such as change management, coaching, team working, innovation and communication will become more important than ever.

It is important to develop leadership in all roles, not just management roles, and involve everyone in becoming world class. At **NHS Dumfries and Galloway**, Sandy Wilkie, head of organizational development, has launched a scheme that offers employees seed funding to implement ideas for improving efficiency or the quality of the patients' experience. As Sandy says, 'in a challenging financial situation, that's a positive way of diverting energy away from anxiety to something more positive'.

Similarly, the UK's **Birmingham City Council** launched its employee engagement programme, Best, in better times. The workshop-based programme has generated tens of thousands of ideas for improving services, and, with the council set to lose 4000 jobs in 2012, Best is providing a framework for communicating with staff and consulting them on new ways of working (Arkin, 2011). Birmingham City Council is also leading the field among local authorities in using strategic workforce planning and organization design to create strong alignment between strategy, structures, systems and processes, as well as to equip people for the challenges ahead.

> Ironically, these times of austerity may prove to be the opportunity that frees up the public sector to banish bureaucracy, introduce innovation and develop creative solutions to the challenges presented by budget cuts.

Ironically, these times of austerity may prove to be the opportunity that frees up the public sector to banish bureaucracy, introduce innovation and develop creative solutions to the challenges presented by budget cuts, such as improving team working and introducing improved business processes. Tough change can help employees to 'pull together' but people have to believe that change is the right thing to do. They need at least to understand why change is needed and how they can help. It's an environment where focusing on engagement is no longer just something good employers do, but something smart organizations rely on as a key enabler of change.

Creating a change-able work environment

Looking ahead, today's tough times teach us that organizations will need change capability – to be able to manage 'business as usual' while also managing change and innovating at the same time. Change capability is reflected in people's attitudes, behaviour, skills and priorities. So how can today's challenges be used to help employees become 'change-able'?

'Business as unusual'

During a downturn, line managers have to juggle both 'business as usual' as well as change. By making change a part of every employee's job, mindsets can be 'morphed' so that change comes to be seen as the norm, not the exception, and it is recognized as the spur to innovation and improved customer service. Leaders need to reshape the work environment and culture to match their unique basis of competitive advantage and enhance performance. They should work to create a shared sense of purpose, setting a clear direction and priorities so that employees know what is required and feel 'empowered' to deliver the right outputs. This involves top management driving forward with purpose and cascading the vision – so that people 'get it' and are ready to respond to the challenges ahead.

Line managers shoulder the day-to-day challenge of maintaining employee morale, and if necessary re-engaging employees, even though they are themselves generally under pressure from every angle. They need to:

- feel supported by top management
- execute tasks, but in an enabling way
- continue to develop people's performance potential
- keep staff motivated and ready for more change
- ensure employees have the skills, authority and resources to do their jobs
- set objectives so that people know what is required, but allow staff to work out how to deliver them without the need for micro-management
- ensure that jobs are 'de-cluttered' of unnecessary bureaucracy so that people can have a clear line of sight to the purpose, mission and goals of the organization through their day job.

Therefore managers need more of a coaching style, to be willing and able to involve staff so that staff can become active change agents. Tips for managers relating to change are shown in Box 10.4.

Box 10. 4 Tips for managers: change

- Bring employees in touch with the changing environment – make sure they know what's happening with competitors, and that they understand the evolving needs of customers.
- Involve people in improving the day job – ask all staff about how they can help innovate and improve products, services and customer relations. Be sensitive to the emotional as well as task elements of the job.
- Equip people for change by giving regular feedback, using just-in-time training and development, and providing coaching where needed.
- Help people to manage workloads and make it easier for them to do demanding jobs by being specific about the key priorities, as well as about what work can be stopped.
- Highlight successes resulting from ideas generated by teamworkers.
- Keep performance management and other people processes simple and user-friendly.
- Maintain developmentally linked incentives for high performers and use non-financial benefits and forms of recognition that matter most to people. Pay extra attention to small gestures such as thanks and feedback, even if constrained budgets prevent you from giving financial rewards.

Keep focused on developing people

A sustained investment in people can also help organizations to maintain their competitiveness and retain valued employees. Employers who are efficient, forward-looking and continue to develop the abilities of their workforce are more likely to be well-positioned for growth when the economy picks up. Therefore, it is important to make sure that the organization's human capital strategies align to create a high-performance culture. This may involve continuing to recruit new talent to bring in missing skills and expertise, even while downsizing.

Managers are the key conduit to growing the abilities of employees, which involves managers spotting opportunities for development, actively coaching the team and providing job shadowing and mentoring. Engaging managers:

> Employers who are efficient, forward-looking and continue to develop the abilities of their workforce are more likely to be well-positioned for growth when the economy picks up.

- give people the chance to change roles and re-energize themselves and the organization
- work at improving the skills and competencies that people really need, focusing in particular on people in new roles
- encourage staff to move between domestic and international divisions, or from one country to another.

They also develop people by involving them in working on real business issues, which allows them to gain new experiences, helps develop different parts of the business, and is also a great motivator. When people are seconded into new roles they feel valued – 'you are the future of the company' – and are more likely to want to empower the next level too.

Provide support to employees

While no organization can guarantee job security, they can help employees cope with stress and anxiety. Simply giving them opportunities to talk – in one-to-ones and in groups – can be enough. Employee assistance programmes may also be needed to help people cope with the impact of the recession, whether or not employees are directly affected by redundancies. Providing meaningful support for staff and managers to help them deal with issues arising from the recession not only shows employees that they are valued, even if their own job may be at risk, but it can also help 'survivor' employees remain productively focused on their work.

Provide a sense of purpose and progress

Frequent and honest communication will be vital for building employee resilience and the engagement needed to help organizations through the downturn. So mark the milestones, celebrate success, stabilize the business and share the benefits. For employees, change can be welcome if they are working in a positive work environment, come to see themselves as part of a winning team, are more capable and empowered because they have learned from their experience, and have the tools to be self-managing. Above all, change can provide opportunities for development and growth, new skills and challenges, new networks, recognition and (with care) a better work-life balance. The potential is there – the delivery of that possibility relies on a shared effort. Leaders, managers and HR have key roles to play, but so too do employees; employee engagement flows up, down and across the organization.

> Above all, change can provide opportunities for development and growth, new skills and challenges, new networks, recognition and (with care) a a better work-life balance.

Focus on a better long-term future

A major leadership role is to think strategically beyond the current challenges and create a sense of a positive future: something to aim for. It is clear that in future, organizations will need to be agile; this requires looking ahead, making market predictions to enable planning and decision making, and being capable of speedy execution. Leaders need to anticipate the big business issues and plot a way through to recovery. Short-term decisions must be taken with the longer term in mind: where will your future sources of revenue come from, how will you innovate and keep close to customers, etc.? HR too needs to anticipate the big people issues, do some workforce planning and work closely with line managers, helping them to (re-)energize and develop their teams. Organizations need to understand their employees' needs as well as they understand their customers', so as to build employer brands that put them ahead of the competition in terms of attracting, engaging and retaining employees.

But in the toughest times, values and organizational integrity are more important than ever for engagement and change-ability. Organizations that keep their word can successfully bring employees through the most challenging business conditions. So to reinforce this, values should be incorporated into appraisals and promotion criteria, and line managers should be recognized for their efforts in engaging employees. Good intent, in the form of work-life balance or diversity policies, should be translated into practice, with issues recognized and addressed. Every effort should be made to close any 'say-do' gap so that the values aren't just something on a slide or poster, but are genuinely reflected in day-to-day behaviours. Leaders and managers in particular should role model the values; 360-degree feedback and survey results should be used to get through to senior managers who might be difficult to reach. Managers should be developed as leaders, giving them access to new tools, techniques and ideas. They need to be versatile, able to judge and deliver what is required when it is needed, such as when it is vital to involve employees and when it is important to direct them. They need the wisdom to know the difference.

Conclusion

So the short-term challenges may prove a blessing in disguise because they signal that, if organizations are not only to recover but also be capable of sustaining performance in ongoing change, it's about doing the right things and doing them even better than usual. It's about recognizing that new capabilities, mindsets and approaches to running business will be needed. It's about managing change with a human touch.

If leaders want people to be willing and able to come with them through change, they must take employee engagement seriously, and understand the link between engagement and performance. They need to recognize the huge positive impact they can have on employee engagement, retention and performance. But rather than attempting to force engagement, it is healthier to encourage it. The two-way nature of this relationship requires that employees also become active players in managing their own engagement, demonstrating both resilience and flexibility. This is the focus of our final chapter.

Checklist: keeping engagement going in tough times

- What people issues do you need to focus on?
- What are the main priorities and what will make the biggest difference?
- If cost-cutting is needed, are there ways to do so while retaining as much of the workforce as possible?
- Do staff understand the challenges at hand and are they involved in the change process?
- Are change initiatives being adequately staffed and planned so they can be managed effectively?
- Is there full and timely communication? Do you allow for two-way exchange?
- How will you know if your people are really committed and engaged?
- Have the staff who are critical to future performance been identified, and how do you plan to retain them?
- Do people have meaningful work?
- Are there regular workload reviews? Are people clear about what work is no longer needed?
- Do employees have adequate resources and support systems?
- Are performance reviews encouraging and do they promote the right behaviours?
- How are recognition and reward being used?
- Is there commitment to diversity and work-life balance policies?
- Have career tracks been developed and do people know about them?
- Do people have the chance for learning and growth so they can grow in their current job and be better positioned for future ones?
- Are learning reviews being conducted?
- Are managers acting as credible leaders?
- Does the 'walk' match the 'talk' on values?

CHAPTER 11

So as we complete this picture of engagement, we're coming back to where we began – the vital importance of employee engagement to business success. Right now, it's difficult to predict when the global economy will recover; after the collapse of Lehman Brothers in 2008, it seemed like a turnaround was beginning in 2010, but developments such as the Eurozone sovereign debt crisis, the tsunami in Japan in 2011 and widespread economic sluggishness have put paid to this. Various economic pundits predict that the global economic situation may only start to stabilize and return towards more sustainable growth from 2015 on. But whenever growth does return, it is likely that knowledge and service-intensive work will play a key part in driving economic recovery, so the engagement of 'knowledge workers' will be crucial for businesses to achieve their full potential.

As the economy becomes more and more driven by knowledge work, engagement becomes the vital lubricant in 'oiling' the 'engine' of high-quality knowledge- and service-intensive performance and productivity. When talented people love what they do and experience 'flow' in the way that Gardner et al. (2001) describe it, they give of their best. In a state of flow, employees are at their most productive and creative. As the famous American photographer Annie Leibovitz puts it, 'when I go into my work, I am transcended' (Galvin, 2011).

So what makes the greatest difference to producing the state of 'flow'? We believe the answer lies in **Scope**, the fourth quadrant of our model. As the word implies, 'Scope' is about freedom, choice, opportunity, space, shaping, planning and organizing. Scope is a two-way phenomenon:

- Employees need Scope, or freedom of action, in their jobs if they are to give of their best. This translates into autonomy, trust, growth and accomplishment, career development, meaning, and purpose.
- Firms (leaders especially) need to provide the parameters that allow employees to do their best work to benefit the business. This translates into designing jobs that are stretching, defining what needs to be done – but leaving the latitude on how to do it, and providing guidelines for performance in the form of values rather than micro-managing. This way, they help to provide purpose (rather than drudgery) in daily work, create development opportunities, encourage lifelong learning and allow people to focus on their tasks and achieve mastery in their work.

So far we have mainly focused on the organization's responsibilities for creating the conditions in which employees are likely to engage: that is, through Connection, providing Support and involving employees through Voice. But at the same time, employees can and do exercise considerable influence over their own destiny and engagement levels, and those of others. We argue that it is in employees' own interests to maintain and grow their engagement levels, and Scope is where this happens. Managers have the dual challenge of engaging others and watching out for their own engagement levels. So in the final part of this book we shall suggest some pointers you might wish to consider personally as possible actions for boosting your own engagement.

Scope concerns both the actions taken by organizations that set employees free to do their best work and also employees feeling engaged in work that serves the organization's interests, not just their own. It is about enlightened self-interest on both sides. In this chapter we shall explore the components of Scope and consider what organizations can do to liberate employees to reach the ultimate level of engagement: when employees experience meaning at work. Putting the specific needs and aspirations of individual employees centre stage therefore complements the broader engagement elements of Connection, Support and Voice.

> Long-term demographic changes mean that employers will be competing in a shrinking labour market.

As we have already seen, there is widespread disengagement in many workplaces today, risking talent flight once the global economy starts recovering. Added to this, long-term demographic changes mean that employers will be competing in a shrinking labour market. With the exception of India, most major economies will undergo a shrinking of their working age population between 2005 and 2050, with the biggest falls (of more than 10 per cent) occurring in South Korea, Spain, Russia, Japan, Italy and China (Hawksworth, 2006). It was back in 1997 that McKinsey & Company coined the phrase 'the war for talent' – but it's a battle that is likely to become more intense in the long run. So let's begin by looking at the talent challenge and how providing Scope may be part of the solution by making your organization a talent 'hub'.

The talent challenge

As work becomes ever more knowledge-intensive, employees' competencies and enthusiasm are a firm's most important resource. People will not only be a source of critical skill and knowledge, but also of sustainable competitive advantage. Talent management, or an organization's ability to attract and retain knowledge workers, and engage them with the work of the firm, is therefore likely to distinguish organizations that survive and thrive from those that fail. Strong professionals are the single biggest differentiator in a knowledge-intensive firm. When employees' talents are harnessed in a way that furthers the goals of the business, as well as those of employees, the possibilities of win-win outcomes multiply. In such a situation, the relationship between employer and employees is symbiotic. There are mutual gains to be had that require mutual efforts.

Managing talent through Scope

Providing Scope is at the heart of the challenge of attracting, engaging and retaining knowledge workers, since it unlocks the latent potential of employees. But we argue that this requires two major shifts in how people are managed. Firstly, organizations need to apply the same disciplines to understanding their workforce as they do their customers – to give themselves a competitive edge in attracting, retaining and engaging employees and channelling their energy and brain power most effectively, they need to understand employees' needs, issues, values and 'buying' patterns. Market research is a well-established activity in most companies, but is employee research? Unless organizations are smarter at monitoring and responding to the pulse of their workforce, they may struggle in the long run.

Secondly, it seems to us that so much talent management activity in companies is really just another name for succession planning – and too often this is not well done anyway. A CIPD survey in 2010 found only 59 per cent of companies undertook talent management activities and only just over half of these thought they were effective (CIPD, 2010b). A plethora of talent processes, tools and software solutions means that companies risk focusing more energy on procedures than on people, and losing sight of what will engage the best people in the first place. We argue that the emphasis should be placed instead on designing processes that can flex to meet the needs of individual employees.

So if talent is so important, what do employees want? The answers can vary by place and by sector, but here are some of the key themes from various global studies.

What attracts future employees?

Towers Watson's survey (2010b) found that the five main drivers for *attracting* employees were:

- competitive base pay
- career advancement opportunities
- challenging work

- convenient work location
- flexible schedule.

The vast majority of employees today are looking to make a difference in an organization that makes a difference in the world. When it comes to recruiting the right people, Towers Watson's study implies that, while salary counts in terms of getting someone 'through the door', corporate purpose also matters. As we saw in Chapter 2, expectations of younger workers are shifting – they tend to look more carefully at employer brands and select future employers on the basis of an organization's reputation for social responsibility. They want to know how what the organization does helps to create a better world and they want to play a part in improving society through their work. They find this **meaningful**. Therefore to maximize recruitment success, firms must commit themselves to creating the right reputation among their preferred target groups of potential employees.

Reputation, like values, must be real, so managers should formulate clear, visible goals for employees and spend time with them, demonstrating that they are serious about putting values into practice rather than just paying lip service.

> To maximize recruitment success, firms must commit themselves to creating the right reputation among their preferred target groups of potential employees.

What engages knowledge workers?

When it comes to *engaging* young professionals, a survey by Mercer LLC (2011) of nearly 30,000 employees aged 16–24 in 17 markets across Asia, Europe and the Americas highlights a global generational workforce shift that will have big implications for employers wishing to engage and retain young workers. The study found that these employees are more mobile than their predecessors and came of age with technology that allows them to share popular culture. They see that loyalty from employers has eroded and they recognize that the employment deal is not about longer-term commitment, so they don't give automatic allegiance to their employer. Workers in this age group are very interested in growth, change and opportunities, in how one job will get them to their next job. They recognize that they must make their own career and that this will entail **lifelong learning**.

This is echoed in findings from a survey of US workers of all ages by Aon Hewitt (2011), which found that the top engagement drivers were:

- clear career path
- being involved in decisions that affect their work
- necessary development
- career development
- team work.

Other studies by providers such as Effectory, Kenexa and Towers Watson, as well as awards companies such as Best Companies, frequently point to leadership, corporate social responsibility (CSR), good supervision and the chance to contribute as key themes in engagement, very much reflecting our view of the importance of Connection, Support and Voice. But **growth opportunities** come out high too – underlining the relevance of Scope in engaging employees.

What retains knowledge workers?

The top five drivers for *retaining* employees in the Towers Watson (2010b) study were:

- the organization's reputation as a great place to work
- satisfaction with the organization's people decisions
- good relations with a supervisor
- understanding potential career track within the organization
- ability to balance work and personal life.

BlessingWhite Research (2011, p. 14) found that the top reason for staying with their employer was that people liked their work, whereas the foremost reason for changing employer was lack of career opportunities. Other studies about knowledge workers emphasize the importance of development as a retention factor. So it's about doing **great work** plus the **chance for career progression**. It's not necessarily the rate of progression that matters, but the fact that career paths are there and have the potential to be realized. Armed with this information, organizations are well positioned to make a significant difference to employee's discretionary effort. It is up to employers to help make this happen.

Components of Scope

In unpacking this kaleidoscope of attraction and retention factors, we detect a hierarchy – with 'flow' most likely at the highest levels of meaning and purpose. When employees embrace the organization's purpose and share its values, they are most likely to perform at their best and experience 'flow', job satisfaction and personal fulfilment. They have a sense of belonging and congruence with the organization and believe they are making a useful contribution to something worthwhile.

Unlike in Maslow's famous 'Hierarchy of Needs' model, where the base level of the pyramid is physiological needs, including safety, we argue that highly skilled knowledge workers are unlikely to suffer from worries over job security since they are more likely to expect to progress their career by moving jobs. However, what is more important for these workers is the chance for development and accomplishment, in roles in which they can grow themselves and the business. This means that the working environment should be conducive to lifelong learning and career development. Employees will expect a fair deal, without which they are unlikely to stay.

> The working environment should be conducive to lifelong learning and career development. Employees will expect a fair deal, without which they are unlikely to stay.

Knowledge workers will also thrive best in situations where they have autonomy and control over their work. The CIPD found that immersion in the job through variety, autonomy and meaningfulness evoked the highest levels of engagement (CIPD Research, 2011b). This means that jobs should be designed to maximize individual discretion, job enrichment and empowerment. Knowledge workers often operate quite individualistically. They must feel they have a role to play, in their own way, or they will leave. They need to be given a shared framework so that they can be themselves, but contribute within agreed parameters. Values and mutual trust should provide the parameters for this freedom, and individual choice should be counter-balanced by a team culture.

In this model (see Figure 11.1), as the Scope hierarchy ascends and the organization successfully meets each of these engagement factors, the organization becomes more attractive to new and potential employees and more engaging to its existing staff.

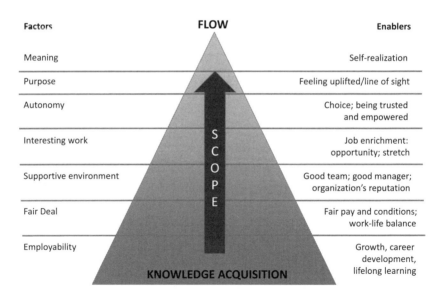

Figure 11.1 Scope and knowledge workers. Source: Holbeche, L.S. & Matthews, G.P.

Identifying future stars

This is a key responsibility of senior managers. In knowledge-intensive firms, highly talented individuals tend to become 'stars' who act as if they have high self-esteem and demand a lot of management attention. They crave management recognition and praise to reassure them that they are on the path for further advancement. They have a voracious appetite for feedback to know how they are doing. Constructive feedback should include praise as well as the deconstruction of weak performances and how these can be improved. Then there needs to be proactive development and coaching.

Not surprisingly, managers tend to pay more attention to the self-promoting, attention-seeking stars at one extreme, and under-performers at the other. Stars who do not get their own way can behave counter-productively, as Ejler et al. (2011, p. 76) point out:

> We know many managers of team-focused knowledge-intensive firms who have even on occasion had to ask star professionals to leave because they have behaved too much like lone wolves.

By only looking at the high potential 'stars', it is easy for managers to overlook the talent that is in front of them. Goffee and Jones (2009) argue that it may be better to build a 'galaxy' of (lesser) lights, since not everyone can be a star and other stable performers are vital to skilfully and efficiently fulfil one assignment after another. These represent the real backbone of a firm and should not be neglected. In this sense, talent management is not just about identifying the high performers or future leaders. It is about looking at the roles in your organization, and all the people you have, ensuring their capabilities are being developed to the full. Then it's about ensuring that they are then being best matched to where they can contribute the most.

Growth and continuous development

A key trend in the labour market is the increasing demand of employees for self-development on the job. This is understandable, since the disappearance of 'jobs for life' makes employability essential. But this doesn't automatically mean going on courses or pursuing promotions. Employees thrive in an open and trusting working environment where there is delegation, personal development and good opportunities for competence development. This is a win-win situation, since development increases employees' value to the firm and also in the labour market.

Managers play the key role in aiding the development of their teams. In their three-year study of outstanding leaders, The Work Foundation found that such leaders love to grow people and use their skills effectively: this unlocks something energizing for the individuals and creates intense loyalty. They also manage people in ways that promote and maximize self-management (Tamkin et al. 2010, p. 60).

Engaging managers are 'experience optimizers'. They are aware what makes their employees tick, and show empathy and understanding in the way they manage them. They facilitate and empower others, build confidence, and offer continuous support, feedback and coaching. They provide opportunities to practise new skills, enable reflection on learning assignments and help balance learning and work.

Good line managers continually invest in people, using everyday projects and extra-role responsibilities to encourage growth, learning and engagement. They make use of all sorts of development tools, not just classroom training but secondments, work shadowing, distance learning, reading, watching DVDs, attending meetings and workshops, workbooks and guides – anything relevant that will help the person develop towards their aims. In knowledge-intensive firms the best opportunity to develop staff comes through real-time project work.

> Engaging managers are 'experience optimizers'. They are aware what makes their employees tick, and show empathy and understanding in the way they manage them.

Engaging managers also follow up with individuals after development activities, ensuring that new skills are being put to good use and developed further, which is a key retention factor. Through dialogue with individuals they formulate new challenges and specific goals to help people make progress from a personal and a career development perspective. For instance, they encourage employees to cope with more variety, such as fixing failing projects, and assuming tasks outside their comfort zone – not only out of fairness but also to ensure that everyone is fresh, challenged and satisfied – so a degree of rotation is required.

Organizations that give their staff the opportunity to use their skills gain multiple benefits. Not only do individuals feel valued and more competent but their learning becomes more widely shared too. And the benefits of sharing learning apply equally well to junior staff, craftworkers and trades specialists as they do to star 'knowledge workers'. For instance, the **New Charter Housing Trust Group** holds skills-sharing lunches during a 'Learning at Work Week', when plasterers, for example, might run a plastering course for people to use their learning in their own home.

Career development and lifelong learning

Many companies provide career development opportunities, such as training, coaching and job-rotation opportunities, or even postings abroad. Sometimes there's a reluctance to make such investments because they will make the employee more marketable, and so potentially at greater risk of leaving. But in practice people who feel they have a positive future ahead of them, and are able to pursue their personal ambition in their organization, are less likely to want to leave. After all, growth and development matter to most employees: in the Towers Watson (2010b) global employee engagement survey, 'My skills and capabilities have improved in the last 12 months' was the second out of 75 drivers. Amabile and Kramer (2010, p. 44) noted that the ability to progress is the top motivator affecting professionals' performance:

> On days when workers have the sense they're making headway in their jobs, or when they receive support to overcome obstacles, their emotions are most positive and their drive to succeed is at its peak. On days when they feel they are spinning their wheels or encountering roadblocks to meaningful accomplishment, their mood and motivation are lowest.

The Corporate Executive Board defines one of the essential roles of senior leaders in building new leadership capability as being an 'experience broker', directing people to career-advancing job assignments. They are not afraid to change things around, moving people into new roles to keep them developing and exposed to new stimuli. They give advice on career progression and development needs. As a senior manager, Krista Baetens describes the importance of understanding what motivates individuals:

> One of my team brought me a card to put on my door which says 'The dream manager'. It's not because I'm the perfect manager at all, but it means the 'manager of the dreams', because what I do with my team is to try and understand what their dreams are – I always ask them because I think that, if I understand their dreams, and I can relate this somehow to what they do and their role in the team, to what we want to achieve then I think that there are no limits to what we can achieve together.

Rather than 'talent hoarding', engaging managers help and encourage staff to apply for promotions and prepare for successful career moves. They act as relationship brokers and career champions, connecting their direct reports to other key leaders, building relationships and enabling learning from the most influential leaders. They ensure that senior colleagues see the employee's long-term potential.

At the professional recruitment consultancy **Goodman Masson**, as part of its 'Your Career' process, everyone in the firm writes a business plan. This document acts as a great structure for managers to support and develop their team members. The business plan includes the individual's personal vision, goals and objectives, their client base, their candidate base, their sales forecast, and how they will build their brand. It's also an opportunity to discuss barriers to progress. Every quarter, the managers use the business plan as a benchmark of progress in the appraisal process.

It's important as well to bear in mind that development is not confined to early in one's career – on the contrary, growth can occur at all career stages, and there should be an emphasis on lifelong learning. While younger employees will see development as key to help them move ahead, older employees may be looking to reorient their career or find a particular way to leave their mark. One way of harnessing these trends is to encourage a mentoring and coaching approach, such as senior managers mentoring line managers and line managers mentoring new managers and employees. This has the benefit of being supportive in nature as well as disseminating the culture throughout the organization. At the **UKRD Group**, the radio and media company, training goes beyond developing skills required for the job and focuses on developing personal qualities. Development activities are not always conventional – they can have a quirky edge, such as a group of managers hearing a talk on leadership by an eminent historian in a historic setting. It's about giving people more life skills to do their jobs effectively and developing their latent skills and talent.

Career development opportunities and customer focus are even more vital in a downturn. Even organizations in a 'strategic holding pattern' must find ways of stretching and motivating key talent that prepare the organization for the upturn. Talent management must remain in focus: build career paths, integrate business-relevant learning and role design. Appelbaum et al.'s study of downsizing (2003) recommended more frequent and more formal performance planning sessions, employee-focused action plans linking career ambitions with specific training, and involving employees in succession planning.

If – exceptionally – employees do decide to leave, smart employers still aim to make their feelings about the company positive so that they turn these employees into ambassadors for the firm. Later, armed with new skills and experiences, re-hiring them may be a win-win possibility. By then, they might be ready for a role that they couldn't have taken on before, and they have the advantage of 'knowing the ropes' and being a good cultural fit.

> The evidence is clear: talent retention is about managers recognizing the need to develop their employees, thinking about the individual ambitions of employees and trying to develop them.

The evidence is clear: talent retention is about managers recognizing the need to develop their employees, thinking about the individual ambitions of employees and trying to develop them. If staff believe they have a worthwhile future in the firm, they will perform in such a way that brings benefits to the organization and grows their capability.

Job design and enrichment

For most employees, their job – and the variety, autonomy and meaning it provides – is a critical engagement factor (CIPD, 2011b). People want a job that is interesting to do, to be treated with respect, to have the chance to get on and a boss who is some help rather than their biggest problem.

As we discussed in Chapter 9, work can have a positive impact on health and psychological wellbeing. David Coats of the Work Foundation points out that 'work is good for you – good work is even better' (Coats and Lehki, 2008). The problem so often lies in jobs that are of poor quality and offer little chance for employees to grow and experience real development. Poor-quality jobs also often have an obscured 'line of sight' to organizational purpose, so that employees may end up feeling that their tasks are not interesting or worthwhile. Many company surveys echo this observation. For example, the **Nationwide Building Society**'s annual employee survey includes five questions designed to measure employees' engagement with both the organization and their own work, and these tend to go hand-in-hand. As the building society's HR and Corporate Affairs Director Graeme Hughes explains, 'if you feel good about the job you are doing and see value in that job, you have confidence in the business'. 'Good' work can enhance wellbeing and so foster greater performance and productivity through having employees who feel psychologically healthy and full of energy at work.

> While good quality work can be good for you, too much work can not only be harmful, it can even be counterproductive for the organization.

But, as with everything, there's a balance – while good quality work can be good for you, too much work can not only be harmful, it can even be counterproductive for the organization. As David Coats warns, 'employers underestimate at their peril the impact on productivity and performance of stress and physical problems which are directly attributable to the experience of the employee in the workplace' (In MacLeod and Clarke, 2009, p. 60).

The impact of the quality of jobs and of the working environment on employees' psychological wellbeing at work is becoming better understood and much can be done to improve matters. A review carried out by the Foresight project (Department for Business Innovation and Skills, 2009) concludes that interventions at three main levels can make a difference:

- work context – management style, organizational justice, workplace support, participation and communication
- work content – key workplace factors such as job demands, control/autonomy, flexible working schedules, and job stability
- individual – training in resilience, stress management and psychological flexibility.

Work context

Building on these categories, we argue that organizations need to customize and shape the work environment and culture to match their unique basis for competitive advantage. Future business priorities should lead to an aligned workforce strategy that helps build the right organization for the future. Tools like the Galbraith 'Star' model or the McKinsey '7-S' model can help create a holistic view of what's needed. But whichever tools are used, the aim should be to answer the following questions:

- What are the key business drivers for the future and how do they differ from the present?
- What are the implications for the people we should employ, the skills they have and the ways they are measured and paid?
- How should the organizational structure change and how should roles alter?
- What are the organization's unique cultural differentiators, and to what extent is the existing culture supporting and driving the behaviours required for success?
- Taken together, are the right ingredients in place to create a high-performance culture? If not, what's missing and what needs to be done?

Empowerment

With respect to work context, empowerment links closely to the overall organizational structure – as we saw in the **Sika** case in Chapter 8, and the need to remove unnecessary work from the system. But management style is perhaps the most crucial factor here, and the manner by which workplace support is provided. Goffee and Jones (2009) suggest some dos and don'ts with respect to getting the best out of knowledge workers (whom they describe as the 'Clevers'):

- **Do** explain and persuade; **don't** tell people what to do.
- **Do** give real-world challenges with constraints; **don't** build an ivory tower.
- **Do** protect them from the rain; **don't** expose them to politics.
- **Do** encourage failure and maximize learning; **don't** train.

Teams

In many knowledge-intensive firms, client work is usually delivered by individuals working directly or indirectly with teams. Team performance is important because it creates development and synergy through knowledge transfer, reflection and flexibility in performing assignments. When a group of people cooperate, critique each other, and develop their projects, quality improves. On the contrary, 'lone wolves' tend not to last long. As Ejler et al. point out (2011, p. 77), this team approach benefits not only the client (since the best brains are brought to bear on a problem) but also individual employees:

> It is our belief that good professionals can gain optimal freedom in a team, provided that they are stimulated and supported when creating results. Since the professionals are the most important asset in knowledge-intensive firms, it is often wise to prioritize the team-based business model for this reason.

Of course, if team work is the espoused policy but incentive schemes reward lone players, the policy is contradictory and does not support the achievement of success. People will soon work out what counts and behave accordingly.

The challenge is to create opportunities and structures that ease the direct communication between professionals in a firm. This could take the form of experience groups, communities of practice

> When a group of people cooperate, critique each other, and develop their projects, quality improves.

(CoPs) and centres of excellence (CoEs), where people meet and share experiences. Others might include clever use of office space; for instance, establishing small café environments where people can meet informally and share knowledge over coffee.

Work content

With respect to job content, engaging managers design roles to ensure that work is delivered efficiently and effectively, and also provide space for individual development. In *The Craftsman* (2008), Richard Sennett makes the point that, in today's short-termist organizations, concepts such as craftsmanship and getting the job right are seen as wasteful and somewhat obsessive. Yet, he argues, every human being wants to do intrinsically useful work, and can become a craftsman in ways that play to their intrinsic motivations – that is, they can learn a skill and adjacent skills deeply, gain pride in achievement, and build their self-respect. However, to truly acquire a craft takes time and requires the craftsman to think, experiment and learn deeply, understanding the relationship between problem solving and problem finding. In the modern world, skills – interpersonal and managerial – are a substitute for craft, and are often acquired in order to compete with others rather than for their own sake. Moreover, the development of skills is often treated as a mechanical exercise, with the learner relieved of having to think through unsolved problems to find solutions since they instead rely on the use of technical and other tools to cut corners in the development and application of a skill. As a result, skill is reduced to mere procedure rather than real knowledge. Sennett suggests that it is only by reaching a more balanced state that the craftsman can focus externally and really build up their own capacity for learning.

As previously discussed, care needs to be taken that job descriptions avoid becoming a straightjacket that hinders growth. Rather than shoehorning the person into a job, it's important to look at how well the job fits the person and enabling team members to have input into what they are doing. This joint process of 'job crafting' then allows for work to become more varied, interesting and challenging. The alternatives – monotony, boredom, absence of challenge – can instead induce stress and disengagement. Proactive job crafting can avoid this as well as ensuring breadth and depth of knowledge across the team.

Autonomy

As products and services become increasingly knowledge-intensive, this creates a demand for autonomous thought processes in the workforce. These days changes happen with considerable speed, so it becomes increasingly difficult to construct bureaucratic systems that are nimble enough to handle everything. Employees must be capable of taking independent action and be willing and able to innovate. This though depends on their being empowered and authorized to act – otherwise, people can become victims of circumstances rather than being in charge of the situation, which in turn will generate stress and burnout.

To enable greater employee autonomy, knowledge-intensive firms typically have minimal hierarchy and considerable delegation of authority to individuals. But how can individuals be trusted to do what is needed? Organizational values can help provide a code of conduct: trusting people to follow agreed behaviours is one way of keeping professionals motivated so that they work in a way that meets the needs and priorities of the firm. But when done right, autonomy is – according to Davenport and Harding (2010, p. 120) – 'a feature of a rewarding job and a reward unto itself'.

> To enable greater employee autonomy, knowledge-intensive firms typically have minimal hierarchy and considerable delegation of authority to individuals.

Challenging goals

Engaging managers also know how to provide the right amount of 'stretch' for their employees – enough to be challenging, but not overwhelming. This is where good performance management comes into play, with regular feedback taking place. It begins, though, with setting effective objectives in the first place. Davenport and Harding of Towers Watson (2010, pp. 168–9) argue that the traditional 'SMART' goals (specific, measurable, agreed, realistic and time-limited) are not enough and they proposes an alternative set of five performance goal criteria using the acronym FAMIC:

- Few in number and focused
- Aligned internally and organizationally
- Build Mastery
- Incremental
- Controllable.

Individual

Today employees have enormous expectations and demands in terms of self-realization, particularly at work, so it is important that they are able to identify with work that is meaningful. This means giving them influence over the work they do, even if there need to be clear guidelines on how they approach this. They want to be involved in decisions about career development, the work they do and how they do it, and they want to feel that they are heard and are consulted. They want influence. Decisions must therefore be discussed before they are set in stone. Even if they don't agree with the final outcome, people will appreciate having had the chance to contribute to the discussion.

Meaning

Engaging managers and leaders bring meaning to life. As we have seen in case studies featured earlier, they focus on passion and on ethical purpose to create a vision that people can feel pride in. They do this authentically rather than for impression management purposes. They understand that mutual gains are immensely important in fuelling engagement and driving constructive behaviour. Delivering the organizational side of the employment relationship requires a 'both-and' mindset, namely:

- *both* trust *and* flexibility
- empowerment *and* accountability
- support *and* challenge
- performance *and* development
- shared risk *and* shared gain.

They therefore build bridges of understanding and create an emotional connection to purpose for people in the work that they do. As Tamkin et al. (2010, p. 4) observe:

> *What is clear is that outstanding leaders have great clarity on how to do things, of how to translate what is on the inside to create impact on the outside. They have a toolkit to create change and plug away at it understanding that growing individual and team capability takes time and effort.*

Box 11.1 features tips for managers relating to creating a 'good work' context.

Box 11.1 Tips for managers: creating a 'good work' context

- Look ahead: conduct workforce planning to understand supply/demand.
- Understand engagement levels, engagement profiles within your organization and turnover risk.
- Identify attraction, retention and engagement drivers for the different parts of your workforce.
- Open up communication with existing staff about what keeps your workers from being engaged.
- Start to take steps to unblock roadblocks to engagement.

- Be prepared to clarify job expectations, provide better resources, etc.
- Communicate meaningfully, speaking with employees at both a rational and emotional level.
- Organize your staff's work in such a way that it is divided into interesting, complete jobs. Avoid dumping all the boring or repetitive work into one job.
- When designing roles, make sure that there are appropriate levels of autonomy, responsibility and accountability built in – along with the appropriate authority, systems and other resources required. Overlaps or 'underlaps' with other roles should be avoided to prevent gaps, frustration or duplication. Make sure that your staff are clear about the main accountabilities of the post and reporting relationships.
- To enrich roles, give people the opportunity for cross-divisional working. Set up innovation groups tasked with tackling long-standing business problems or thinking of new business ideas. Make it possible for people to achieve 'mastery' at something of value.
- Allow for job rotation within a team where there are repetitive or less interesting elements, or between teams to foster cross-organizational learning and collaboration.
- Make sure that staff are able to cope with the demands of their jobs, both in terms of capability and workload.
- Give high performers additional opportunities and expanded portfolios to keep them stretched and motivated.
- Keep in mind the needs of potentially more vulnerable staff, such as young workers, employees with disabilities or women returning after maternity leave.

Physician, heal thyself!

If you are a manager, you have the twin tasks of engaging other people and managing your own engagement levels. Managers are expected to be positive, even when the going gets tough. But this can be draining, and people soon become aware if the enthusiasm is being faked – or is generally lacking.

So how engaged are you? It's important to keep a watching brief on your own enthusiasm, motivation and commitment. You can't be there for everyone else if you don't look after yourself first. So take time to take stock of how you feel, what's working, what isn't and what needs to change. Work-wise, that means thinking about the job you do and how you see your career progressing. But it also means thinking about your private life – is it a resource that energizes you or something that makes you want to escape into work instead? What do you want to stop doing, start doing or do differently to balance out the things you feel are missing?

This isn't a one-off exercise or something that can be quickly done. A different point of view – from a partner or close friend, for example – can help to provide perspective and challenge your thinking. But awareness and reflection can bring you different options so that, if one option proves difficult, another might be pursued instead. Maybe it's a major decision like a change of career direction – or simply

> So take time to take stock of how you feel, what's working, what isn't and what needs to change.

a commitment to do a bit more to improve your health, like taking the stairs rather than the elevator at work. Choices should be realistic and ones you feel most committed to. Then work out who else will be affected by what you plan to do, and what actions you need to take to mitigate the risk of harm to others or of backsliding when you are under pressure.

After this, it's about taking action – moving beyond good intentions. Actions may need to be phased, so planning helps. If you want to lose weight, for instance, it is all too easy to revert to unhealthy eating patterns when you are under stress: recognizing the risk is the first step to putting contingencies in place to strengthen your resolve, or to get you quickly back on track. Planning helps you set realistic 'stepping stones' that can realistically be achieved, and also helps you see when you are making progress towards your key goals. When progress is being made, it is important to recognize and celebrate this. Most of all, planning helps you take control of your own situation and address your own needs.

Taking stock

- Connection
  - So what is your purpose? What matters most to you?
  - How much are you able to pursue this purpose through your work?
  - To what extent are your values and those of your organization in sync?
  - When did you last experience meaning at work? What was happening?
  - If things are out of skew, what needs to shift for you to connect more?
- Support
  - How well do you cope with change? How resilient do you feel?
  - How much do you strive to maintain optimum health – physical, emotional and mental wellbeing?
  - To what extent do you feel accepted by others and part of a collegial network?
  - How well do you support others and how well are you supported by others, especially your boss?
  - If you are currently giving or getting less help than you would wish, how else can you strengthen your support levels?
- Voice
  - How well informed, consulted and involved do you feel?
  - How much do you feel able to influence others?
  - How open are you to new ideas?
  - How well connected are you?
  - If you are less influential than you wish to be, how can you strengthen your ability to influence others and shape your destiny?
- Scope
  - Do you have a job in which you can pursue your dreams?
  - How engaged are you? Which aspects of engagement – intellectual, social, emotional – are you most happy with? Which do you want more of?
  - How confident are you about your own abilities?
  - Do you have strengths that are underused? If so, can you find ways to use them more?
  - What, if anything, do you want to pursue in more depth, and why? How can you make this happen?

- How proactive are you in managing your own development and taking charge of your own life?

Then, having taken stock, it's about making choices. Above all, don't complain – do something!

Making choices

Connection

Know yourself and your values

The most important work you can do as a manager is to know yourself and to take care of yourself, recognizing that you are a unique individual. Your state of 'being' is more important than exactly what you do. No two managers work in exactly the same way; each brings their own unique perspective, experience and wisdom. So it's important to recognize and work with your natural style, be clear about your values, recognize other people's values, and see how your values sync with organizational values.

Whenever you prepare to work with your team in a challenging situation, you might want to ask yourself how good you are feeling about yourself and your situation. Whatever assumptions, intentions or attachment to particular outcomes that we bring into a team meeting can affect the meeting. This is especially so if we are not aware of (or fail to acknowledge) our assumptions, intentions, and desired outcomes.

> The most important work you can do as a manager is to know yourself and to take care of yourself, recognizing that you are a unique individual.

The work of a leader or manager is to begin with oneself, to make genuine contact. We encourage you to start from where you are, and develop your consciousness and awareness about yourself. Take whatever path works for you to do this work and make time to do the work of knowing the self from the inside out, going deeply to see what is there. One way of doing this is to explore 'who am I, and who am I not?'

- What I do – my 'doing':
  - tools and techniques
  - my skills and learnt abilities
  - competencies
  - role and job title.
- Who I am – my 'being':
  - my values
  - my assumptions about people/reality/change/etc
  - the kind of person I fundamentally am
  - my natural self.

This is about getting the bigger picture, reflecting on what you've achieved so far in your life and what you want to do, or who you want to be, now. We encourage you to work actively to develop your intuition. This will benefit the groups of people you work with and will benefit you. You will 'be' differently. The art of managing for engagement requires a different way of 'being' rather than 'doing'.

Having and sharing a vision

An outcome of the 'taking stock' exercise above should be that you are clear about your own future direction. Assuming it's remaining with your current organization, is it clear how your role fits in? Are you completely up to speed on the internal and external trends driving your business, so you can decide better what to do as a leader and be able to articulate this to your team? Although your organization may have an overarching vision, think about one for your own group as a way of motivating yourself and others. To be a leader, it's about acting with congruence and authenticity, or aligning 'being' and 'doing'. It's about 'walking the talk' on values and building your presence, personal power and influence.

Voice

Since no person is an island, it is important to be in touch with, and know what is going on and also to be able to communicate well with, and influence other people.

Setting communication boundaries

In today's frenetic world, when it is all too easy to mistake being busy for being effective, it is important to set your own boundaries about how you want communication to work for you (such as email, electronic, personal) and stick to them. Here are some suggestions:

- Be assertive over what you need. Request information you require, establish ground rules, negotiate if necessary.
- Prioritize one-to-ones. Determine the time needed, contract with individuals, summarize and finish – then follow up.
- Check if meetings are always necessary; ask 'can I achieve this another way?' If it's a team meeting, make it valuable, using the tips for building engaged teams in Chapter 9.
- Avoid getting your personal and work life completely blurred – for example, let people know whether or not you intend to answer emails when on holiday. Keep at least some of your own traditions and priorities sacrosanct.
- Remember that nobody's indispensable. Check if you need to be involved or can delegate the task – and potentially provide a developmental opportunity for a member of your team.

Bringing other people with you

At the same time, your ability to lead other people effectively depends on your ability to bring them with you. This involves understanding your audience, convincing others and influencing them, as well as being influenced by them. Influencing – the actions that attempt to modify, affect or change someone else's behaviour, attitudes, feelings or ideas – is a two-way activity that occurs all the time in relationships. Most influencing is concerned more with the process (for example, listening or building trust) than with the content, and much influencing behaviour is outside the awareness of both parties. Therefore, to

> Most influencing is concerned more with the process (for example, listening or building trust) than with the content, and much influencing behaviour is outside the awareness of both parties.

Table 11.1 Key influencing skills

Influencing skill	The ability to ...
Observation	Pay attention to the process messages, such as non-verbal behaviour
Interpretation	'Read' process messages
Listening	Hear what is said, and what is implied or not said
Feedback	Offer feedback to the other person about what you see, interpret, hear and feel
Awareness	Be aware of yourself moment by moment, particularly of patterns of behaviours (such as not listening) that are counter-productive
Choices	Recognize that whatever the situation you are dealing with at the moment, you can change your own feelings and behaviour
Self-confidence	Feel confident about yourself in the face of resistance or conflict
Timing/judgement	Know when to give feedback and when not to, or when to use choice 'A' or choice 'B'; if this is not the right time, be flexible, and pursue your influencing intentions at a better moment
Intuition	Trust your own feelings or 'hunches' about the likely patterns of another person's behaviour

be more influential, you need to identify potentially valuable opportunities to increase your influence and use a wide range of influencing skills congruent with your values and beliefs. The key influencing skills are shown in Table 11.1.

Building your networks

Being connected with others can be crucial to your effectiveness. But with so much work to do, there's a risk of being stuck in an office rather than getting out and about. By networking more actively, you'll:

- be more aware of what's going on
- anticipate better what to do

- influence others who can be important stakeholders in your projects
- discover opportunities, information, resources or advice that can help you in your job.

Map out who you know and who you don't know well but ought to get to know better. Think about how you can develop these collaborative relationships internally and externally – for example, a chat over coffee or meeting someone for lunch rather than retreating to a sandwich at the desk. Some organizations are not terribly sociable, but others may rely as much on 'who you know' as on 'what you know' – in which case, not spending time wisely here is simply going to hold you back.[1]

Being open to new ideas

Sometimes, usually quite unwittingly, our ideas and way of thinking gets stuck in a rut. We assume that our experience has taught us a lot about how things work, and this may be true – but our experience may also have made us more closed-minded towards other possibilities or interpretations. Given that things change quickly, our way of thinking can become a set of blinkers that limit our options. When we are unaware and stuck in a rut, we become less influential and more of a blocker. People learn to work round us.

> Visiting unfamiliar places, joining new networks and reading outside your normal boundaries can help you gain insight into how other people think and view the world through different lenses.

So challenge yourself to learn something new, meet new people and get some variety in your regular routines. Visiting unfamiliar places, joining new networks and reading outside your normal boundaries can help you view the world through different lenses and gain insight into how other people think. This is about challenging your own assumptions, so that you can alter them if they are restricting your options.

Support

This is about getting the support you need to be to be healthy and effective.

Managing your energy

It is difficult to be authentic in managing others if you are not working to optimize your own wellbeing. Are you satisfied with your own work/life balance? Is your personal energy being spent getting what you want from life? Where is your personal energy going?

Do you feel you have control over your situation? If not, we encourage you to learn to manage your energy. This requires that you make contact with your beliefs to understand whether you have any energy drains. How are your beliefs informing your reality? Do you see yourself as a victim of circumstances or as a co-creator of your own life? What adjustments do you need to make to lead the life you want to lead? What support might you need to make the most of your energy?

A simple way to get in touch with energy drains is to pay attention to your thoughts throughout the day. Every time you have a negative thought (an energy waster) – whether it is about unresolved issues, your current situation or fears of the future – make a note that you are having that negative thought. As you get better at spotting and stopping negative thoughts, reward yourself with something positive that you will enjoy.

Then be very clear about what you are and what you are not available for. We can choose lives where we are available for things that bring us joy and we are not available for things that do not.

Resourcing yourself

Check in with your body. How well are you supporting your body to be healthy? Do you lead a life that is life-nurturing or life-depleting? We recommend that you maintain daily practices of good absorbable nutrition so that your whole system receives optimum nourishment. Make time for some exercise each day; even a short walk can boost energy levels. Take a break at lunchtime.

Plan for a better balance. Set yourself some achievable objectives for improvement and monitor your progress regularly to keep on course. Be prepared for busy periods and plan regular breaks. Make sure your own needs are balanced alongside those of the job. Renew yourself by developing and pursuing interests outside work. Prioritize that special time-limited exhibition or show when it's in town. Change scene when you can: get out into the countryside or to a city you've always wanted to visit. Enjoy the fresh energy and renewed vigour you gain from these.

Getting the support you need from others

This is about you becoming even more effective at delivering results for the organization and for yourself.

Develop a good working relationship with customers, both external and internal. Involve customers from the outset, clarify expectations and establish service-level agreements that are deliverable. Be clear what you need to do and what other people need to do, so delegate upwards, sideways or downwards, as appropriate. Don't do other people's jobs for them – empower others by making sure they have the scope, skills, resources, information and authority they need to do the job. Ask for solutions (not just problems), provide any guidance and coaching required and review progress.

Make sure you also manage your boss. Agree your contract with him or her: both what they need from you and what you need from them. Challenge and support your boss, establish frontiers and planned reviews. Make sure these are delivered, so that you get the information and support you need.

Scope

The stock-taking and suggestions throughout this chapter are intended to help you to think strategically about your own situation, wants and needs. Having done so, we suggest that you do the following.

Set personal goals for improved effectiveness

Think about when you are at your best – when and where did you last feel a sense of 'flow'? Perhaps this is an area you could develop further, or maybe there are new skills you want to master. Scope is also about gaining a heightened sense of accomplishment that can both bolster a sense of self-worth as well as self-confidence (see below).

Establish key goals and priorities – brainstorming with a trusted person can help. Ask others for feedback and then apply some 'soft' project management discipline to help you deliver your own dream.

Your plan should incorporate a goal of improving, maintaining or enhancing your personal effectiveness. Build your personal resource plans, such as the (uninterrupted) time you will need. Apply time management practices that work for you, such as daily 'to do' lists with time allocated. Maximize 'bonus' time and use your prime time to pursue the most important activities. Map out dependencies, outputs, critical paths and simultaneous activity. Look ahead and predict crises or other things that might take you off-track. Build in risk management or mitigation of these derailers.

Plan in your achievements. Use a learning log to review progress: always carry a notebook, recording device or mobile phone with voice recorder. Evaluate your success against objectives and reward yourself! Raise your profile in the way you want it to be raised.

Increase your confidence

Get things done and show persistence. We admire people who never give up. Leaders who persevere and insist that their legitimate demands are met will win respect, however grudging.

> Use a learning log to review progress: always carry a notebook, recording device or mobile phone with voice recorder.

Develop a 'can do' ethos. This liberates energy and mobilizes the team. Effective teams are confident, able to take initiatives, overcome obstacles and win despite difficulties. When problems are identified, team members feel that they can be resolved. Opportunities are recognized and exploited. The behaviour of the team manager, and other opinion leaders, is a key factor in creating this kind of team climate so display self-confidence, relish challenges and take a few risks. Turn 'failure' into a learning opportunity and maintain your determination to win.

In summary: managing your own engagement

In the last few pages we've given you some suggestions about how you can manage your own engagement, and have included a final checklist below for you as well. Given how busy many managers are, it might seem a tall order – if not a counsel of perfection – to do all of these things. We know the demanding world that's out there. But we would encourage you to make some time for this, because a combination of greater self-awareness and working on those areas of most concern to you can pay off both professionally and privately. By addressing your own engagement level, your job can become more energizing and you can help your organization as well.

Checklist: performing under pressure

The acid test of our model is what happens when you are performing under extreme pressure. We suggest that you do the following:

- Remain connected:
  - remind yourself about your job purpose – why am I here?
  - set priorities – importance and urgency
  - acknowledge your responsibility to move things forward
  - don't try to do everything – be clear about what you can stop doing, what you need to start doing and what can be simply maintained.
- Keep actively involved:
  - find out what's happening and communicate with others
  - if you are a team leader, at least involve others in decisions about the 'how' if not the 'what' and the 'why'.
- Give and get support:
  - know what happens to your personality and to others' when you are under stress (use psychometric tests, coaches, etc.)
  - observe how others are doing and be prepared to flex your style to provide what others need
  - think about what support you need and ask clearly for it.
- Keep control over your own destiny:
  - take decisions faster – avoid procrastination by going for the 60:40 rule rather than 80:20
  - get back on track as soon as possible
  - celebrate success
  - reflect on and celebrate the progress and learning that you and others have made.

Conclusion

Employee engagement distinguishes sustainably successful organizations from others. Engagement creates a mutually beneficial, long-term relationship between employees and employers. The return on engagement (ROE) is a more committed workforce with a greater intention to stay, employees who are willing to exert their discretionary effort and be more innovative, and so create satisfied customers and good business results.

What produces engagement will vary according to circumstances. We know that what most people want, most of the time, falls mainly into the three fundamental drivers: intellectual, social and emotional. We recognize that what individuals want at any given time may change, and that external events in these challenging economic times may cause employees to be less aspirational and more focused on basic needs, such as job security. We also recognize that these drivers are profoundly impacted by people's perceptions of how they are treated, either fairly, inclusively and as adults, or as expendable chattels. And as innovation expert Cris Beswick reminds us:

> *Engagement isn't something in itself, it's not an individual ingredient that can be bottled and labelled and so is no panacea. When you understand that engagement is a witch's brew of elements common to every organization – like leadership, direction, vision, shared ownership and voice, to name but a few – that's when you realize, like any great chef, that the quality of the ingredients is the defining factor.*

Given this complex mix, we have proposed that the 'ingredients' that fall into our model's categories of Connection, Support, Voice and Scope provide a rule of thumb about where employee engagement initiatives might make most difference.

We hope, too, that by now you need no further convincing about the importance of engagement for organizations, and the challenge this has for existing assumptions about how people should be led. For us, this starts at the top of organizations, and we concur with the report published in 2010 by the UK's National School of Government (Hockey and Ley, 2010), which interviewed leaders and organizations in the private, public and NGO sectors and identified several common characteristics of engaging leadership as well as the behaviours that should go along with them:

- **Open and honest** – shares bad news as well as good, wants employees to do the same: admits mistakes.
- **Approachable** – encourages people to speak up and say what they feel.
- **Visible and accessible** – has an open-door policy for all employees, undertakes frequent visits to interact with people working off-site.
- **Leads by example** – is interested in employees' work and has an involvement in the business.
- **Empowering** – trusts people, encourages responsibility and innovation.
- **Collaborative** – works with teams and individuals to solve problems.
- **Treats people well** – gets to know employees, meets their needs.
- **Humble** – rank is not relevant, no ego, not looking for compliments.
- **Coaches** – understands the work and helps employees improve their performance.
- **Trustworthy** – fulfils commitments made.

But while senior leaders should role model these behaviours, in practice they apply to managers and leaders at all levels. For us, engaging managers are ones who have gone beyond the traditional 'stick and carrot' approach of the transactional leader and can adopt a more transformational leadership style.

That means using our model as a compass to see where engagement is heading in your organization, and where you may need to tack or change course. It means addressing all four quadrants:

- **Connection** – helping others see the way ahead and how they can contribute to making it happen, as well as helping them identify with the organization by setting an example in terms of your own ethical behaviour.
- **Support** – being attuned to others' individual needs and showing consideration and empathy. It calls for encouragement, coaching and real recognition of others.

- **Voice** – allowing others to have their say and keeping them 'in the loop'.
- **Scope** – empowering others, providing challenge and room to grow, and fostering (rather than stifling) initiative and creativity.

As with all successful recipes, balance is everything. Of course, it is possible to overdo some ingredients and neglect others: for instance, if people have Scope but little Voice, they are likely to act like mavericks or hermits, or relate more to peers externally than connect with the organization. If they are too involved they may lose interest in delivery. If they lose Support, they are likely to become risk-averse or politicized. Moreover, what people need may change as their career (or age) advances. Senior managers usually want more Scope than Support. Certain professions require specific emphasis; for instance, in clinical teams working in intensive care, high involvement by team members can be critical to patient survival.

> As with all successful recipes, balance is everything.

However, in general we're arguing for a balance of ingredients. Engagement is a dynamic and fragile phenomenon and we are dealing with unique individuals. Connection is the red thread running throughout engaged workforces: the benefit, if you get it right, is that you get more out of people and people get more out of work. There is no excuse not to pay attention; you can measure engagement and take action to improve it. In Chapters 8–11 we have tried to set out some key steps you can take in each of the four quadrants; these different action areas are summarized in Figure 11.2.

Ultimately, it means placing people at the centre of everything: as an asset, not a cost; as an opportunity, not a challenge. Authenticity is crucial in order to create trust in the first place, and fairness of treatment so as to sustain it. So while measurement is vital, simply running periodic engagement surveys and offering token follow-up are not the answer. It means an ongoing dialogue between managers and employees based on open, straight exchange. Of course, this isn't easy: the MacLeod Report (MacLeod and Clarke, 2009) reported one chief executive as saying that 'balance sheets don't answer back. The risk of listening is that you may hear things you don't want to hear.' But we would contend that, however uncomfortable the feedback might be, there

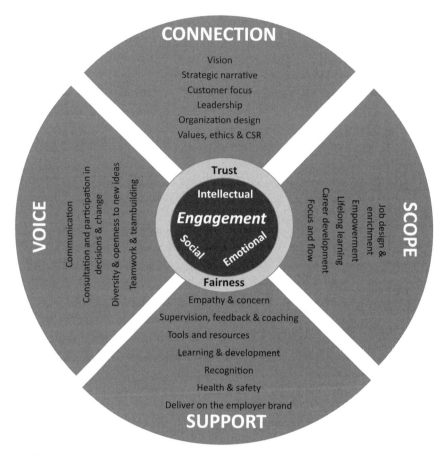

Figure 11.2 Employee engagement model: action areas. Source: Holbeche, L.S. & Matthews, G.P.

is more to be gained by hearing it and taking action than ignoring it and letting disengagement spread.

We've talked about what you can do to manage your engagement level, but also about what you can do to engage others. Above all, employee engagement is a shared endeavour that requires active partnership between employers and employees. As economies eventually recover, employee engagement will be a strong foundation on which to build a new employment relationship between employers and employees – based on mutual commitment, responsibility, obligations, needs, risks and benefits.

No longer can we be 'average' or even pretty good at how we do what we do. We must strive to be absolutely exceptional at the key things that build amazing places to work. The means of getting there are in our grasp. We just need to step up to the challenge so that we – and our organizations – can become engaged.

Notes

1 A useful test to help you assess your organization's culture and its degree of sociability and solidarity can be found in Goffee and Jones, 1998.

ANNEX 1

The model of the core employee engagement drivers that we have shown, built around Connection, Support, Voice and Scope, is to a high degree reflected in the key engagement drivers identified by major surveys of employee engagement.

Gallup

Gallup's Q^{12} survey is based on 12 statements that, based on their research, best predict employee engagement. While Gallup were not willing to grant permission to republish the questions, our review of the Q12 would suggest that ten of them align closely to the model we have proposed and only two are less clearly related. Five of the 12 statements relate to Support, which is not surprising given their supervisor-centric perspective.

Kenexa

Kenexa's latest survey work has generated a top 10 list of engagement drivers globally. Except for the last of these (10. 'Quality and improvement are top priorities'), these again fit into the four overall drivers proposed by our model.

Engagement element	Kenexa top 10 engagement driver
Connection	1. Confidence in organization's future
	8. Leadership has communicated a motivating vision
	9. Organization's corporate responsibility efforts increase overall satisfaction
Support	3. Organization supports work-life balance
	4. Contribution is valued
	7. Safety is a priority
Voice	–
Scope	2. Promising future for one's self
	5. Excited about one's work
	6. Opportunity for growth and development

Towers Watson

Towers Watson's latest global workforce study is not publicly available but the previous one (from 2007/08) largely validates our model, with all but two (5. 'Organization quickly resolves customer concerns' and 6. 'Set high personal standards') of the top 10 global drivers of engagement being matched.

Engagement element	Towers Watson global workforce study
Connection	1. Senior management sincerely interested in employee wellbeing 3. Organization's reputation for social responsibility
Support	9. Good relationship with supervisor
Voice	4. Input into decision making in my department
Scope	2. Improved my skills and capabilities over the last year 7. Have excellent career advancement opportunities 8. Enjoy challenging work assignments that broaden skills 10. Organization encourages innovative thinking

ANNEX 2

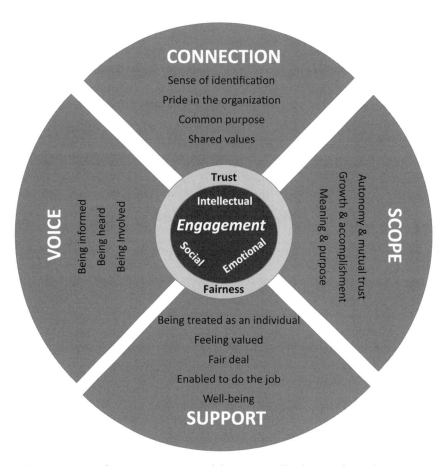

Figure A2.1 Employee engagement model. Source: Holbeche, L.S. & Matthews, G.P.

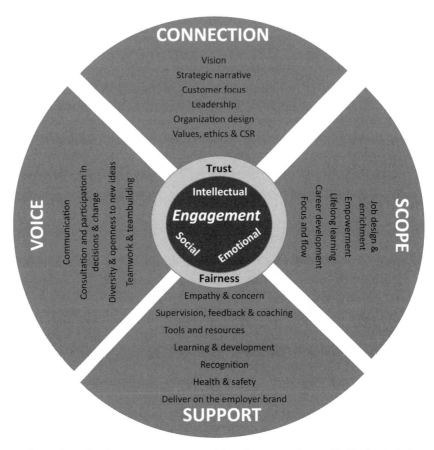

Figure A2.2 Employee engagement model: action areas. Source: Holbeche, L.S. & Matthews, G.P.

BIBLIOGRAPHY

Accenture Institute for High Performance (2011) *What Executives Really Need to Know about Employee Engagement*, June 2011; summarized in Hastings, R.R., *Study Explores Mysteries of Employee Engagement*, SHRM, 26 October 2011.

Aitken, G., Marcs, N., Purcell, J., Woodruffe, C. and Worman, D. (2006) *Reflections on Employee Engagement*, London: CIPD.

Alfes, K., Truss, C., Soane, E.C., Rees, C. and Gatenby, M. (2010) *Creating an Engaged Workforce*, London, CIPD.

Allen, K.E. and Cherrey, C. (2000) *Systematic Leadership: Enriching Meaning in Our Work*, Lantham, MD: University Press of America.

Amabile, T.M. and Kramer, S.J. (2010) 'What really motivates workers', *Harvard Business Review*, vol. 88, no. 1 (January/February), pp. 44–5.

Aon Hewitt (2010) *Engagement 2.0: Focus on the Right People. Build the Excitement. Preserve the Passion*, Deerfield, IL: Aon Hewitt.

Aon Hewitt (2011) *Trends in Global Employee Engagement*, Deerfield, IL: Aon Hewitt.

Appelbaum, S. and Donia, M. (2001) 'The realistic downsizing preview: a management intervention in the prevention of survivor syndrome (part 2)', *Journal of Career Development International*, vol. 6, no.1.

Appelbaum, S.H., Lopes, R., Audet, L., Steed, A., Jacob, M., Augustinas, T. and Manolopoulos, D. (2003) 'Communication during downsizing of a communications company', *Corporate Communications: An International Journal*, vol. 8, no. 2, pp. 73–96.

Arkin, A. (2011) 'Is engagement working?', *People Management* magazine, 24 October.

Ashton, J. (2010) 'Rewards that beat money', *The Sunday Times*, 6 June.

Augier, M. and Teece, D.J. (2005) 'Reflections on (Schumpeterian) leadership: A report on a seminar on leadership and management education', *California Management Review*, vol. 47, no. 2, pp. 114–36.

Axelrod, R.H. (2011) *Terms of Engagement: New Ways of Leading and Changing Organizations*, San Francisco, CA: Berrett-Koehler.

Baker, K. (2010) 'Employee engagement guidance prepares business for recovery', *Personnel Today online*, 23 March.

Bains, G. et al. (2007) *Meaning Inc: The Blueprint for Business Success in the 21st Century*, London: Profile Books.

Balain, S and Sparrow, P. (2009) *Engaged to Perform: A New Perspective on Employee Engagement*, Centre for Performance-Led HR, Lancaster University Management School, White Paper 09/04, May.

Bardwick, J.M. (2007) *One Foot out the Door: How to Combat the Psychological Recession that's Alienating Employees and Hurting American Business*, New York, NY: AMACOM.

Basu, S. (1999) *Corporate Purpose: Why it Matters More than Strategy*, New York, NY: Garland Publishing.

Bates, S. (2004) 'Getting engaged', *HR Magazine*, vol. 49, no. 2, pp. 44–51.

Beer, S. (2002) 'What is cybernetics?', *Kybernetes*, vol. 31, no. 2, pp. 209–219.

Bevan, S., Cowling, M., Horner, L., Isles, N. and Turner, N. (2005) *Cracking the Performance Code*, London: The Work Foundation.

Blau, P.M. (1964) *Exchange and Power in Social Life*, New York, NY: Wiley.

BlessingWhite Research (2008) *The State of Employee Engagement*, Skillman, NJ: BlessingWhite Research.

BlessingWhite Research (2011) *Employee Engagement Report 2011 – Beyond the Numbers: A Practical Approach for Individuals, Managers, and Executives*, Skillman, NJ: BlessingWhite.

Brown, P., Lauder, H. and Ashton, D. (2010) *The Global Auction: The Broken Promises of Education, Jobs and Rewards*, New York, NY: Oxford University Press.

Bridges, W. (2003) *Managing Transitions: Making the Most of Change* (2nd edn), Da Capo Press.

Buckingham, M. and Coffman, C. (1999) *First, Break All the Rules: What the World's Greatest Managers Do Differently*. New York, NY: Simon and Schuster.

Bunting, M. (2004) *Willing Slaves: How the Overwork Culture is Ruling Our Lives*, HarperCollins.

Buytendijk, F. (2006) 'The five keys to building a high-performance organization', *Business Performance Management*, pp. 24–30.

Cheese, P. in Mayson, H. (2011) 'Boardroom boss', *Edge*, London: The Institute of Leadership and Management.

CIPD (2010a) *Developing Positive Employee Relations*, Building Productive Public Sector Workplaces series, August, London: CIPD.

CIPD (2010b) *Learning and Talent Development: Annual Survey Report 2010*, London: CIPD.

CIPD (2011a) *Building the Business Case for Managing Stress in the Workplace*, London: CIPD.

CIPD (2011b) 'Diversity in the workplace: an overview', factsheet. Available from: http://www.cipd.co.uk/hr-resources/factsheets/diversity-workplace-overview. aspx#link_0 (accessed 30 January 2012).

CIPD Research (2009) Employee Outlook survey, June, London: CIPD.

CIPD Research (2010) Employee Outlook survey, January, London: CIPD.

CIPD Research (2011a) Employee Outlook survey, October, London: CIPD.

CIPD Research (2011b) *Locus of Engagement: Understanding what Employees Connect with at Work*, Research Insight, London: CIPD.

Coats, D. and Lehki, R. (2008) *'Good Work': Job Quality in a Changing Economy*, The Work Foundation. Available from: http://workfoundation.org/assets/docs/publications/197_good_work_final2.pdf (accessed 30 January 2012).

Collins, J. and Porras, J.I. (1994) *Built To Last: Successful Habits of Visionary Companies*, New York: HarperCollins.

Collins, J.C. (2001) *Good to Great: Why Some Companies Make the Leap ... and Others Don't*, New York: Harper Collins.

The Conference Board (2006) *Employee Engagement: a Review of Current Research and its Implications*, The Conference Board.

Cormack, J. (2011) Presentation at CIPD OD Conference, London, September.

Corporate Leadership Council (2004) *Driving Performance and Retention through Employee Engagement*, Corporate Executive Board.

Covey, S.M.R. and Merrill, R. (2006) *The Speed of Trust*, Simon and Schuster.

Coyle-Shapiro, J. and Kessler, I. (1998) 'The psychological contract in the UK public sector: employer and employee obligations and contract fulfilment', in Havlovic, S.J. (ed.) *Academy of Management Best Paper Proceedings* (NPS, 1–7).

Coyle-Shapiro, J. and Kessler, I. (2000) 'Consequences of the psychological contract for the employment relationship: a large scale survey', *Journal of Management Studies*, vol. 37, no. 7, pp. 903–930.

Cruise O'Brien, R. (2001) *Trust: Releasing the Energy to Succeed*, Chichester: John Wiley and Sons.

Csikszentmihalyi, M. (1998) *Finding Flow: The Psychology of Engagement with Everyday Life*, Basic Books.

D'Annunzio-Green, N. and Francis, H. (2005) 'Human resource development and the psychological contract: great expectations or false hopes?', *Human Resource Development International*, vol. 8, no. 3, pp. 327–44.

D'Aveni, R. (1994) *Hyper-competition*, Free Press.

Davenport, T.O. and Harding, S.D. (2010) *Manager Redefined: The Competitive Advantage in the Middle of Your Organization*, San Francisco. Jossey-Bass.

Davis, S. (1984) *Managing Corporate Culture*, Cambridge, MA: Ballinger.

Dawson, J. (2009) *Health and Wellbeing of NHS Staff: A Benefit Evaluation Model*, London: The Work Foundation, Aston Business School and RAND Europe.

De Baere, S. and Baeten, X. (2008) 'Royal Bank of Scotland improves employee engagement with new flexible benefits tool', *Newsline*, WorldatWork.

Department for Business Innovation and Skills (2009) *Mental Capital and Wellbeing, Foresight.* Available from: www.bis.gov.uk/foresight/our-work/projects/current-projects/mental-capital-and-wellbeing/reports-and-publications (accessed 30 January 2012).

Department for Business Innovation and Skills (2011) 'Employee engagement – an overview', Business Link. Available from: http://tinyurl.com/7zs5ezz (accessed 30 January 2012).

Devine, M., Hirsh, W., Garrow, V., Holbeche, L. and Lake, C. (1997) *Mergers and Acquisitions: Getting the People Bit Right,* Horsham: Roffey Park.

Dulewicz, C., Young, M. and Dulewicz, V. (2005) 'The relevance of emotional leadership for leadership performance', *Journal of General Management,* vol. 30, no. 3 (Spring).

Ejler, N., Poulfelt, F. and Czerniawska, F. (2011) *Managing the Knowledge-intensive Firm,* London: Routledge.

Ellsworth, R.R. (2002) *Leading with Purpose: The New Corporate Realities,* Stanford University Press.

Erickson, T. (2010) *What's Next, Gen X? Keeping Up, Moving Ahead and Getting the Career You Want,* Harvard Business School Press.

Fennell, E. (2011) 'We're a long-term chauffeur, not a cab for the night', *The Times,* 10 August.

Flade, P. (2003) *Great Britain's Workforce Lacks Inspiration,* Gallup Press.

Flade, P. (2006) 'Unlocking customer service excellence', *Gallup Management Journal,* 12 January.

Flade, P. (2008) 'Employee engagement drives shareholder value', *Director of Finance,* 13 February.

Francis, H., Holbeche, L.S. and Reddington, M. (2012) *People and Organisation Development: A New Agenda for Organisational Effectiveness,* London: CIPD.

Friedman, M. (1982) *Capitalism and Freedom* (2nd edn), University of Chicago Press.

Furbini, D.D., Price, C. and Zollo, M. (2007) *Mergers: Leadership, Performance and Corporate Health,* Basingstoke, Palgrave Macmillan.

Gallup Study (2005) 'Feeling good matters in the workplace', *Gallup Management Journal.*

Gallup Consulting (2010) *What is Your Engagement Ratio?,* Gallup.

Galvin, C. (2011) 'Starless horizons', *The Sunday Times Magazine,* 6 November, p. 59.

Gardner, H., Csikszentmihalyi, M. and Damon, W. (2001) *Good Work: When Excellence and Ethics Meet,* New York: Basic Books.

Gebauer, J. and Lowman, D. (2008) *Closing the Engagement Gap: How Great Companies Unlock Employee Potential for Superior Results,* New York: Penguin.

Gentry, W.A., Weber, T.J. and Sadri G. (2010) *Empathy in the Workplace: A Tool for Effective Leadership,* White Paper, Center for Creative Leadership.

Gifford, J., Finney, L., Hennessy, J. and Varney, S. (2010) *The Human Voice of Employee Engagement: Understanding What Lies Beneath the Surveys,* Horsham: Roffey Park Institute.

Gobillot, E. (2007) *The Connected Leader*, London: Kogan Page.

Goffee, R. and Jones, G. (1998) *The Character of a Corporation: How Your Company's Culture Can Make or Break Your Business*, Profile Books.

Goffee, R. and Jones, G. (2005) 'Managing authenticity, the paradox of great leadership', *Harvard Business Review*, December.

Goffee, R. and Jones, G. (2006) *Why Should Anyone Be Led By You?*, Harvard, MA: Harvard Business School Publishing.

Goffee, R. and Jones, G (2009) *Clever: Leading Your Smartest, Most Creative People*, Boston, MA: Harvard Business Press.

Goleman, D. (2005) *Working With Emotional Intelligence*, Bantam Books.

Goleman, D., Boyatzis, R. and McKee, A. (2002) *Primal Leadership*, Boston: Harvard Business School Press.

Gostick, A. and Elton, C. (2007) *The Carrot Principle: How the Best Managers Use Recognition to Engage Their People, Retain Talent and Accelerate Performance*, New York, NY: Free Press.

Gratton, L. (2007) *Hot Spots: Why Some Companies Buzz with Energy and Innovation – And Others Don't*, London: Financial Times/Prentice Hall.

Great Places to Work Institute (2010) *Trust: The Key to Enhanced Business Performance and accelerated recovery*, GPWI.

Guest, D.E. (1997) 'Human resource management and performance: a review and research agenda', *The International Journal of Human Resource Management*, vol. 8, pp. 263–76.

Guest, D.E. (2002) 'Human resource management, corporate performance and employee well-being: building the worker into HRM', *The Journal of Industrial Relations*, vol. 44, no. 3, pp. 335–58.

Guest, D.E. and Conway, N. (1997) *Employee Motivation and the Psychological Contract*, London: Institute for Personnel and Development, CIPD.

Hackman, J.R. and Oldham, G.R. (1976) 'Motivation through the design of work: test of a theory', *Organizational Behavior and Human Performance*, vol. 16, pp. 250–79.

Hakanen J.J., Bakker A.B. and Schaufeli, W.B. (2006) 'Burnout and work engagement among teachers', *Journal of School Psychology*, vol. 43, pp. 495–513.

Hamel, G. (2009) 'Moonshots for management', *Harvard Business Review*, no. 91, February.

Hamel, G. and Breen, B. (2007) *The Future of Management*, Boston: Harvard Business School Press.

Hammer, M. and Champy, J. (1993) *Reengineering the Corporation: A Manifesto for Business Revolution*, Harper Business.

Harris Poll (2010) Harris Interactive.

Harter, J.K., Schmidt, F.L. and Hayes, T.L. (2002) 'Business-unit-level relationship between employee satisfaction, employee engagement and business outcomes: a meta-analysis', *Journal of Applied Psychology*, vol. 87, no. 2, pp. 268–79.

Haudan, J. (2008) *The Art of Engagement: Bridging the Gap Between People and Possibilities*, New York, NY: McGraw-Hill.

Hawksworth, J. (2006) 'The world in 2050: How big will the major emerging market economies get and how can the OECD compete?', PricewaterhouseCoopers, March.

Hay Group (2010) *Giving Everyone the Chance to Shine: How Leading Organizations Use Engagement to Drive Performance Cost-effectively*, Philadelphia: Hay Group.

Hay Group (2011) *Climate Change and Environmental Impact, Leadership 2030*, London: Hay Group.

Health and Safety Executive (2007) *Managing the Causes of Work-related Stress*, London: Office of Public Information.

Heger, B.K. (2007) 'Linking the employment value proposition (EVP) to employee engagement and business outcomes: preliminary findings from a linkage research pilot study', *Organization Development Journal*, vol. 25, no.2 (Spring), pp. 121–31.

Heintzman, R. and Marson, B. (2006) *People, Service and Trust: Links in the Public Sector Service Value Chain*, Canadian Government Executive.

Herriot, P. and Pemberton, C. (1995) *New Deals: The Revolution in Managerial Careers*, Chichester: Wiley.

Herzberg, F.I. (1987) 'One more time: how do you motivate employees?', *Harvard Business Review*, vol. 65, no. 5, Reprint 87507, September/October, pp. 109–20. http://www.facilitif.eu/user_files/file/herzburg_article.pdf

Hockey, J. and Ley, I. (2010) *Leading for Engagement: How Senior Leaders Engage Their People*, National School of Government, Sunningdale Institute.

Holbeche, L.S. (2009) *The Changing Nature of Employee Relations*, unpublished paper.

Holbeche, L.S. (2005) *The High Performance Organization*, Oxford: Butterworth-Heinemann.

Holbeche, L.S. and Springett, N. (2005) *The Search for Meaning at Work*, Horsham: Roffey Park.

Huselid, M. (1995) 'The impact of human resource management practices on turnover, productivity, and corporate performance', *Academy of Management Journal*, vol. 38, no, 3, pp. 635–72.

Hutton, P. (2009) *What Are Your Staff Trying to Tell You? Revealing Best and Worst Practice in Employee Surveys* (revised edn), Sutton. Brand Energy Research Ltd.

Hutton, W. (2010a) *The Landscape of Tough Times*, London: The Work Foundation.

Hutton, W. (2010b) *Them and Us: Changing Britain – Why We Need a Fair Society*, Little, Brown & Co.

Hutton, W. (2011a) 'Staff lead the focus on recovery', *The Sunday Times*, 6 March.

Hutton, W. (2011b) 'Executive pay phenomenally out of kilter', *Dods Politics Home*, 4 December.

IABC Research Foundation and Buck Consultants (2011) *Employee Engagement Survey 2011*, San Francisco: Buck Consultants, LLC.

IDS (2009) *HR Study 892 – Employee Engagement*, April, London: IDS (ISSN 0308–9339).

IDS (2010) *HR Study 910 – Employee Engagement Surveys*, January, London: IDS (ISSN 0308–9339).

ILM and Ashridge Business School (2011) *Great Expectations: Managing Generation Y*, London: Institute of Leadership and Management.

Jameson, H. (2009) *IPA Guide to Workforce Engagement*, London: IPA.

Jenkins, C. and Sherman, B. (1979) *The Collapse of Work*, Eyre Methuen.

Kerber, K. and Buono, A.F. (2005) 'Rethinking organizational change: reframing the challenge of change management', *Organizational Development Journal*, vol. 23, no. 3 (Fall), pp. 23–38.

Khan, W.A. (1990) 'Psychological conditions of personal engagement and disengagement at work', *Academy of Management Journal*, vol. 33, no. 4, p. 692.

Kirn, S.P., Rucci, A.J., Huselid, M.A. and Becker, B.E. (1999) 'Strategic human resources at Sears', *Human Resource Management*, vol. 38, no. 4 (Winter), pp. 329–35.

Kübler-Ross, E. (1969) *On Death and Dying*, New York, NY: Macmillan.

Kuh, G.D. (1991) 'Characteristics of involving colleges', in Kuh, G.D. and Schuh, J.H. (eds) *The Role and Contribution of Student Affairs in Involving Colleges*, pp. 11–29, Washington, DC: NASPA.

Kuh, G.D. and Whitt, E.J. (1988) *The Invisible Tapestry: Culture in American Colleges and Universities: ASHE-ERIC Higher Education Report Series, No. 1*, Washington, DC: Association for the Study of Higher Education.

Lambert, A. (2010) *Employee Engagement and Organisational Performance*, London: CRF (Corporate Research Forum).

Lawler III, E.E. and Worley, C.G. (2011) *A Suggestion for Creating Effective Sustainable Organizations: Get Rid of Job Descriptions*, CEO Publication G 11–05 (593), Center for Effective Organizations.

Leonard, S. (2011) 'Keeping the brightest on board', *The Sunday Times*, 6 March.

Lorenzi, P. (2004) 'Managing for the common good: prosocial leadership', *Organizational Dynamics*, vol. 33, no. 3 (August), pp. 282–91.

Macey, W.H. and Schneider, B. (2008) 'The meaning of employee engagement', *Industrial and Organizational Psychology*, vol. 1, pp. 3–30.

Macey, W.H., Schneider, B., Barbera, K.M. and Young, S.A. (2009) *Employee Engagement: Tools for Analysis, Practice, and Competitive Advantage*, Chichester: Wiley Blackwell.

MacLeod, D. and Brady, C. (2007) *The Extra Mile: How to Engage Your People to Win*, London: Financial Times/Prentice Hall.

MacLeod, D. and Clarke, N. (2009) *Engaging for Success: Enhancing Performance through Employee Engagement* ('The MacLeod Report'), London: Department for Business, Innovation and Skills.

MacNeill, R. (2011) 'Employee engagement in decline', *Hotel Industry Magazine*, hotel-industry.co.uk, 24 October.

Marks, A. and Scholarios, D. (2004) 'Work life boundary, reciprocity, and attitudes to the organization, the special case of software workers', *Human Resource Management Journal*, vol. 14, no. 2, pp. 54–74.

Marshak, R.J. (2004) 'Morphing: the leading edge of organizational change in the twenty-first century', *Organization Development Journal*, vol. 22, no. 3, pp. 8–21.

Maslach, C. and Leiter, M.P. (2008) 'Early predictors of job burnout and engagement', *Journal of Applied Psychology*, vol. 93, pp. 498–512.

Maslach, C., Schaufeli, W.B. and Leiter, M.P. (2001) 'Job burnout', *Annual Review of Psychology*, vol. 42, pp. 397–422.

Maslow, A. (1954/1987) *Motivation and Personality* (3rd revised edn), Hong Kong: Longman Asia.

Melcrum Publishing (2005) *Employee Engagement: How to Build a High-performance Workforce. An independent Melcrum Research Report Executive Summary*, Melcrum Publishing.

Mercer (2011) *What's Working Survey*, July, Mercer.

Michelman, P. (2004) 'Methodology – how great managers manage people', *Harvard Management Update*, 1 August, Boston: Harvard Business School Publishing.

Millward, D. (2009) 'Bentley car firm builds furniture to stave off recession job losses', *Daily Telegraph*, 3 March.

The Mind Gym (2011) *The Engaged Employee: How to Keep Your People Flourishing Whatever the Weather*, London: The Mind Gym.

Moorcroft, D. (2006) 'Realizing RBC's new vision for employee communication', *SCM*, vol. 10, no. 6 (October/November).

Nicholson, N. (2011) in Saunders, A. 'Rebuilding management's good name', *Management Today Online*, 1 May.

Norman, S., Luthans, B. and Luthans, K. (2005) 'The proposed contagion effect of hopeful leaders on the resiliency of employees and organizations', *Journal of Leadership and Organizational Studies*, vol. 12, no. 2.

ORC International (2011) *Global Perspectives Survey*, London: ORC International.

Packard, D. (1995) *The HP Way: How Bill Hewlett and I Built Our Company*, Harper Business.

Pearson, E. (2011) 'Cost of ineffective management tops £19billion', CMI, 30 November. Available from: http://www.managers.org.uk/practical-support/management-community/professional-networks/cost-ineffective-management-tops-%C2%A319-bi (accessed 28 January 2012).

Peters, T. and Waterman, R. (1982) *In Search of Excellence*, New York: Harper Row.

Pink, D. (2009) *Drive: The Surprising Truth about What Motivates Us*, Riverhead.

Porter, M. and Kramer, M.R. (2011) 'Creating shared value', *Harvard Business Review*, January.

PricewaterhouseCoopers (2008) *Managing Tomorrow's People*, PWC.

Pryce-Jones, J. (2010) *Happiness at Work: Maximizing your Psychological Capital for Success*, Chichester: Wiley-Blackwell.

Purcell, J., Hutchinson, S., Kinnie, N., Rayton, B. and Swart, J. (2003) *Understanding the Pay and Performance Link: Unlocking the Black Box*, London: CIPD.

Quantum Workplace (2011) *The Impact of Manager Effectiveness on Employee Engagement*, Quantum Workplace.

Raelin, J.A. (2005) 'We the leaders: in order to form a leaderful organization', *Journal of Leadership and Organizational Studies*, vol. 12, no. 2.

Robbins, S.P. (1999) 'Lay-off survivor sickness: a missing topic in organizational behaviour', *Journal of Management Education*, vol. 23, no. 1, pp. 31–43.

Robertson, I. and Cooper, C. (2011) *Well-being: Productivity and Happiness at Work*, Palgrave MacMillan.

Robinson, D., Hooker, H. and Hayday, S. (2007) *Engagement: The Continuing Story*, Brighton: Institute for Employment Studies.

Robinson, D., Perryman, S. and Hayday, S. (2004) *The Drivers of Employee Engagement*, Brighton: Institute for Employment Studies.

Roffey Park (1998–2012) *The Management Agenda*, Horsham: Roffey Park.

Rousseau, D.M. (1990) 'New hire perceptions of their own and their employer's obligations: a study of psychological contracts', *Journal of Organizational Behavior*, vol. 11, pp. 389–400.

Rousseau, D.M. (2000) *Psychological Contract Inventory Technical Report*, Pittsburgh, Pennsylvania: Carnegie Mellon University.

Saks, A.M. (2006) 'Antecedents and consequences of employee engagement', *Journal of Managerial Psychology*, vol. 21, no. 7, pp. 600–619.

Salter, C. (2008) 'Google', Fast Company, 1 March. Available from: www.fastcompany.com/magazine/123/google.html (accessed 30 January 2012).

Saunders, M. (2011) *Employee Engagement*, White Paper series, London: Mind Gym.

Scase, R. (2006) *Global Re-mix: The Fight for Competitive Advantage*, Kogan Page.

Schein, E.H. (1999) *The Corporate Culture Survival Guide: Sense and Nonsense About Culture Change*, San Francisco, CA: Jossey Bass.

Schein, E.H. (2004) *Organizational Culture and Leadership* (3rd edn), San Francisco, CA: Jossey Bass.

Seijts, G.H and Crim, D. (2006) 'What engages employees the most or, the ten C's of employee engagement', *Ivey Business Journal*, March/April, pp. 1–5.

Sennett, R. (1998) *The Corrosion of Character: The Personal Consequences of Work in the New Capitalism*, New York, NY: W.W. Norton & Co.

Sennett, R. (2008) *The Craftsman*, Yale University Press.

Sergiovanni, T. and Corbally, J. (eds) (1984) *Leadership and Organizational Culture*, Urbana, IL: University of Illinois Press.

SHRM (2011a) *Developing and Sustaining Employee Engagement*, The Society for Human Resource Management (SHRM).

SHRM (2011b) 'Employee job satisfaction: the external forces influencing employee attitudes', *Workplace Visions*, no. 4 (November).

Sibson, S. (2006) *Rewards of Work Study*, The Segal Group.

Siebert, S. (2011) *The UK Family Business Sector*, Report for Institute for Family Business, February.

Sims, R.R. (1994) *Ethics and Organizational Decision-making: A Call for Renewal*, Westport, CT: Quorum Books.

Sparrow, P.R. (1996) 'Transitions in the psychological contract in UK banking', *Human Resource Management Journal*, vol. 6, no. 4, pp. 75–92.

Sparrow, P.R. and Cooper, C.L. (2003) *The Employment Relationship: Key Challenges for HR*, Oxford: Butterworth-Heinemann.

Springett, N. (2009) *Shared Purpose and Sustainable Performance*, Shaping the Future research paper, London: CIPD.

Standing, G. (2011) *The Precariat: The New Dangerous Class*, London: Bloomsbury Academic.

Storey, J., Wright, P.M. and Ulrich, D. (eds) (2008) *The Routledge Companion to Strategic Human Resource Management*, London: Routledge

Tamkin, P., Pearson, G., Hirsh, W. and Constable, S. (2010) *Exceeding Expectation: The Principles of Outstanding Leadership*, London: The Work Foundation.

Terkel, S. (1974) *Working*, Pantheon Books (Random House).

Totterdill, P. (2002) *Developing New Forms of Work Organisation: The Role of the Main Actors*, The Work Institute, Nottingham Trent University.

Totterdill, P. (2010) *Workplace Innovation: Europe 2020's Missing Dimension?*, Report of a workshop hosted by DG Employment, Social Affairs and Equal Opportunities, 23 June, Nottingham, UKWON.

Towers Watson (2000) *WorkUSA 2000: Employees Commitment and the Bottom Line*, research report, January, Towers Watson.

Towers Watson (2008) *Closing the Engagement Gap: A Roadmap for Driving Superior Business Performance*, Towers Watson.

Towers Watson (2010a) *2009/2010 Communication ROI Study Report*, New York, NY: Towers Watson.

Towers Watson (2010b) *Driving Business Results Through Continuous Engagement*, Watson Wyatt 2008/2009 WorkUSA Report.

Truss, K., Soane, E.C. and Edwards, C. (2006) *Working Life: Employee Attitudes and Engagement*, London: CIPD.

Tsui, A.S., Pearce, J.L., Porter, L.W. and Tripoli, A.M. (1997) 'Alternative approaches to the employee-organization relationship: does investment in employees pay off?', *Academy of Management Journal*, vol. 40, no. 5, pp. 1089–1121.

Tubbs, S.L. and Schulz, E. (2006) 'Exploring a taxonomy of global leadership competencies and meta-competencies', *Journal of American Academy of Business*, Cambridge, vol. 8, no. 2 (March), pp. 29–35.

Vance, R.J. (2006) *Employee Engagement and Commitment: A Guide to Understanding, Measuring and Increasing Engagement in Your Organization*, Alexandria, VA: SHRM Foundation.

Victor, B. and Stephens, C. (1994) 'The Dark Side of the New Organizational Forms', *Organization Science*, vol. 5, no. 4, pp. 479–82.

Walker, B. (2011) 'Simple pleasures', *Professional Manager*, May/June, pp.18–23.

Whitt, E.J. (1997) 'Don't drink the water? A guide to encountering a new institutional culture', in Whitt, E.J. (ed.) *College Student Affairs Administration*, pp. 516–23, Needham Heights, MA: Simon and Schuster.

Whittington, J.L. and Galpin, T.J. (2010) 'The engagement factor: building a high-commitment organization in a low-commitment world', *Journal of Business Strategy*, vol. 31, no. 5, pp. 14–24.

Wiley, J., Kowske, B.J. and Herman, A.E. (2010) *Developing and Validating a Global Model of Employee Engagement*, White Paper, Kenexa High Performance Institute.

Wiley, J.W. (2010a) *Driving Success Through Performance Excellence and Employee Engagement*, Minneapolis, MA: Kenexa Research Institute.

Wiley, J.W. (2010b) *Strategic Employee Surveys*, San Francisco, CA: Jossey-Bass.

Wood, Z. and Wearden, G. (2009) 'John Lewis staff delighted with 13% bonus', *The Guardian*, 11 March.

The Work Foundation (2010) *Understanding the Deal: Placing the Employee at the Heart of the Employment Relationship*, London: The Work Foundation.

Yarker, J., Lewis, R. and Donaldson-Feilder, E. (2008) *Management Competencies for Preventing and Reducing Stress at Work*, London: Health and Safety Executive.